11-36

THE GREAT CIRCLE

THE
GREAT
CIRCLE

American Writers and the Orient

BEONGCHEON YU

Wayne State University Press
Detroit, 1983

12/1984
gen'l

Library of Congress Cataloging in Publication Data
Yu, Beongcheon.
  The great circle.

  Includes bibliographical references and index.
  1. American literature—Oriental influences.
2. American literature—History and criticism.
3. Civilization, Oriental, in literature. 4. Exoticism
in literature. I. Title.
PS157.Y8 1983   810'.9'325   83–14811
ISBN 0–8143–1737–5

To my family,
Yung Jai, Vincent, Vera, and Hyatt

Here individuals of all nations are melted
into a new race of men, whose labours and
posterity will one day cause great changes in
the world. Americans are the western
pilgrims, who are carrying along with them
that great mass of arts, sciences, vigour, and
industry which began long since in the east;
they will finish the great circle.

—Crèvecoeur, *Letters from an American Farmer*

Contents

Preface

Now that the project has been completed, I feel that this was a "logical" book for me to write, and my friends seem to think that it was a "natural" subject for me to tackle. But the truth is that the original impulse came to me by accident during my first Fulbright stint in Korea (1965–67). As I recall, it came during the routine question-and-answer period that followed one of my lectures to student groups. "But, sir, what do these American writers know about us?" asked a young man in a voice unceremoniously loud and impatient. There was a moment of awkward silence in the hall. Fortunately, I had ready a few names, such as Emerson, Fenollosa, Hearn, Eliot, and Pound. The audience was impressed, of course, but I myself was even more impressed with my own list. The experience set me thinking seriously about these and other writers in terms of an American response to the Orient.

This interest continued to grow after my return to the States, as I repeatedly tested its potential significance in a graduate seminar. While defining and redefining its form and content with my students, I went ahead with my reading. The present study developed largely out of this process of teaching and reading.

According to *Webster's Second International Dictionary*, Orientalism means, among other things, "imitation or assimilation of that which is Oriental, esp. in religious or philosophical thought, or in art." In other words, it is a cultural phenomenon which appears in architecture, literature, music, painting, philosophy, religion, and other creative endeavors. In literature, that is, in Western literature, it has evolved over the centuries into a distinct, rich, and enduring tradition. American literary Orientalism, to be sure, is one of those traditions which we inherited from European literature, but our writers have transformed it into something uniquely American, a significant part of the American experience.

The Orient has a wide geographical and cultural range, encircling half the world, from the Mediterranean to the Pacific. In this study, however, I have confined myself to three major traditions—Indian, Chinese, and Japanese—since they are directly relevant to my inquiry. In its history of one and a half centuries American literary Orientalism has involved several generations of writers—creative artists and thinkers—from Emerson, Thoreau, and Whitman down to Salinger, Kerouac, and Snyder. In order to stress the representative I have eliminated some writers, such as Alcott, Robinson, Amy Lowell, Steinbeck, Rexroth, and Ginsberg, from my original list. Most of the time I have concentrated on those writers who responded intensely to the Orient, matured significantly in the process, and thereby contributed to the furtherance of this particular tradition. In general I have adopted a biographical approach, and if, with certain writers, I seem to have belabored the familiar and the obvious, that is because I have wished to examine the role of the Orient in the total drama of their careers, properly and without making exaggerated claims, and to suggest the possibility of reevaluating their art and thought from a fresh perspective.

For this project I am deeply indebted to all those scholars who have explored the field, especially Frederic Ives Carpenter, Arthur Christy, Earl Miner, Van Meter Ames, and Lawrence W. Chisolm. Without their pioneering efforts I could not possibly have undertaken to write this book. In a more personal way I am grateful to Donald Gallup, David G. Hoch, C. T. Hsia, Hugh Kenner, Thomas Parkinson, Angela Jung Palandri, Barend van Nooten, and Gary Snyder, all of whom graciously responded to my various queries; to those graduate students who helped me with their critical insights; and to my long-time friends Daniel and Mary Hughes, who read through the entire manuscript and offered many valuable suggestions. It only remains for me to note that a Wayne State University faculty fellowship for the summer of 1978 enabled me to initiate the actual writing of this book.

Acknowledgments

Chapter 6 of this book is based on my longer study, *An Ape of Gods: The Art and Thought of Lafcadio Hearn,* copyright © 1964 by Wayne State University Press. A portion of Chapter 9 is based on my article "The *Gita,* the *Comedy,* and Eliot," *The English Language and Literature,* Nos. 51–52 (1974), pp. 227–47.

My thanks go to the following for permission to use copyrighted material:

Coyote's Journal, for quotations from "The Hump-Backed Flute Player," copyright © 1971 by James Koller and Gary Snyder.

Faber and Faber Ltd., for quotations from T. S. Eliot, *Collected Poems 1909–1962, Murder in the Cathedral, The Family Reunion, The Cocktail Party, The Confidential Clerk,* and *The Elder Statesman;* and from Ezra Pound, *Collected Shorter Poems, The Classic Noh Theatre, The Great Digest, The Unwobbling Pivot, The Classic Anthology Defined by Confucius,* and *The Cantos of Ezra Pound.*

Farrar, Straus & Giroux, Inc., for quotations from T. S. Eliot, *The Elder Statesman,* copyright © 1959.

Four Seasons Foundations, for quotations from *Riprap & Cold Mountain Poems,* copyright © 1965 by Gary Snyder; and *Six Selections from Mountains and Rivers Without End Plus One,* copyright © 1970 by Gary Snyder.

Harcourt Brace Jovanovich, Inc., for quotations from T. S. Eliot, *Collected Poems 1909–1962, Four Quartets, Murder in the Cathedral, The Family Reunion, The Cocktail Party,* and *The Confidential Clerk,* copyright 1935, 1936 by Harcourt Brace Jovanovich, Inc., copyright © 1939, 1943, 1950, 1954, 1963, 1964 by T. S. Eliot, copyright 1967, 1971, 1978 by Esme Valerie Eliot.

Harvard University Press, for quotations from *Buddhism in Translations,* translated by Henry Clarke Warren, copyright © 1953; and *The Confucian Odes,* translated by Ezra Pound, copyright © 1954.

New Directions Publishing Corporation, for quotations from *Confucius,* copyright 1947, 1950 by Ezra Pound; *The Confucian Odes,* 1959; *The Classic Noh Theatre of Japan,* copyright 1959 by New Directions Publishing Corporation; and *The Cantos of Ezra Pound,* copyright 1934, 1937, 1940, 1948, © 1959, 1962 by Ezra Pound.

Gary Snyder, for quotations from *Myths & Texts,* copyright © 1960 by Gary Snyder; *The Back Country,* copyright © 1968 by Gary Snyder; and *Regarding Wave,* copyright © 1970 by Gary Snyder; and *Turtle Island,* copyright © 1974 by Gary Snyder.

Peter Owen Ltd., for quotations from *The Confucian Analects,* translated by Ezra Pound.

Random House, Inc., for quotations from Eugene O'Neill, *The Iceman Cometh,* copyright 1946; *Nine Plays,* copyright 1952; and *The Plays of Eugene O'Neill,* vols. 1 and 3, copyright 1947, copyright 1946.

ACKNOWLEDGMENTS

The Vedanta Society of Southern California, for quotations from *The Upanishads,* translated by Swami Prabhavananda and Frederick Manchester, copyright 1957; and *The Song of God: Bhagavad-Gita,* translated by Swami Prabhavananda and Christopher Isherwood, copyright 1972.

Yale University Press, for quotations from Eugene O'Neill, *A Long Day's Journey Into Night,* copyright 1956 by Yale University Press.

PROLOGUE

Orientalism as a Literary Tradition

"Oh, East is East, and West is West, / And never the twain shall meet." Kipling could not have said this so cavalierly had he but paused for a moment to think of the contact between India and Greece that is said to have existed long before the Christian era. Pythagoras, for instance, traveled widely, studying the esoteric teachings of the Egyptians, Assyrians, and Brahmans. Metempsychosis, one of his doctrines, was in all likelihood influenced by Indian thought, though Herodotus traced it to Egypt. Herodotus himself, a near contemporary of Gautama Buddha, knew a great deal about India. Socrates, according to one source, conversed with learned visitors from India; when he explained his philosophy as an inquiry into human affairs, one Indian visitor burst out laughing: "How could a man grasp human things without first mastering the Divine?"[1] Better known was the case of Plato, who accepted metempsychosis matter-of-factly; his utopian scheme, especially, including his fable of the three metals, seems as Indian as it was Greek.

Alexander died too young to realize his imperial dream of unifying Asia and Europe, but his invasion of India in 326 B.C. did break down the barrier between East and West, heralding a new era of cultural fusion. Plotinus, the founder of Neoplatonism, joined a military expedition to the East so that he might have firsthand knowledge of Indian philosophy. Centering on the mystical doctrine of emanation and absorption, Neoplatonism thus showed striking resemblances to the Vedanta; insisting on the abstension from sacrifices and animal food, it also had obvious similarities to Buddhism. In the cosmopolitan city of Alexandria the Buddhists were a familiar presence, as Clement of Alexandria noted repeatedly: "The Greeks stole their philosophy from the barbarians."[2] This early contact between East and West may account for quite a few parallels between Christian and Buddhist parables and miracles.

After the fall of Alexandria in A.D. 642, the contact continued into the Middle Ages, with the Arabs acting as mediators between East and West—until 1258, when their center, Bagdad, was destroyed by the Mongols. Through the Arabs, Indian myths, fables, and folktales found their way into Europe, springing up in unlikely works, such as Gottfried von Strassburg's *Tristan and Isolde*, Boccaccio's *Decameron*, and Chaucer's *Canterbury Tales*. Perhaps the most intriguing example of this migration of tales was *Barlaam and Josaphat*, often called the first religious romance published in a Western language. According to this story, the young Indian prince Josaphat was profoundly touched by various forms of human misery and suffering, so much so that he accepted Christianity and renounced the world. Translated from the original Greek into Arabic, and therefrom into a number of European languages, the legend became immensely popular. In the sixteenth century Josaphat was finally made a Christian saint, although it is now evident that he was really the Bodhisat, or Bodhisattva, and that his story merely embellished Gautama Buddha's Great Renunciation.[3]

These isolated cases have been told over and over again in order to prove the historical contact between East and West. However interesting in themselves, they did not constitute Orientalism as a literary trend, as a literary tradition. That had to wait until the Renaissance. Outstanding among those works which set the trend was Sir Thomas More's *Utopia* (1516). Presented as an account by one Raphael Hythloday of his fantastic voyage, *Utopia* belonged to a new genre of travel literature which was catering to the reading public still excited over the recent feats of Columbus and Vasco da Gama. As its title suggests, *Utopia* also stood in another, longer tradition of utopian literature. By fusing Plato's *Republic* and Saint Augustine's *City of God*, More envisioned an ideal commonwealth, at once Christian and humanistic, located not in heaven, where his predecessors had placed theirs, but on earth—in the spirit of the Renaissance. And by contrasting the actual and the ideal, *Utopia* continued still another literary tradition, that of satirical allegory. Partly for his personal safety, and partly for his desired effect, More chose to have a returning traveler relate his experience in the "nowhere land," making an implicit and explicit criticism of the existing conditions in England.

When these various genres and traditions were combined, the so-called imaginary, philosophic, or allegorical voyage was born. The popularity of this new genre in ensuing generations produced numerous accounts of earthly paradise: Andreae's *Christianopolis* (1619), Campanella's *City of the Sun* (1623), Bacon's *New Atlantis* (1627), and Harrington's *Oceana* (1656).[4] What made More's *Utopia* especially significant, however, was its geographical location. Inasmuch as Hythloday was supposedly in the service of Vespucci, More could have placed his ideal commonwealth somewhere west of Europe—in the Atlantic, as Bacon was to do a century later, or even in the New World. Instead, he let Hythloday find it in the opposite direction, in the Gulf of Persia. In so doing More provided a new direction for the new genre, or set it in the proper direction, namely, the East.

As More undoubtedly knew, the East had long evoked a cluster of rich associations. Still fresh in memory were Columbus's repeated search for a passage to India, which resulted in his discovery of the New World, and Vasco da Gama's success in doubling the Cape of Hope and reaching India from the other direction. In each case India already stood for what Milton was later to call the gorgeous East. And farther beyond India were China and Japan, whose fabulous wealth Marco Polo had earlier magnified to mythic proportions. Turning eastward for his utopia, More, in a way, exploited the ancient maxim: *Ex oriente lux, ex occidente lex.*

Although the origin of this maxim was obscure, what it signified was unmistakable. In terms of the Mediterranean, the Orient meant Israel, the home of two religions, Judaism and Christianity, and the Occident meant Greece and Rome, the sources of the material, scientific, and rational spirit. In due time the Orient began to extend beyond Israel. More's *Utopia* marked this signal moment when the European imagination crossed its medieval boundary and entered the realm of moral and spiritual wealth. A history of Orientalism is therefore a history of the expanding definition of the term *Orient*—a history of its ever-expanding image mirrored in the consciousness of the Occident.

During the sixteenth and seventeenth centuries the image of the Orient was largely Near Eastern, because the Arabs were the only medieval link between East and West. The Middle East continued to dominate the popular imagination, as is apparent in More's *Utopia*, and, indeed, in the whole range of English literature from Marlowe's *Tamburlaine the Great* (1590) to Dryden's *Aureng-Zebe* (1676) and Rowe's *Tamerlane* (1702). When Shakespeare made Othello of Moorish origin he was in his own way capitalizing on the general trend of his time.[5]

The eighteenth century, however, witnessed a dramatic shift in the overall image of the Orient. China became almost synonymous with the Orient as the Chinese vogue, *chinoiserie*, swept through Europe, turning persons of taste and culture into addicts to things Chinese—from porcelain to architecture, from textiles to landscaping, from colored wallpapers to tea drinking. Like any other fashion, it often ran to extremes, as with a certain crazed English duchess who consented to marry only after having been assured that her bridegroom was the Emperor of China.[6] Although much of this Chinese vogue was ephemeral, Chinese motifs, designs, and decorations eventually led to the emergence of the rococo style.

The Chinese vogue turned out to be greater and farther-reaching in the intellectual sphere. Confucius suited the rationalistic temper of the century admirably. To the *philosophes* of the Enlightenment, Chinese civilization seemed to embody Reason better than any other civilization in history; Confucianism in particular seemed to approximate the sort of natural religion they were advocating—free from rituals, dogmas, and superstitions. Leibnitz, a leading philosopher of the period, declared: "I almost think it necessary that the Chinese missionaries should be sent to us to teach us the aim and practice of natural theology, as we send missionaries to them to instruct them in revealed theology."[7] More aggressive and even subversive was Christian Wolff. When he said of China that "in the Art of Governing, this Nation has ever surpassed all others without exception," he was reportedly ordered to leave the University of Halle within twenty-four hours, "under pain of immediate death."[8]

Ironically, the Jesuits, active in China since 1600, were originally responsible for what amounted to intellectual idolatry. In their reports home they extolled the Confucian state as a way of justifying their own missionary work. Although they were apparently sincere, they did not realize that they were in effect supplying munitions to their mortal enemies, the free-thinking Deists. In his *Philosophical Dictionary* (1764) Voltaire eulogized Confucius: "I have read his books with attention; I have made extracts from them; I have never found in them anything but the purest morality, without the slightest tinge of charlatanism." Elsewhere he wrote no less enthusiastically: "The happiest period, and the one most worthy of respect which there has ever been on this earth, was the one which followed his laws."[9]

Reflecting the relativistic spirit of the period, Orientalism continued to thrive in new literary genres—the mock-spy sketch and the Oriental tale. Here, at least, China claimed no monopoly, sharing popularity with other Oriental countries. In 1704 *Arabian Nights* became available in English, inspiring many imitations. In 1721 Montesquieu's *Persian Letters* appeared, and five years later Swift sent his ever-roaming Gulliver to Japan, among other Oriental countries. Goldsmith, in his *Citizen of the World* (1762), created the imaginary Chinese philosopher Lien Chi Altangi as a device to satirize English customs and manners. In this field Voltaire also proved to be an old hand. Besides his Oriental tales, such as "Zadig" and "The Good Brahmin," he wrote *Candide* (1759). Given his enthusiasm about China, it is curious that he let his much-suffering hero settle near Constantinople. But *The Orphan of China* (1755), which he adapted from a translation of the Yuan drama, was as much Chinese as it was neoclassical.[10]

Arthur O. Lovejoy suggested that this Chinese vogue, with its accent on irregularity, undermined the classical tradition and helped pave the way for Romanticism;[11] it was India, however, that fascinated European Romantics as they came to discover it through the pioneering efforts of

18

Sanskrit scholars. (The East India Company had been active since 1600, securing English leadership in this area.) In 1785 Charles Wilkins brought out his translation of the *Bhagavad-Gita*, the first Sanskrit work ever to be rendered in English. During the same decade Sir William Jones, a great pioneer of Sanskrit studies and comparative philology, also brought out, among other translations, the English versions of the *Laws of Menu* and Kalidasa's dramatic masterpiece *Shakuntala*. These works, along with those of another great Indologist, H. T. Colebrooke, found avid readers in England and America—Emerson and Thoreau among them. (Upon reading a German translation of Jones's *Shakuntala*, Goethe wrote a poetic homage to the Indian dramatist, as well as his prologue to *Faust*. His *West-Eastern Divan*, a series of lyrics inspired by a study of Persian poetry, appeared in 1819.)

In the meantime, the German poet and philosopher Friedrich von Schlegel, having learned Sanskrit while detained in Paris during the Napoleonic Wars, published *On the Language and Wisdom of the Indians* (1808), as H. G. Rawlinson put it, "the most important event of its kind since the rediscovery of the treasures of classical Greek literature at the Renaissance."[12] Sanskrit poetry, thus made available, inspired Schiller, Heine, and others. Similarly, Indian philosophy impressed German Transcendentalists. Schopenhauer, who independently came to know the *Upanishads*, declared: "That incomparable book stirs the spirit to the very depths of the soul. From every sentence deep, original, and sublime thoughts arise, and the whole is pervaded by a high and holy and earnest spirit. Indian air surrounds us, and original thoughts of kindred spirits. And oh, how thoroughly is the mind here washed clean of all early engrafted Jewish superstitions, and of all philosophy that cringes before these superstitions!" And once again referring to the *Upanishads* he concluded: "It has been the solace of my life, it will be the solace of my death."[13] Here Schopenhauer was speaking of his personal response to India, and at the same time he was also speaking for many of his contemporary intellectuals.

Turning to England, we can only conjecture to what extent the Orient, through Germany, influenced Coleridge, Carlyle, and other English Romantics. There seemed to be much of India in Wordsworth and Shelley, especially in their pantheism. The Orient was more visible in Landor's *Gebir* (1798), Southey's *Thalaba* (1801) and *Curse of Kehama* (1810), and Moore's *Lalla Rookh* (1817), all of which exploited the current vogue. No exception was Byron, who not only wrote his Turkish poems *Giaour* and *The Bride of Abydos* but also said in 1813 with his usual shrewdness: "Stick to the East; the oracle, Stael, told me it was the only poetical policy. The North, South, and West have all been exhausted.''[14] This trend eventually culminated in Fitzgerald's *Rubáiyát* of Omar Khayyám (1859) and Arnold's *Light of Asia* (1879), two of the best-known works that caught the changing mood of the Victorian world.

During the second half of the nineteenth century Europe's image of the Orient expanded beyond China, finally absorbing Japan. With Japan's emergence on the international scene, Orientalism reached its outermost limits—an outcome anticipated since Marco Polo's account of Japan as a veritable El Dorado. Now the Japanese vogue began to excite Europe.[15] Unlike the Chinese vogue of the previous century, however, it had little to do with religion or philosophy; it was basically aesthetic. Gauthier, the Goncourt brothers, and Zola, among others, prized their collections of Japanese *objets d'art*. Edmond de Goncourt wrote monographs on the Japanese artists Utamaro and Hokusai. Popular Japanese color prints came as a revelation to Toulouse-Lautrec and other French artists, as it did to Whistler, an American living in Europe. In music there were Gilbert and Sullivan's *Mikado* (1885) and Puccini's *Madame Butterfly* (1904). And in literature Loti and Hearn both brought Japan closer to the Western audience. Without Fenollosa, another American, Yeats could not have written his Noh plays; nor could Pound have become the kind of poet he was.

Although Orientalism completed its cycle with Japan, the outermost East, there are no signs that it has been exhausted. Quite the contrary. Pound's interest in China may remind us of that of the eighteenth-century *philosophes*, and Eliot's interest in India, while much more restrained, is just as enduring as Pound's. The Orient still looms large in the works of Conrad, Forster, Claudel, Hesse, and Huxley. At one time or another it touched a number of unlikely writers, such as Strindberg, Mann, Malraux, Orwell, Brecht, and Greene. Moreover, the Orient now ranges from Japan to Burma, from China to India. Involving so many different writers and so many different trends, modern Orientalism defies any hasty attempt to find a general pattern in its manifestations, the kind of pattern which characterized the Orientalism of previous periods and centuries. All that can be said for the moment is that it is vitally alive.

As an offshoot of European Orientalism, America's response to the Orient has shown the same general pattern of steady expansion, allowing for its own peculiar circumstances. The early Puritans were perhaps too preoccupied with the immediate business of settling in the New World to share fully the growing European interest in the Orient. Exclusive in religious conviction and parochial in cultural taste as they were, they nonetheless became conscious of the idea of the Orient. Anne Bradstreet wrote of her husband's love, which she prized more than ''all the riches that the East doth hold.'' And Cotton Mather, true to his reputation as a Puritan intellectual, displayed a vision capable of extending beyond Europe, encompassing the whole range of the Orient, from Persia to India to Japan.

In the eighteenth century, however, the Orient came closer to America, whose response began to deviate in a significant way from that of Europe. Such was the case with Franklin and with Jefferson, both acknowledged sons of the Enlightenment. Franklin knew Sir William Jones personally, wrote ''An Arabian Tale''—about a Mohammedan hermit pondering the mystery of Providence—and apparently entertained the notion of reincarnation, as his own epitaph suggests. But as might be expected, it was China, Confucian China, that engaged his fertile mind. In 1749 he urged George Whitefield to continue preaching among the greatest. ''On this principle,'' Franklin explained, ''Confucius, the famous Eastern reformer, proceeded. When he saw his country sunk in vice, and wickedness of all kinds triumphant, he applied himself first to the grandees; and having, by his doctrine, won *them* to the cause of virtue, the commons followed in multitude. The mode has a wonderful influence on mankind; and there are numbers who, perhaps, fear less the being in hell, than out of the fashion. Our most western reformations began with the ignorant mob; and when numbers of them were gained, interest and party views drew in the wise and great.''[16] He compared both methods only to stress his point: the double advantage of using them together for speedier reforms. In 1784 Franklin again referred to China, expressing his dislike of establishing ranks of nobility: ''Thus among the Chinese, the most ancient, and from long Experience the wisest of Nations, honour does not *descend*, but *ascends*. If a man from his Learning, his Wisdom, or his Valour, is promoted by the Emperor to the rank of Mandarin, his Parents are immediately entitled to all the same Ceremonies of Respect from the People, that are establish'd as due to the Mandarin himself; on the supposition that it must have been owing to the Education, Instruction, and good Examples afforded him by his Parents, that he was rendered capable of serving the Public.''[17] His argument was that, whereas the ascending honor is useful to the state, the descending honor benefits only those offspring who have no share in obtaining it. It was typical Franklin.

Jefferson, too, was interested in Sir William Jones's legal works and proud to possess a copy of his *Shakuntala*. (It is worth noting that Sir William's sympathy with the American cause of liberty won him many friends on this side of the Atlantic, and this in turn helped draw them to the Orient.[18]) For his proposed educational system as ''the key-stone of the arch of our government,'' Jefferson may have consulted the Chinese examination system.[19] One of the principal architects of the new republic,

21

he set his heart on opening the trade route to the Orient, and it was said that to this end he commissioned the expedition of Lewis and Clark (1803–6), which marked the beginning of the westward movement. Indeed, this notion of a passage to the Orient was "one of the ruling conceptions of American thought about the West," as Henry Nash Smith pointed out, and obsessed many of the champions of western expansion.[20]

Already manifest in Franklin and Jefferson was this sense of America as a historic experiment—a sense of determination to search far and wide, to appropriate anything and everything useful, even from the Orient, in order to make a success of their common undertaking, the creation of a new nation, a new civilization which would inherit the world. If this pioneering spirit characterized the American response to the Orient, it also distinguished the cycle of American Orientalism from that of its European parent. After all, America was a New World, discovered as Columbus searched for a passage to India, a climactic moment in the westward course of human civilization. In this respect Americans were certainly "a new race of men whose labours and posterity will one day cause great changes in the world," as Crèvecoeur observed prophetically in 1782. "Americans," he further pointed out, "are the western pilgrims, who are carrying along with them that great mass of arts, sciences, vigour, and industry which began long since in the east; they will finish the great circle."[21] Take, for instance, the Transcendentalists. Emerson, Alcott, Thoreau, and Whitman all shared one thing in common: an openness toward the Orient. To that extent they were a part of the overall Romantic Movement. What was unique about their response, however, was the total absence of literary exoticism and cultural dilettantism. At once existential and mythical, they responded to the Orient as a mandate of history, as a matter of birthright. Whatever separate paths they pursued, it was the Orient that helped clarify their sense of direction. By translating Columbus's passage to the Orient into a symbolic return to the source of light, the source of life, they all set a singularly American pattern of Orientalism for ensuing generations to follow.

PART ONE

ONE

Emerson

Past attempts to define the New England Transcendental movement have been too belletristic, too parochial to do justice to the collective dreams of that remarkable generation. What we need now is a larger perspective—for it was more than a literary movement, more than a religious movement—a perspective capable of accommodating the wide range of endeavors the generation undertook, from the *Dial* to the Transcendental Club, from Brook Farm, Fruitlands, to antislavery activities. In short, New England Transcendentalism was a cultural revolution which completed the long process initiated by the Founding Fathers of the Republic and, going back even farther, by the band of Puritans aboard the *Mayflower* in search of a new haven that would promise a freer, fuller, and more satisfactory way of life.

A new haven, a new country, and a new culture—it is this vision of a Brave New World that set the whole generation afire. Looking back at the period 1820–40, Emerson wrote in "Historic Notes of Life and Letters in New England":

> The key to the period appeared to be that the mind had become aware of itself. Men grew reflective and intellectual. There was a new consciousness. The former generations acted under the belief that a shining social prosperity was the beatitude of man and sacrificed uniformly the citizen to the state. The modern mind believed that the nation existed for the individual, for the guardianship and education of every man. This idea, roughly written in revolutions and national movements, in the mind of the philosopher had far more precision; the individual is the world.

No wonder the era has been called the American Renaissance.[1]

Awakening to its own possibilities, the generation eagerly turned to the world at large for nourishment, inspiration, and guidance: to Coleridge, Wordsworth, and Carlyle in England; to Kant, Jacobi, Fichte, Schelling, Goethe, and Richter in Germany; to Montaigne, George Sand, Mme de Staël, and Cousin in France; to Swedenborg in Scandinavia; to Plato and his Alexandrian followers in the classical world; and even to the Orient. It seems as though provincial New England had suddenly decided to go "cosmopolitan," ready to absorb whatever might stimulate its *élan vital*. What saved it from being torn asunder by these divers forces from the four quarters of the world was its growing conviction that it was heir to the whole world. Here again it was Emerson who best represented this generation by gathering all these forces in his person. To be sure, he was its most articulate spokesman, as his friend Alcott put it, "the master-mind of our country and time."[2]

Ralph Waldo Emerson's Orientalism is a subject which has been treated repeatedly and is now well worn. Throughout his writings Oriental deities, sages and saints, religious and literary classics appear familiarly, as familiarly as their Western counterparts. His voluminous journals abound in Oriental references and allusions, not to mention his annual reading lists, which often include Oriental books. Some of his poems, such as "Brahma," "Maia," and "Hamatreya," and also some of his essays, such as "The Over-Soul," "Compensation," "Illusions," and "Fate," are often cited as the incontestable proofs of his saturation with the Orient. And then there is his preface to the American edition of Saadi's *Gulistan*. For good reason Emerson has been regarded as the first Orientalist, and indeed the Orientalist *par excellence*, of American literature.

Emerson's interest in the Orient was no secret to his contemporaries. We have only to recall the controversy stirred by the magazine publication of his poem "Brahma." Soon after Emerson's death, W. T. Harris remarked on this aspect of his thought: "He delights in the all-absorbing unity of the Brahman, in all-renouncing ethics of the Chinese and Persian, in the measureless images of the Arabian and Hindoo poets." Some Indian scholars went further, claiming his soul, as when Protap Chunder Mozoomdar concluded his memorial tribute: "Yes, Emerson had all the wisdom and spirituality of the Brahmans. Brahmanism is an acquirement, a state of being rather than a creed. In whomsoever the eternal Brahma breathed his unquenchable fire, he was the Brahman. And in this sense Emerson was the best of Brahmans." There were others, of course, who flatly rejected such an extravagant claim. Among them, John Jay Chapman retorted: "The East added nothing to Emerson, but gave him a few trappings of speech."[3]

Another generation had to pass before two sober, scholarly assessments appeared: F. I. Carpenter's *Emerson and Asia* (1930) and Arthur Christy's *Orient in American Transcendentalism* (1932). While covering the whole range of Asian traditions which interested Emerson, from Arabian literature to Indian philosophy and from Persian poetry to Confucian ethics, Carpenter concentrated on his debts to the wisdom of the Brahmans. Emerson's early interest in Plato, Carpenter suggested, led him to the

Neoplatonists, notably Plotinus, and then on to Brahmanism. That is, Emerson reached India by way of Neoplatonism, which was "the fusion of Greek Platonism with a mysticism brought from the Orient by way of Alexandria." Even so, Carpenter further suggested, he became "an Orientalist in earnest" only in 1845,[4] which means that the Orient came much too late to play a direct role in shaping Emerson's philosophy. Christy, on the other hand, stressed the contemporary intellectual milieu which stimulated Orientalism in England and America. As he surveyed various Oriental traditions in terms of Emerson's readings, he found Confucian influences in his ethical writings and Persian influences in his poetry. Emerson's doctrines, especially those of the Over-Soul, Compensation, and Illusion, he related to the corresponding Hindu doctrines of Brahman, karma, and maya.[5] Christy thus agreed with Carpenter about the primacy of India in Emerson's Orientalism.

Since their publications in the early 1930s, *Emerson and Asia* and *The Orient in American Transcendentalism* have become standard works, exerting a significant impact on subsequent Emerson scholarship. Stephen Whicher's *Freedom and Fate* (1953), for instance, dramatized Emerson's inner life with its two crises, one from 1830 to 1832 and the other from 1838 to 1844, during which Emerson the Transcendentalist turned into Emerson the humanist. Although the Orient had played no part in his Transcendentalism, it did help him face his humanistic period, Whicher argued. And in dating Emerson's Oriental readings he merely reiterated his authorities: "As Carpenter and Christy have shown, Emerson's readings in Buddhism did not begin to 'take' until nearly 1846; the frequency of references after that indicates the depth of their influence then on his thought."[6]

This later dating of Emerson's Oriental readings did not go unchallenged, however. Questioning the current view, some Indian scholars suggested that Emerson's exposure to the Orient, especially to India, well preceded the publication of his essay *Nature*. Based on his early readings of contemporary magazine articles on Indian subjects, Man M. Singh argued that at the age of eighteen Emerson was already an Orientalist.[7] More recently, Kamal K. Shukla and J. P. Rao Rayapati have also argued the case along similar lines, in spite of their varying conclusions.[8] Supporting these attempts to date Emerson's exposure early in life was Kenneth Walter Cameron's edition of "Indian Superstition," the poem Emerson composed as an assignment for the Harvard College Exhibition of 1821. By analyzing the text and outlining contemporary Orientalism at Harvard and in Massachusetts, Cameron proved that Emerson's interest in India began much earlier than was generally believed.[9]

In the meantime there have been new attempts to reexamine Emerson's thought from a broader Oriental perspective, specifically in terms of Taoism and Zen Buddhism, both of which have in recent years been gaining popularity in the West. In his seminal study Carpenter wrote: "It is striking that he [Emerson] never seems to have come in contact with Taoism—a philosophy which would doubtless have been more congenial to him than that of Confucius." In this Carpenter was not alone. Lin Yutang also, noting some parallel insights of both Laotzu and Emerson, suggested that their epigrams "can be better understood through an understanding of the transcendentalism" of both. Citing Emerson along with the Taoist commentator Chuangtzu, Lin declared: "For the above Emersonian paradoxes, the reader will be able to find exact, and sometimes verbal, parallels in the selections from Chuangtse. Emerson's two essays, 'Circles' and 'The Over-soul,' are completely Taoist, and one appreciates them better after reading the relativity of opposites: 'One man's beauty is another's ugliness; one man's wisdom, another's folly.' And Emerson quoted some Yankee farmer speaking a typical Taoist proverb: 'Blessed be nothing. The worse things are, the better they are.' "[10]

Because of what Taoism and Zen Buddhism have in common,[11] Emerson is logically susceptible to Zen interpretations; in 1962 Van Meter Ames's *Zen and American Thought* and Robert Detweiler's "Emerson and Zen" appeared. With his general thesis that Zen has great affinities with American thought, Ames called Emerson one of its major representatives, an "American Bodhisattva." Taoism, which contributed to the development of Zen in China, would seem in his opinion closer to Emerson than Hinduism. On the other hand, Detweiler, comparing Zen and Transcendentalism, observed that Emerson came close to Zen in three respects: self-reliance, intuitional experience, and the miracle of the moment. Continuing further in this direction Donald D. Eulert found, among other things, the haiku quality in Emerson's style and thought.[12]

By now it should be clear that the Oriental influence on Emerson was primarily Indian—Indian religion and philosophy. Emerson's exposure to Arabian literature was confined largely to Persian poetry, in which he took such delight that he wrote an enthusiastic preface for Francis Gladwin's translation of Saadi's *Gulistan*. He translated Hafiz and Saadi from German, and saw in the latter his ideal poet. His love of Persian poetry, especially its spirit of abandon, made its way into his own poetic practice.[13] Although his reading was limited to the Confucian classics, Emerson understood that Confucius is central to Chinese civilization, and as he grew more interested in the problem of human conduct, he often turned to Confucius, whom he called the "glory of the nations," "sage of the

Absolute East.''[14] It is, therefore, perfectly legitimate to discuss Emerson's Orientalism in terms of Indian, Persian, and Chinese influences.

To relate Emerson to Taoism and Zen Buddhism, however, is to speak no longer of "influence" but of "parallels." Although Emerson read some Buddhist works, he knew nothing about Zen, much less about haiku poetry, for both were as yet unheard of in the contemporary West. As for Taoism, there is no evidence that he ever heard of it or its founder, Laotzu, much less that he read the *Tao Te Ching* and Chuangtzu's commentaries.[15]

The extent of "influence" is usually measured in terms of reading; thus has Emerson's Orientalism been studied. And yet we often seem to forget his warnings: "It is the necessity of my nature to shed all influences" and "Shake off from your shoes the dust of Europe and Asia."[16] These statements, paradoxical as they may sound, ring true, considering Emerson's personal habit of reading. His was a special, creative way of reading, which he recommended in "The American Scholar." A lifelong practitioner of this art of creative reading, Emerson read books "for the lustres" they could offer[17]—for confirmation of those intimations in which his mind was singularly rich. And these intimations in time matured into parallels, even influences. As Alcott said, Emerson "found himself there," in those books he read.[18]

There is little doubt that this reading habit was dictated by the peculiar quality of Emerson's mind. Introverted and introspective, Emerson was never an egotistical narcissist who saw his own shadow everywhere. As Alcott noted once again, there was something tender, almost feminine about Emerson.[19] His was a receptive nature full of "wise passiveness."[20] Well aware of his own nature, he, in effect, strove to cultivate it through his reading, one of his most valued areas of experience. "For good reading," wrote Emerson, "there must be, of course, a yielding, sometimes entire, but always some yielding to the book. Then the reader is refreshed with a new atmosphere and foreign habits." By yielding he could absorb or let himself be absorbed into whatever he was reading. Emerson reminded himself not to read too critically, lest it interfere with this slow process of absorption. With this in mind he also advised: "Keep a thing by you seven years, and you shall find use for it. You will never waste knowledge." "We form no guess, at the time of receiving a thought, of its comparative value."[21] (Hence he called his journals his savings bank.) His was the kind of mind on which no experience, small or large, was wasted.

Everything indicates that Emerson matured slowly.[22] Far from being precocious, he was a slow learner who had to take his time. His Orientalism also developed slowly in its early stages. When the young Emerson wrote down in his journal Professor Everett's eloquence: "All tends to the mysterious east,"[23] we might expect him to have turned into an all-out Orientalist. Such was not the case, however, as his college exhibition poem, "Indian Superstition," indicates. The gist of this poetic exercise is that India, though long infested with political corruption and religious superstition, will eventually restore its old glory of learning with the aid of the American spirit of freedom. There is little that suggests Emerson's later love of India. Rather, we find a proud lover of democracy and freedom, upholding America as superior to the erstwhile "Queen of the East," now dishonored in universal misery. What characterizes the poem as a whole is the young poet's mixed reaction to India, a strange mixture of fascination and aversion.[24]

This pattern of fascination and aversion, attraction and resistance, was evident in his developing concept of God. Emerson started with the traditional Christian notion of individual souls as unique and of God as a Person; yet, through his reading, he became intrigued by the old Pythagorean doctrine of *anima mundi*, "into which the Soul of the individual was absorbed and afterwards emanated again."[25] With this question of absorption-emanation continuing to haunt him, Emerson once again observed that moral law sanctions the Platonic notion that the individual soul is "but an emanation from the Abyss of Deity, and about to return whence it flowed." Upon returning from his trip to Florida, he wrote in his journal for October 1827: "There prevailed anciently the opinion that the human mind was a portion of the Divinity, separated for a time from the infinite mind, and when life was closed, reabsorbed into the Soul of the world; or, as it was represented by a lively image, Death was but the breaking of a vial of water in the ocean. But this portion of the Divine mind in childhood and youth they thought was yet pure as it was from God and yet untainted by the impurities of this world. There was much truth in the beautiful theory."[26]

Whether or not Emerson owed what was to be his doctrine of the Over-Soul to the Greek sources, he at last came close to the Hindu concept of Atman and Brahman. In any case this notion of absorption-emanation did undermine his inherited Christian notion of God as a Person. Soon after having been admitted to the Divinity School, Emerson wrote to his Aunt Mary: "Anthropomorphism is, or has been, a bugbear of a word, and yet it wraps up in its long syllables a sound and noble doctrine."[27] Somewhat defensive, he reassured himself of the basis upon which to rest his cherished belief in the personality of God. By 1830, however, he had ceased to conceive of God as a Person. God, he wrote, is "the individual's own soul carried out to perfection," or "the substratum of all souls.''[28] Still, the question persisted until after the publication of *Nature*. As late as 1837, Emerson kept at the familiar question: ''But is God a person?'' His answer was: ''No, that is a contradiction; the personality of God. A person is finite personality, is finiteness.'' And in the following year he wrote again: ''I say, that I cannot find, when I explore my own consciousness, any truth in saying that God is a person, but the reverse. I feel that there is some profanation in saying, He is personal. To represent him as an individual is to shut him out of my consciousness.''[29] From then on, the term *God* began to be taken over by his doctrine of the Over-Soul, newly coined to accommodate his twin notions: the absorption-emanation of the individual soul and the impersonality of God.

Whether the doctrine of the Over-Soul derived from the Greek or the Indian sources remains a moot question in Emerson studies, the kind of question almost impossible to settle, given the subtle and complex quality of Emerson's mind. The fact is that it took twenty years for these ideas to mature. This long and slow process of maturation resulted from Emerson's groping efforts to discover his own being by shedding or shaking off all sorts of conventional notions he had inherited. His reading was his way of unlearning what he had learned. On this matter Emerson and Alcott saw eye to eye, as the latter said: ''The Oriental Scriptures, we agree, are to be given to the people along with the Hebrew books, as a means of freeing their faith from the Christian superstitions.''[30]

Emerson pursued this process of self-liberation as he outgrew his cherished religious and philosophical notions, and at last he found his own consciousness, his own mind, which was now to serve as his guide. He would accept whatever his consciousness accepted and reject whatever it rejected. Neither metaphysical nor theological, his approach would be psychological. Although he continued to entertain a few doctrines of his own—those of life, polarity, use, and the like—they were never meant to be dogmas, but remained tentative, experimental, and pragmatic.[31] ''At bottom he had no doctrine at all,'' as George Santayana pointed out.[32]

Oriental religion and philosophy were peculiarly well suited to a mind such as Emerson's, and this point cannot be overemphasized. The Orient, with all its diverse traditions, produced what Emerson called ''the *first* philosophy, that of mind,'' which stressed not so much systems and dogmas for their own sake as the wisdom of life. Religion was philosophy, and philosophy was religion, that is, in the traditional Orient. Because of this constant merging of religion and philosophy, the Orient had a special appeal to Emerson, who lamented their ''unhappy divorce.''[33] In search of the wisdom of life, Oriental religious philosophy or philosophical religion is concerned primarily with the individual's authentic experience as its starting point; it seeks knowledge not for information but for transformation, because the latter alone ensures liberation in that it aims at release via enlightenment rather than salvation via faith.[34] Such a religion of liberation was most congenial to Emerson, who needed to shed all influences in order to discover his original nature whole and intact.

Furthermore, Oriental religion tends toward mysticism as it insists on the one in many, the many in one, and thus the ultimate unity of the universe.[35] A monistic world view, embracing all levels of human experience, it would eminently qualify for what Emerson called the philosophy of identity. In this mysticism he found the identity of all religions. As he stated in 1836, "This is the effervescence and result of all religions; this is what remains at the core of each, when all forms are taken away. This is the Law of Laws, Vedas, Zoroaster, Koran, golden verses of Pythagoras, Bible, Confucius." If, as Emerson said in 1839, the perception of identity is "a good mercury of the progress of the mind," it also signaled the enormous distance he had traveled since setting out for the mysterious East. And this philosophy of identity was what his so-called Master Key finally unlocked for him.[36]

Speaking of the young Emerson, Christy wrote: "He turned both inward and Eastward"[37]—an apt comment on Emerson's twofold journey of self-discovery. It is a journey he could perhaps have undertaken alone, without those "lustres" from the Orient, but there is no doubt that they helped him see his way more clearly and keep his progress steadier and more confident.[38]

On June 10, 1835 Emerson wrote in his journal: "I endeavor to announce the laws of the First Philosophy. . . . Every one of these propositions resembles a great circle in astronomy. No matter in what direction it be drawn, it contains the whole sphere."[39] Needless to say, he was referring to his essay *Nature*, whose publication in the following year turned out to be a momentous event in the history of American literature. A sort of Transcendental manifesto, it was highly programmatic in its attempt to integrate, or rather reintegrate God and man, mind and matter once and for all—on the ground of nature. Their reintegration is possible, Emerson believed, because nature is their common matrix.

In upholding nature as an ideal norm Emerson was voicing the thought shared by the Romantics, such as Wordsworth, Coleridge, Carlyle, Schelling, and Goethe, all of whom he read in his particular way. But the reintegration had to be completed with his doctrine of identity, and this doctrine of identity had in turn to be authenticated by his own perception, his own experience, which was now the final authority for Emerson. Take, for instance, his ecstasy in the woods: "Standing on the bare ground—my head bathed by the blithe air and uplifted into infinite space—*all mean egotism vanishes. I become a transparent eyeball; I am nothing; I see all; the currents of the Universal Being circulate through me; I am part or parcel of God''* (italics added). Just before this passage Emerson also wrote: ''In the woods, we return to reason and faith. There I feel that nothing can befall me in life—no disgrace, no calamity (leaving me my eyes), which nature cannot repair.''[40] Whether in the woods or at the common, the experience points to the same kind of fearful ecstasy. More than anything else, Emerson valued this kind of experience, to which he referred variously as ''a certain wondering light,'' ''certain moments,'' and ''a certain brief experience,''[41] for these mystical experiences, no matter how rare and transitory, assured him of the truth of universal identity. As he noted: ''Every man has had one or two moments of extraordinary experience, has met his soul, has thought of something which he never afterwards forgot, and which revised all his speech, and moulded all his forms of thought.''[42]

Later in the same essay Emerson spelled out his view thus: ''The world proceeds from the same spirit as the body of man. It is a remoter and inferior incarnation of God, a projection of God in the unconscious. But it differs from the body in one important respect. It is not, like that, now subjected to the human will. Its serene order is inviolable by us. It is, therefore, to us, the present expositor of the divine mind. It is a fixed point whereby we may measure our departure. As we degenerate, the contrast between us and our house is more evident. We are as much strangers in nature as we are aliens from God.'' In this scheme God, having already discarded His anthropomorphic image, stands on the verge of merging with the Universal Mind, the Over-Soul; by reabsorbing God nature becomes divine once again, serving as the ultimate norm, authority, and source. Hence Emerson's advice: Study nature. Not only does its constancy indicate the extent of man's deviation from his original wholeness, which is Emerson's way of saying that man did indeed fall from the Garden of Eden, but its divinity helps him restore his own. So in those privileged moments of mystical ecstasy we do realize our original relation to the universe.

Emerson's doctrine of nature, however, while sustaining his overall outlook on life, underwent a deepening process—as is apparent in ''The Method of Nature'' (1841) and ''Nature'' (1844)—by accepting growth as the central fact of nature. In this process Emerson came close to science (as we know, he embraced evolutionism without qualms) and at the same time to the Orient. After all, the term *Brahman* derived from the Sanskrit root *brih-*, ''grow,'' and the term *Tao* can best be understood in terms of ''growing.''[43] Emerson's doctrine of nature does indeed resemble the Taoist doctrine of nature as man's ideal norm. As Huston Smith noted, the term *Tao* has a threefold meaning: transcendental as the way of ultimate reality; immanent as the way of the universe; and practical as the way of life.[44] As Emerson's doctrine of the Over-Soul corresponds to the first meaning of Tao, so does his doctrine of nature contain the second and third meanings. And if Taoism points to nature as the ultimate norm embodying its mode of operation *"wei wu wei"*—"creative quietitude" in Smith's translation[45]—it is certainly not far from Emerson's doctrine of nature as the foundation of his philosophy. In "Country Life" (1858), one of his later essays, Emerson wrote: "Nature is vast and strong, but as soon as man knows himself as its interpreter, knows that Nature and he are from one source, and that he, when humble and obedient, is nearer to the source, then all things fly into place, then is there a rider to the horse, an organized will, then Nature has a lord." All this is profoundly Taoistic. Even the last passage, with its hint of the familiar catchword "Conquest of Nature," is not objectionable since what it means is: Obey nature if you wish to use her.

It is this doctrine of use that helped Emerson deal with the age-old question of good and evil, not by confronting it in a conventional way but rather by using it for the soul's growth. As he said in the essay "Experience," "life is no dialectics." In other words, life is not a problem calling for a logical solution but an experience to be used for attaining a new perspective. This essentially pragmatic attitude also enabled Emerson to deal with his dilemma of Reason and Understanding, the ideal and the real. He once confessed in frustration: "A believer in Unity, a seer of Unity, I yet behold two." His task was not to reject the ideal for the real or to reject the real for the ideal, but to domesticate the ideal in the real, or rather to accommodate both in life. The task, though a slow process, resulted in his doctrine of double consciousness which accepted man's double nature, an earthbound creature capable of partaking in the ideal. *"Dualism,"* wrote Emerson in 1851, "I see but one key to the mysteries of human condition, but one solution to the old knots of fate, freedom and foreknowledge; the propounding, namely, of the double consciousness."[46]

In insisting on man's bipolarity as the basis of his unity, this doctrine is undoubtedly Transcendental. It was, as shall be seen, the very mode of perception subscribed to by Thoreau and Whitman, even by Melville and Poe in their Transcendental moments.[47] With Emerson, it was no mere doctrine; it was an article of faith he attempted to live by. His success in the attempt was borne out by Lowell's lines: "A Greek head on right Yankee shoulders, whose range / Has Olympus for one pole, for t'other the Exchange" and "So perfect a balance there is in his mind." He was not only deeply committed to the spiritual but also involved with the mundane, as his biographers chronicled.

Emerson seemed full of contradictions, aloof and passionate at the same time. One Emerson spoke of the death of his son Waldo as "a beautiful estate—no more," and another Emerson spoke of his wife Ellen's death: "There is one birth, and one baptism, and one first love."[48] These apparent contradictions were resolved in his doctrine of double consciousness. In his essay "The Tragic" (1844) Emerson wrote: "He has seen but half the universe who never has been shown the House of Pain." In pointing out pain as a fact of life he sounded authentic because he spoke from experience, not parroting, say, the Buddhist belief that suffering is the first law of life. Yet Emerson went beyond this tragic view of life when he declared in the same essay: "All sorrow dwells in a low region. It is superficial; for the most part fantastic, or in the appearance and not in things. Tragedy is in the eye of the observer, and not in the heart of the sufferer." Emerson did not deny the existence of pain as a phenomenon, as a human experience. His point was simply that pain does not belong to the upper region of the Reason, that is, there is no tragedy in Heaven. In that journal entry of March 19, 1835 describing his ecstatic experience in the woods he referred to Ellen's death: "Yet when she was taken from me, the air was still sweet, the sun was not taken from my firmament, and however sore was that particular loss, I still felt that it was particular."[49] In 1848, when returning to the *Bhagavad-Gita*, he had every reason to call it "the first of books,"[50] for he found his doctrine of double consciousness confirmed in the dialogue between Arjuna and Krishna, an attempt to reconcile heaven and earth in terms of man's binary nature. When Emerson, in "Natural History of Intellect," insisted on the kind of detachment which "consists in seeing it under a new order, not under a personal but a universal light," he really was speaking the same language Krishna uses, describing his divine vision:

My face is equal
To all creation,
Loving no one
Nor hating any.[51]

Emerson's doctrine of double consciousness is a Transcendental affirmation of man's duality, of his capacity to experience the absolute and the relative, heaven and earth, eternity and time. And if, said Emerson, the "invincible tendency of the mind" is to unify, unification is assured in those moments of mystical ecstasy. They all attest to the inexhaustible richness of every moment, the only point where eternity and time intersect. "A moment is a concentrated eternity: All that ever was is now."[52] Here is Emerson's doctrine of the Here and the Now, which he expounded with increasing emphasis.

This doctrine also had a long history, starting with his characteristic declaration of 1825: "My business is with the living." Even in his early sermons Emerson stressed the *carpe diem* theme. "One well spent hour is the proper seed of heaven and eternity." Again, "The great art which religion teaches, is the art of conducting life well, not only in a view to future well-being, but in the very best manner, if there were no future state."[53] In urging his congregation to let their religion have a direct bearing on their daily conduct, Emerson was perhaps paraphrasing the biblical command not to be anxious about the morrow. But then the question he asked himself was "How shall I live?" Emerson's response was his doctrine of the Here and the Now, and once again he turned to nature as his model. As he wrote in his essay "Circles": "In nature every moment is new; the past is always swallowed and forgotten; the coming only is sacred."

All of Emerson's doctrines thus culminated in the art of living well. And this art of living succeeds or fails, depending upon what one may make of every new, unique, and therefore unrepeatable moment—a fact which makes living forever experimental, as experimental as every artistic creation. Every moment must be lived for its own sake. To express this secret of living Emerson often resorted to his favorite metaphor, skating. As he wrote in the essay "Experience":

> To fill the hour—that is happiness; to fill the hour and leave no crevice for a repentance or an approval. We live amid surfaces, and the true art of life is to skate well on them. Under the oldest mouldiest conventions a man of native force prospers just as well as in the newest world, and that by skill of handling and treatment. He can take hold anywhere. Life itself is a mixture of power and form, and will not bear the least excess of either. To finish the moment, to find the journey's end in every step of the road, to live the greatest number of good hours, is wisdom. It is not the part of men, but of fanatics, or of mathematicians if you will, to say that, the shortness of life considered, it is not worth caring whether for so short a duration we were sprawling in want or sitting high. Since our office is with moments, let us husband them. Five minutes of to-day are worth as much to me as five minutes in the next millennium. Let us be poised, and wise, and our own, today.

Even in "Fate," one of his later essays, he returned to the same metaphor: "But learn to skate, and the ice will give you a graceful, sweet, and poetic motion."[54]

This art of skating, Emerson believed, provides the only means of gliding across the bottomless depths of reality, of a life stripped of all its illusions of comfort and security. When this means of survival becomes the art of life, necessity turns into freedom. "We think," says D. T. Suzuki, "Nature is brute fact, entirely governed by the laws of absolute necessity; and there is no room for freedom to enter here. But Zen would say that Nature's necessity and Man's freedom are not such divergent ideas as we imagine, but that necessity is freedom, and freedom is necessity."[55] In reconciling freedom and necessity in terms of his doctrine of the Here and the Now, Emerson came singularly close to Zen and its insistence on the miracle of the moment.

Once having turned to his so-called mysterious East, "learning's El Dorado," Emerson never lost this sense of mystery.[56] No doubt it was one of those romantic dreams peculiar to youth, yet this one Emerson never outgrew, as is apparent in "mine Asia," a term of endearment he used for his wife Lidian.[57] On the contrary, the Orient continued to grow in his mind and in time became one of the main sources of his intellectual and spiritual nourishment.

Therefore, Emerson regretted all the more the absence of Orientalism from the intellectual life of England, as he duly noted in his journal for August 1849, two years after his second trip there.[58] And in *English Traits* (1856) he voiced the same criticism: "By the law of contraries, I look for an irresistible taste for Orientalism in Britain. For a self-conceited modish life, made up of trifles, clinging to a corporeal civilization, hating ideas, there is no remedy like the Oriental largeness. That astonishes and disconcerts English decorum. For once, there is thunder it never heard, light it never saw, and power which trifles with time and space." He then called attention to the impassioned appeal Warren Hastings had made to his own countrymen while recommending a translation of the *Bhavagad-Gita*. This passage, coming after a survey of contemporary English letters, was obviously intended to serve as Emerson's friendly advice for the English people to heed if they were to revitalize their decaying culture. Since Oriental religion and philosophy, such as the *Gita* exemplified, had liberated him from cultural provincialism, Emerson was convinced the remedy would work with them, too.

Yet the advice came from a deeper source, his Transcendental conviction that the world is one.[59] And by "the law of contraries" he further believed that East and West are complementary and therefore need each other in making the world truly whole again. This complementary relationship of East and West he implied in his domestic term "mine Asia." If the essay "Plato" represented the culmination of Emerson's lifelong interest in the Greek philosopher, it also represented the culmination of his Orientalism. Emerson's failure to distinguish the Platonic and the Neoplatonic has been noted, but the fact remains that in Plato Emerson saw the ideal philosopher. In Plato, too, he "found himself," to use Alcott's words. Upholding his own doctrine of identity, Emerson wrote:

> Meantime, Plato, in Egypt and in Eastern pilgrimages, imbibed the ideas of one Deity, in which all things are absorbed. The unity of Asia and the detail of Europe; the infinitude of the Asiatic soul and the defining, result-loving, machine-making, surface-seeking, opera-going Europe—Plato came to join, and, by contact, to enhance the energy of each. The excellence of Europe and Asia are in his brain. Metaphysics and natural philosophy expressed the genius of Europe; he substructs the religion of Asia, as the base.

Finally, according to Emerson, Plato was "a balanced soul" which absorbed East and West.

In this essay Emerson not only contrasted East and West but also suggested their complementariness. One of the earliest modern pioneers in this area, he anticipated the recent trend in world philosophy. With a greater breadth of philosophical and religious knowledge, with a greater sense of expectation and urgency, an increasing number of thinkers have in recent years called for a universal synthesis along lines similar to Emerson's.[60] Plato suggested to Emerson the necessity, and the possibility, of such a synthesis—a synthesis which insisted on the balanced world as well as the balanced soul. Just as he called Plato "a balanced soul" for uniting East and West, so we are justified in calling him balanced for the same reason.

This is not to say, however, that East and West merely coexist in Emerson's thought, for they are no longer separable and distinguishable, having been fused in his slow process of self-discovery. Attesting best to this happy fusion is "Brahma," a short poem of four stanzas, sixteen lines which Emerson wrote at the height of his intellectual and artistic maturity. No other American poem of comparable length has elicited so much critical discussion as this one:

> If the red slayer think he slays,
>   Or if the slain think he is slain,
> They know not well the subtle ways
>   I keep, and pass, and turn again.
>
> Far or forgot to me is near;
>   Shadow and sunlight are the same;
> The vanished gods to me appear;
>   And one to me are shame and fame.

They reckon ill who leave me out;
  When me they fly, I am the wings;
I am the doubter and the doubt,
  And I the hymn the Brahmin sings.

The strong gods pine for my abode,
  And pine in vain the sacred Seven;
But thou, meek lover of the good!
  Find me, and turn thy back on heaven.

Ever since its publication of 1857 in the first number of the *Atlantic Monthly*, critics have been sharply divided over the poem's meaning. Some, taking the cue from its title, have read it in terms of Hinduism. For its probable source they have searched the whole range of Indian religious classics from the *Upanishads* to the *Laws of Menu*, from the *Vishnu Purana* to the *Gita*. While disagreeing over Emerson's ultimate source, these critics have all pointed out that the idea expressed therein is unmistakably Indian.[61] Other critics, despite its obvious Oriental imagery, have read the poem strictly as an expression of Christian thought, whether it be New England Puritanism or older theological traditions.[62]

As for Emerson himself, he initially called the poem "Song of the Soul," and, much amused over the puzzlement it excited, suggested that Jehovah in place of Brahma would do just as well. His scattered journal entries clearly indicate that the poem was intended not so much to render any particular religious position as to articulate once and for all personal insights that had matured over the years—his mystical vision of identity—in the kind of imagery he thought most fitting, and in the kind of paradox he needed to express the inexpressible.[63]

In this sense "Brahma" should not be treated as a poetic curio. As Christy pointed out long ago, it is "the crystallization of Emerson's Oriental interests," "the high water mark of that flood of Orientalism which inundated Concord during the second quarter of the last century and baffled the practical Yankee villagers."[64] At the same time it is more than that. More than Indian, more than Christian, it is Emersonian in that the poem epitomizes Emerson's art and thought. This he knew instinctively. Indifferent to the ridicule and parody it had suffered at the hands of critics, indifferent also to his publishers' well-meaning counsel, Emerson insisted that "Brahma" be retained in his *Selected Poems* of 1876, whatever else had to go.

TWO

Thoreau

In his memorial essay "Thoreau," Emerson had a few unforgettable things to say about his younger friend: that he was "a speaker and actor of the truth"; that "no truer American existed than Thoreau." Emerson also noted his love of nature, his "rare, tender and absolute religion," and, ruefully, his lack of ambition. Emerson prefaced the essay with observations on Thoreau's problem of vocation, or rather his refusal to choose one: "He was a protestant. He declined to give up his large ambition of knowledge and action for any narrow craft or profession, aiming at a much more comprehensive calling, the art of living well." Indeed, the art of living well—a Transcendental obsession. Here Emerson revealed himself as much as he did Thoreau, for the problem of vocation was also the young Emerson's, as we know.[1] Here Emerson, better than anyone else, defined the quintessence of Thoreau: he was an artist in the largest sense of the term, an artist of life—according to Jung, the most distinguished and rarest of all human endeavors.[2]

Although a memorable tribute, the essay, especially its alleged emphasis on Thoreau's asceticism, offended many of his admirers. Yet even these die-hard Thoreau partisans who have done much to disengage their man from Emerson could not change the fact of their friendship. Not only did Thoreau consciously and unconsciously appropriate some of his mentor's personal mannerisms, but his writings echoed many of Emerson's doctrines—those of nature, double consciousness, the Here and the Now—so often that we may indeed be tempted to accept Lowell's charge that Thoreau's works were but strawberries from Emerson's own garden. But we had better remember their friend Alcott's comparison of them in terms of wine and venison.[3] After all, they were two separate individuals, Transcendental individualists at that.

Temperamentally, Thoreau was direct, intense, uncompromising, and often petulant. In his memorial essay Emerson said: "There was somewhat military in his nature not to be subdued, always manly and able, but rarely tender, as if he did not feel himself except in opposition. He wanted a fallacy to expose, a blunder to pillory, I may say required a little sense of victory, a roll of the drum, to call his powers into full exercise." Emerson's choice of a military metaphor is apt in view of Thoreau's own

40

statement: "Whatever your sex or position, life is a battle. . . . Men were born to succeed, not to fail."[4] Intellectually, too, Thoreau was quite different from Emerson. As his friend William Ellery Channing observed, metaphysics was his aversion.[5] That is, Thoreau's mode of thinking was remarkably free from metaphysical abstraction. Although Emerson had a small number of working doctrines, Thoreau had even fewer. These similarities and differences Emerson himself noted in 1863, two years after Thoreau's death: "In reading him, I find the same thought, the same spirit that is in me, but he takes a step beyond, and illustrates by excellent images that which I shall have conveyed in a sleepy generality."[6]

In many ways Emerson prepared the way for Thoreau; and most certainly he came to the Orient through Emerson. Once initiated, however, Thoreau took his characteristic plunge, without hesitation, without vacillation. That pattern of fascination and aversion which characterized the young Emerson's attitude toward the Orient was altogether absent in Thoreau. In 1841, after reading the *Laws of Menu*, Thoreau wrote: "When my imagination travels eastward and backward to those remote years of the gods, I seem to draw near to the habitation of the morning, and the dawn at length has a place." The following year he again wrote: "When I look back eastward over the world, it seems to be all in repose. Arabia, Persia, Hindostan are the land of contemplation. . . . Was not Asia mapped in my brain before it was in any geography? In my brain is the Sanskrit which contains the history of the primitive times." And in 1850 he also wrote of the *Vedas*: "One wise sentence is worth the state of Massachusetts many times over."[7] From these scattered utterances we can gather a few things. First, his favorite metaphors, "dawn" and "morning," recall Emerson's "To the East again, where the dawn is";[8] second, Thoreau's land of contemplation echoes Emerson's contrast of East and West; and third, Thoreau's journey "eastward and backward" stands in contrast to Emerson's "inward and Eastward," in Christy's phrase.[9] It would seem no mere coincidence that Thoreau's friendship with Emerson, his intellectual development, and his interest in the Orient all coalesced in the 1840s, perhaps the most crucial decade of his career.

While making no mention of Thoreau's Orientalism as such, Emerson, in his memorial essay, spoke of his younger friend's patience: "He knew how to sit immovable, a part of the rock he rested on, until the bird, the reptile, the fish, which had retired from him, should come back and resume its habits, nay, moved by curiosity, should come to him and watch him." With this habit of his in mind, Moncure D. Conway, who knew Thoreau and the Hindus, likened his friend to a yogi. With specific reference to Thoreau at Walden, he wrote: "Like the pious Yogi, so long motionless whilst gazing on the sun that knotty plants encircled his neck and the cast snake-skin his loins, and the birds built their nests on his shoulders, this poet and naturalist, by equal consecration, became a part of the field and forest."[10] Thoreau very likely owed this well-known habit of contemplation to his Oriental reading. Whatever the case, Channing, a close companion of Thoreau for years, wrote about his Oriental reading: "His East Indian studies never went deep, technically: into the philological discussion as to whether ab, ab, is Sanscrit, or 'What is Om?' he entered not. But no one relished the Bhagvat Geeta better, or the good sentences from the Vishnu Purana. He loved the Laws of Menu, the Vishnu Sarma, Saadi, and similar books."[11]

A more eloquent witness is Thoreau's own writings. Besides those "Ethnical Scriptures" which he culled from Hindu, Buddhist, and Confucian books for the *Dial*,[12] and *The Transmigration of the Seven Brahmans*, a translation he made from a French anthology of Hindu literature, there are *A Week on the Concord and Merrimack Rivers*, *Walden*, and his voluminous journals, all of which bespeak his interest in the Orient.

In spite of this, some modern scholars doubted Thoreau's debts to the Orient. Mark Van Doren, for one, observed that "the total influence of Oriental philosophy upon Thoreau was neither broad nor profound," and that he "took figures and sentences, not ideas, from his Oriental reading."[13] But most Thoreau scholars have taken the matter more seriously. Although there were several early attempts to relate Thoreau to India, Christy was the first to present a full-scale study of his Orientalism. In *The Orient in American Transcendentalism* (1932) Christy, noting Emerson's role in the young Thoreau's initiation into Oriental thought, pointed out that his interest, like his mentor's, centered on India, and that he also "used the Hindus to bolster his own thought." While critical of Confucian ceremonialism, Hindu asceticism, and Hindu pessimism, Thoreau learned from the Hindus, Chinese, and Persians a mystical love of nature. Interpreting his Walden experiment from this particular perspective, Christy concluded that Thoreau's ultimate place in American literature is "with the mystics."[14] Christy's has ever since been accepted as the most authoritative work on Thoreau's Orientalism—the standard opinion to which all later scholars turned, whether in agreement or disagreement.

Thoreau's Orientalism, thus established as a significant aspect of his thought, has continued to interest scholars. In *The Shores of America* (1958) Sherman Paul suggested that Emerson's renewed interest in the Orient was no doubt stimulating to Thoreau just as Thoreau's interest was stimulating to Emerson. But "judging by the use that was made of Oriental literature Thoreau was probably more indebted to it than Emerson. For although Emerson found the Hindu doctrines of the soul and karma con-

genial to his thought, Thoreau captured their spirit, their insistence on
behavior and the way of life.'' Paul went on to single out the *Gita* and
especially the *Laws of Menu* as the most important Oriental works that
Thoreau read at the time he was wrestling with the problems of vocation
and the conduct of life.[15] More recently William Bysshe Stein, in a series
of exegeses, has explored Thoreau's Indian connections. In ''The Hindu
Matrix of *Walden*: The King's Son,'' for instance, he analyzed in detail
the second chapter of *Walden* in terms of the *Samkhya Karika*, specifically
its parable of the king's son. ''Structurally,'' argued Stein, ''it culminates
his references to the Hindu sources of the inspiration that shapes his
experience on Walden Pond. His choice of this particular text from *The
Samkhya Karika* beautifully displays his sophisticated understanding of
Indian religious thought.''[16]

As with Emerson, there has been another trend relating Thoreau to Zen
and Taoist traditions. His mystical love of nature, more than anything
else, made him susceptible of Zen interpretations. D. T. Suzuki likened
him to the Japanese poets Saigyo and Basho, while noting the ''cosmic
feeling'' in *Walden*. Van Meter Ames examined him from the same perspective: ''an intense man rather than a complete one.''[17] Especially
suggestive was his chapter title ''Thoreau: Taoist in America.'' (This shift
of emphasis from Zen to Taoism is not at all surprising in view of their
early alliance in ancient China.)

Ames, incidentally, was not the first to notice the Taoist aspect of
Thoreau. Lin Yutang wrote in 1937: ''Thoreau is the most Chinese of all
American authors in his entire view of life. . . . I could translate passages
of Thoreau into my own language and pass them off as original writing by
a Chinese poet, without raising any suspicion.'' Again, in 1948, he specifically noted Thoreau's affinity with Taoist though. Comparing Laotzu
and Chuangtzu in a Taoist perspective, Lin declared that Chuangtzu was
''like Thoreau, with the ruggedness and hardness and impatience of an
individualist.''[18] Sherman Paul made a similar suggestion: ''One wonders
what Thoreau would have done with Lao-tzu's *Tao Tê Ching*'' and ''the
central idea of an organic conduct of life—that whether or not one sub-
scribes to Spirit, one must go with the current of life, not against it. Here
the wisdom of Lao-tzu would have supported Thoreau.'' Lyman V. Cady,
having investigated Confucian quotations in *Walden*, ventured the same
view. While concluding that Thoreau for the most part used Confucian
materials in a non-Confucian way, Cady could not but note the striking
affinity between Thoreau's and Taoist writings: their nature mysticism,
their love of the simple and primitive, their distaste for conventions and
governmental interference, and their repeated use of paradox. ''If,'' concluded Cady, ''Thoreau could find materials to illustrate his ideas from

the Confucian literature, with which on the whole he had no deep affinity, how joyously and literally would he have brought forth the rich ore to be found in the deep lode of Chinese Naturism in the writing of Lao-Chuang school of the Tao had he but known of them!''[19]

In his recent study of this subject T. Y. Chen was more specific and positive. Observing that in style and thought Thoreau was close to Laotzu and even closer to Chuangtzu, Chen examined the similarity between Thoreau's parable of the artist of Kouroo and Chuangtzu's of the royal carpenter Ch'ing. As for the question of Thoreau's access to Taoist writings, Chen went so far as to single out M. G. Pauthier's French translation of the *Tao Te Ching* as Thoreau's probable source. As he noted: "Although my findings are sufficient to convince myself that Thoreau must, in one way or another, have been acquainted with Taoism, the spirit of scholarship keeps me from making an absolutely positive conclusion."[20]

As with Emerson, we are confronted with a peculiar situation. Significant parallels abound between Thoreau's and Taoist thought, yet there is no evidence whatever that Thoreau had even heard of Taoism. Nowhere did Thoreau, or Emerson, mention Taoism, Laotzu, or Chuangtzu. Knowing as we do their habit of recording their current interests and reading, we must assume for the time being that neither man had any knowledge of Taoism. Until someone comes up with the missing link, the similarities between Thoreau and Taoism, however remarkable, should be treated as ''parallels'' rather than influences.''[21]

Thoreau's first book, *A Week on the Concord and Merrimack Rivers* (1849), was no ordinary travelog. More than an account of the two-week-long boat excursion he and his brother, John, took in the early fall of 1839, it was really an autobiography. In order to write it Thoreau ransacked his own journals covering the period 1837–48; into the book's weekly cycle he compressed not just those two weeks but rather those eleven years, the first phase of his career. Emerging as a Transcendental voyager of life or a Transcendental artist of life, Thoreau touched on a wide range of topics close to his heart—from art to life, from poetry to science, from Chaucer to Goethe, and from East to West—as might be expected of one for whom reading and thinking occupied a significant portion of life.

True to Thoreau's boasting that he was "better acquainted with those [scriptures] of the Hindus, the Chinese, and the Persians than of the Hebrews," *A Week* reveals a great number of Oriental references and allusions. Buddha, Confucius, and the Persian poets Hafiz and Saadi mingle with Indian dance and Chinese tea—all reflective of the author's widening horizons. The "Monday" chapter in particular is Oriental, centering on his reading of Hindu classics—the *Vedas*, *Vishnu Purana*, *Vishnu Sarma*, *Laws of Menu*, and *Bhagavad-Gita*, the last two of which he called "the noon-tide philosophy" of India, "the better part of our thoughts."

Judging from Thoreau's journals, the *Laws of Menu* was certainly the first Hindu book that opened his eyes to the Orient. While he was reading it during the spring and summer of 1841 Thoreau was wrestling with the problem of vocation, in particular, and with the problem of the conduct of life, in general. As Paul suggested, the *Laws of Menu* did more than any other book to shape his outlook on life.[22] And, remembering what it had done for him at the threshold of his career, Thoreau, in *A Week*, paid his tribute:

> This of Manu addresses our privacy more than most. It is a more private and familiar, and at the same time a more public and universal, word than is spoken in parlor or pulpit nowadays. As our domestic fowls are said to have their original in the wild pheasant of India, so our domestic thoughts have their prototypes in the thoughts of her philosophers. We are dabbling in the very elements of our present conventional and actual life; as if it were the primeval conventicle, where how to eat, and to drink, and to sleep, and maintain life with adequate dignity and sincerity were the questions to be decided. It is later and more intimate with us even than the advice of our nearest friends. And yet it is true for the widest horizon, and read out of doors has relation to the dim mountain line, and is native and aboriginal there. Most books belong to the house and street only, and in the fields their leaves feel very thin. They are bare and obvious, and have no halo nor haze about them. Nature lies far and fair behind them all. But this, as it proceeds from, so it addresses, what is deepest and most abiding in man. It belongs to the noontide of the day, the midsummer of the year, and after the snows have melted, and the water evaporated in the spring, still its truth speaks freshly to our experience.

A great compendium of orthodox Hindu life which details social, ritual, and religious prescriptions, the *Laws of Menu* no doubt had a special appeal for the young Thoreau, determined as he was to live his life as art.

But the *Bhagavad-Gita* elicited more than a tribute from Thoreau. As we remember, Emerson called the *Gita* "the first of books," and Alcott, in turn, called it "the best of all reading for wise men," indeed the "best of books." Emerson rediscovered the *Gita* in 1845 and Alcott was reading

it the following year.[23] Thoreau most certainly read it, too. His passage
on the *Gita*, twice as long as his tribute to the *Laws of Menu*, stands as
perhaps the most extended Transcendental reaction to this religious classic. Consisting of generous extracts and comments, the passage evinces
Thoreau's characteristic excitement of discovery. It is obvious that the
Gita meant to him something more urgent than, something quite different
from, the *Laws*.

With the statement: "The wisest conservatism is that of the Hindus,"
Thoreau begins to compare Hinduism and Christianity, or rather begins to
stress what he calls the "sublime conservatism" of Hinduism by way of
Christianity, which is "humane, practical, and, in a large sense, radical."
If the New Testament stands for pure morality, the *Gita*, "the best of the
Hindu scriptures," aspires to pure intellectuality. After quoting from
Warren Hastings's prefatory letter recommending Charles Wilkins's
English translation, Thoreau quickly turns this question of morality versus
intellectuality into that of action versus contemplation. The Oriental philosophy, says Thoreau, "only assigns their due rank respectively to Action
and Contemplation, or rather does full justice to the latter. Western philosophers have not conceived of the significance of Contemplation in their
sense." Rather than develop this into the East-West contrast as Emerson
does in his essay "Plato," Thoreau urges fellow Americans to take advantage of their New World and heed the message of the *Gita*. "*Ex
oriente lux* may still be the motto of scholars, for the Western world has
not yet derived from the East all the light which it is destined to receive
thence."[24]

The lengthy extracts from the *Gita* clearly indicate that here Thoreau is
grappling with the heart of the *Gita*, namely, Krishna's message of selfless action in terms of Hindu doctrines of work and renunciation. As
Thoreau quotes, "He who may behold as it were inaction in action, and
action in inaction, is wise amongst mankind. He is a perfect performer of
all duty." While coming so close to the heart of the *Gita*, Thoreau finds
himself ill at ease with what it seems to suggest: the primacy of contemplation over action. In response to Krishna's repeated reminder, "I am the
same to all mankind," Thoreau challenges with a series of questions:

> This teaching is not practical in the sense in which the New
> Testament is. It is not always sound sense in practice. The Brah-
> man never proposes courageously to assault evil, but patiently to
> starve it out. His active faculties are paralyzed by the idea of
> caste, of impassable limits, of destiny and the tyranny of time.
> Krishna's argument, it must be allowed, is defective. No suffi-
> cient reason is given why Arjuna should fight. Arjuna may be
> convinced, but the reader is not, for his judgment is *not* "formed

upon the speculative doctrines of the Sankhya-sastra." "Seek an asylum in wisdom alone"; but what is wisdom to a Western mind? The duty of which he speaks is an arbitrary one. When was it established? The Brahman's virtue consists in doing, not right, but arbitrary things. What is that which a man "hath to do"? What is "action"? What are the "settled functions"? What is "a man's own religion," which is so much better than another's? What is "a man's own particular calling"? What are the duties which are appointed by one's birth? It is a defense of the institution of caste, of what is called the "natural duty" of the Kshetree, or soldier, "to attach himself to the discipline," "not to flee from the field," and the like. But they who are unconcerned about the consequences of their actions are not therefore unconcerned about their actions.

Here Thoreau is going over Krishna's message once again point by point, as though trying to make sure he understands it right, and he finally comes to his own problem of reconciling contemplation and action. He puts it: "The things immediate to be done are very trivial. I could postpone them all to hear this locust sing. The most glorious fact in my experience is not anything that I have done or may any hope to do, but a transient thought, or vision, or dream which I have had. I would give all the wealth of the world, and all the deeds of all the heroes, for one true vision. But how can I communicate with the gods, who am a pencil maker on the earth, and not be insane?" He is torn between the "one true vision" he is seeking more than anything else and those multitudinous trivialities which constitute his daily life, a frustrating dilemma familiar to all Transcendentalists. As we have already seen, Emerson attempted to resolve it with his doctrine of double consciousness. To him it posed no special difficulty. By insisting that for the American scholar action is subordinate, though essential, and that knowledge itself is a form of action, he managed to neutralize their possible conflict. No such solution was acceptable to Thoreau, for he was born to act as much as to speak the truth—in Emerson's words, "a speaker and actor of the truth." Studying the *Bhagavad-Gita* made Thoreau fully aware of the fundamental pattern of his life, a creative tension between contemplation and action which was to dramatize both his subsequent writings and his career.

Although *Walden* (1854) contains nothing comparable to the *Gita* passage of *A Week*, there is still a score of Oriental references scattered throughout, side by side with those to Western classics. Most of the Chinese and Indian reference did not appear in the original version but were added later, according to J. Lyndon Shanley, probably during 1850–51.[25] Yet it has been suggested that the entire book is unmistakably Hindu or even profoundly Taoistic.

Walden, like *A Week*, is autobiographical. While compressing his two-year Walden residence into one year-long cycle, Thoreau also plundered his own journals from the period 1839–54. In every way *Walden* is a superior work. If *A Week* seems rather artificial and mechanical in its weekly progression, *Walden* is organic in structure, as organic as nature. It is a book of nature in both form and spirit. With it, Thoreau realized Emerson's doctrine of nature, his call for a book that would smell of pines.

There is something inevitable in Thoreau's having built his cabin on the woodland purchased by Emerson the previous year, for the Walden experiment was Thoreau's response to Emerson's challenge: "Why should not we also enjoy an original relation to the universe?"[26] And true to Emerson's notion of nature's circularity, Thoreau also came to see Walden as his central symbol. What could be more circular than a pond? Thoreau's experiment in living does indeed revolve around Walden, the source of life which never runs dry and promises renewal.

In the central chapter "The Ponds" Thoreau explores Walden—its topology, its ecology, its lore, and its poetry—with a Transcendental thoroughness not dissimilar to Melville's cetological discourse or Whitman's catalog method. Although there are several ponds, some larger than Walden, it is Walden on which Thoreau concentrates, not just because he happens to be living there but also because it is representative. "Lying between the earth and the heavens, it partakes of the color of both." Reminding us that Walden is as sacred as the Ganges, he proposes to call it "God's Drop," as Emerson once did.[27] More than anything else, it is the purity of Walden that appeals to Thoreau:

> Though I am acquainted with most of the ponds within a dozen miles of this centre, I do not know a third of this pure and well-like character. Successive nations perchance have drank at, admired, and fathomed it, and passed away, and still its water is green and pellucid as ever. Not an intermitting spring! Perhaps on that morning when Adam and Eve were driven out of Eden Walden Pond was already in existence, and even then breaking up in a gentle spring rain accompanied with mist and a southerly wind, and covered with myriads of ducks and geese, which had not heard of the fall, when still such pure lakes sufficed them. Even then it had commenced to rise and fall, and had clarified its waters and colored them of the hue they now wear, and obtained a patent of heaven to be the only Walden Pond in the world and

distiller of celestial dews. Who knows in how many unremembered nations' literatures this has been the Castalian Fountain? or what nymphs presided over it in the Golden Age? It is a gem of the first water which Concord wears in her coronet.

Walden, with all its creatures, has remained pure; man alone fell. Walden, Thoreau's symbol of nature, serves as what Emerson calls "the present expositor of the divine mind—"a fixed point whereby we may measure our departure."[28] But we need not despair of our departure, of our fall, for Walden can restore our original purity through nature's capacity for self-renewal; by partaking of nature's process we can recover our lost purity, our lost innocence. Thoreau's daily bathing in Walden is a rite whereby he attempts to approximate the whole process and identify with nature itself. He finally resorts to poetry:

> It is no dream of mine,
> To ornament a line;
> I cannot come nearer to God and Heaven
> Than I live to Walden even.
> I am its stony shore,
> And the breeze that passes o'er;
> In the hollow of my hand
> Are its water and its sand,
> And its deepest resort
> Lies high in my thought.

Man's original innocence is recovered in such a moment of mystical identification with nature. Yet this restatement of the Transcendental vision has a personal ring. As Thoreau progresses through the chapter "The Ponds," he becomes more poetic, intimate, and personal. "Why, here is Walden, the same woodland lake that I discovered so many years ago," he writes, referring to his first childhood glimpse of Walden. Thoreau did not just go to live by Walden; he returned to Walden. By returning to Walden, he realized his wholeness. Indeed, *Walden* is Taoistic, profoundly so, because nature, water, and infancy comprise three primal symbols of Taoism.[29]

In keeping with his initial promise to report on the result of his Walden experiment, Thoreau sets forth what he has learned: "If one advances confidently in the direction of his dreams, and endeavors to live the life he has imagined, he will meet with a success unexpected in common hours." Lest his readers should miss his point, Thoreau then turns to his fable of the artist of Kouroo for illustration:

There was an artist in the city of Kouroo who was disposed to strive after perfection. One day it came into his mind to make a staff. Having considered that in an imperfect work time is an ingredient, but into a perfect work time does not enter, he said to himself, It shall be perfect in all respects, though I should do nothing else in my life. He proceeded instantly to the forest for wood, being resolved that it should not be made of unsuitable material; and as he searched for and rejected stick after stick, his friends gradually deserted him, for they grew old in their works and died, but he grew not older by a moment. His singleness of purpose and resolution, and his elevated piety, endowed him, without his knowledge, with perennial youth. As he made no compromise with Time, Time kept out of his way, and only sighed at a distance because he could not overcome him. Before he had found a stick in all respects suitable the city of Kouroo was a hoary ruin, and he sat on one of its mounds to peel the stick. Before he had given it the proper shape the dynasty of the Candahars was at an end, and with the point of the stick he wrote the name of the last of that race in the sand, and then resumed his work. By the time he had smoothed and polished the staff Kalpa was no longer the pole-star; and ere he had put on the ferule and the head adorned with precious stones, Brahma had awoke and slumbered many times. But why do I stay to mention these things? When the finishing stroke was put to his work, it suddenly expanded before the eyes of the astonished artist into the fairest of all the creations of Brahma. He had made a new system in making a staff, a world with full and fair proportions; in which, though the old cities and dynasties had passed away, fairer and more glorious ones had taken their places. And now he saw by the heap of shavings still fresh at his feet, that, for him and his work, the former lapse of time had been an illusion, and that no more time had elapsed than is required for a single scintillation from the brain of Brahma to fall on and inflame the tinder of a mortal brain. The material was pure, and his art was pure; how could the result be other than wonderful?

This fable signals the climax of *Walden*. At this climactic moment Thoreau has no other recourse than the parable or fable, man's oldest literary form embodying his vision of life. This fable of the artist of Kouroo is perhaps the most fitting symbol of Thoreau as an artist of life.

In this fable Christy found "a veiled suggestion of the reason [Thoreau] went to Walden, of his indifference to criticism and the social standards of his time"—"an allegory of Thoreau's own life, of his love for the Beautiful, the True, and the Good, and of his search for Perfection." Paul also noted: "In order to affirm the open prospects of the eternal present, he had fashioned *Walden*, as he himself had lived, after the example of the artist of the city of Kouroo." While ascribing the place name, the staff, the pure spirit of the artist, etc., to the *Laws of Menu* and the *Gita*, Paul nonetheless pointed out that it is "obviously his own work, full of revisions, with his characteristic pun ['lapse' and 'elapsed'], with transparent personal allusions such as the desertion of his friends."[30]

The fable, which was apparently added to the fifth version of *Walden*, is Thoreau's own creation.[31] There is so much of Thoreau in it. As early as September 17, 1839, he had written in his journal under the heading "The Wise Rest":

> Nature never makes haste; her systems revolve at an even pace. The bud swells imperceptively, without hurry or confusion, as though the short spring days were an eternity. . . . Why, then, should man hasten as if anything less than eternity were allotted for the least deed? Let him consume never so many aeons, so that he go about the meanest task well, though it be but the paring of his nails. . . . The wise man is restful, never restless or impatient. . . . As the wise is not anxious that time wait for him, neither does he wait for it.

And in his journal for July 16, 1851: "It is the love of virtue makes us young ever. That is the fountain of youth, the very aspiration after the perfect."[32] These and many other passages in his writings figure forth an ample portrait of Thoreau, who demanded of himself nothing less than perfection. He was also quick to appreciate virtue in others: when he saw a stonecutter splitting Westford granite for fence posts ("I suspect that these tools are hoary with age, as with granite dust"), when he called George Minott "the most poetical farmer" he knew ("He does nothing with haste and drudgery, but as if he loved it. He makes the most of his labor, and takes infinite satisfaction in every part of it"), when he praised Reuben Rice for mastering "that rare art of living" ("he lives so thoroughly and satisfactorily to himself. . . . His life has been not a failure but a success"), and when he quoted M. Miles in approval: "I have handled a good deal of wood, and I think that I understand the *philosophy* of it."[33] These examples bring to mind Chuangtzu's master artisans who have attained Tao, the great secret common to all their arts and trades.[34]

And yet the fact remains that to illustrate his own secret, the secret he had learned from the Walden experiment in particular and from life in general, Thoreau turned to his beloved India. Kouroo, the city he chose for his ideal artist, was a perfect setting in that it was the battleground celebrated in the *Mahabharata*, the very site of the *Gita*'s immortal dialogue between Arjuna and Krishna. After all, the *Gita* best articulates the essence of Indian religious wisdom that whoever remains faithful to his true nature and performs his duty to perfection can win eternity while on earth.[35] If the fable is thoroughly Indian, it is also Thoreauvian. In this fable Thoreau's vision and Indian wisdom are so well blended that they are no longer distinguishable. Once again, India came to help him, in the shaping of this fable symbolic of his career as an artist of life.

In the chapter "Solitude" of *Walden* Thoreau wrote:

> By a conscious effort of the mind we can stand aloof from actions and their consequences; and all things, good and bad, go by us like a torrent. We are not wholly involved in Nature. I may be either the driftwood in the stream, or Indra in the sky looking down on it. I *may* be affected by a theatrical exhibition; on the other hand, I *may not* be affected by an actual event which appears to concern me much more. I only know myself as a human entity; the scene, so to speak, of thoughts and affections; and am sensible of a certain doubleness by which I can stand as remote from myself as from another. However intense my experience, I am conscious of the presence and criticism of a part of me, which, as it were, is not a part of me, but spectator, sharing no experience, but taking note of it; and that is no more I than it is you. When the play, it may be the tragedy, of life is over, the spectator goes his way. It was a kind of fiction, a work of the imagination only, so far as he was concerned. This doubleness may easily make us poor neighbors and friends sometimes.

This passage has elicited various comments. Edward Rose, for instance, called such a mental condition "a kind of healthy schizophrenia which only a Romantic Transcendentalist would be able to survive." Walter Harding noted Thoreau's constant awareness that "he was never able to lose himself completely in any emotion"—"an interesting psychological problem."[36] But the experience Thoreau is speaking of is typically Upanishadic. The passage reminds us of a parable in the *Upanishads*, the parable of two birds—inseparable friends—clinging to the same tree, one eating the sweet fruit and the other merely looking on—in Tagore's words, "an image of the mutual relationship of the infinite being and the finite self." As Tagore further explains: "The delight of the bird which looks on is great, for it is a pure and free delight. There are both of these birds in man himself, the objective one with its business of life, the subjective one with its disinterested joy of vision."[37] The *Gita* itself is in a way the dialogue between the infinite (Krishna) and the finite (Arjuna). Thoreau must have read in the thirteenth chapter of Wilkins's translation of the *Gita*, on the so-called field and its knower, about "that superior being, who is called Maheswar, the great God, the most high spirit, who in this body is the observer, the director, the protector, the partaker," and also the following passage: "Some men, by meditation, behold, with the mind, the spirit within themselves; others, according to the discipline of the *Sānkhyă* (contemplative doctrines), and the discipline which is called *Kărmă-yŏg* (practical doctrines); others again, who are not acquainted with this, but have heard it from others, attend to it. But even these, who act but from the report of others, pass beyond the gulf of death."[38] Interesting in this connection is Thoreau's "conscious effort of the mind," which attests to his awareness that these various disciplines were meant to yoke the finite and the infinite, and also to his practice of his own kind of yoga. After all, Thoreau himself confided to H. G. O. Blake in 1849: "To some extent, and at rare intervals, even I am a yogi."[39] And all this may recall Emerson's journal entry of 1837:

> The victory is won as soon as any Soul has learned always to take sides with Reason against himself; to transfer his Me from his person, his name, his interest, back upon Truth and Justice, so that when he is disgraced and defeated and fretted and disheartened, and wasted by nothings, he bears it well, never one instant relaxing his watchfulness, and, as soon as he can get a respite from the insults or the sadness, records all these phenomena, pierces their beauty as phenomena, and, like a God, oversees himself. . . . Keep the habit of the observer, and, as fast as you can, break off your association with your personality and identify yourself with the Universe. Be a football to Time and Chance, the more kicks, the better, so that you inspect the whole game and know its uttermost law.[40]

Thoreau's "conscious effort of the mind" and Emerson's art of disengagement, it is clear, shared the same mystical source, the Transcendental vision of bipolarity.[41]

Thoreau's conscious doubleness informs *Walden* as a whole. True to its Transcendental double vision, the book concerns the village of Concord as much as it does Walden Pond. As is evident in the arrangement of its chapters, the village and the country, civilization and nature alternate. This structural pattern is altogether justified in and necessitated by Thoreau's overall intent: "Is it impossible to combine the hardiness of these savages with the intellectualness of the civilized man?" Or as he relates his own experience in the chapter "Higher Laws": "I found in myself, and still find, an instinct toward a higher, or, as it is named, spiritual life, as do most men, and another toward a primitive rank and savage one, and I reverence them both. I love the wild not less than the good.'' With specific reference to Thoreau's doubleness, Richard Drinnon commented: ''It was one of his great achievements to go beyond the polarities of 'Civilization and Barbarism'—alternatively attractive poles which drew most of Thoreau's contemporaries helplessly back and forth like metal particles—to come close to a creative fusion.''[42]

As we recall, Thoreau first articulated this tension in *A Week*, in terms of his personal dilemma of action versus contemplation, Christianity versus Hinduism, and the Occident versus the Orient. This dilemma constituted the most characteristic pattern of his career, as when he wrote of the intimate tension between art and life: ''My life has been the poem I would have writ, / But I could not both live and utter it.'' Thoreau had to both live and utter it, and he did just that. In this sense, his overnight stay in jail was no mere episode, but marked a crucial turning point in his career. The incident occurred during his residence at Walden, as if to restrain Thoreau from running to one extreme, contemplation, and to complete his experiment in what might be called the Transcendental double vision, an experiment which resulted in ''Civil Disobedience'' and *Walden*.

This familiar pattern still persisted in his post-Walden years, both in his career and in his writings. On the one hand, Thoreau made exploratory trips to Cape Cod and the Maine woods, farther into primitive nature; on the other, he became deeply involved with society over the issue of slavery. Accordingly, his writings also fell into two groups: travelogs, such as *Cape Cod* and *The Maine Woods*, and antislavery polemics, such as ''Slavery in Massachusetts.'' (In neither group does the Orient appear any longer, understandably enough.) If the one portrayed Thoreau as a man of disengagement, detachment, and contemplation, the other portrayed him as a man of involvement, commitment, and action. In this creative tension lay the secret of Thoreau's success as an artist of life.[43] And he defined and strove to master this tension with the aid of India, what he called *Ex oriente lux*.

THREE

Whitman

According to the Transcendental genealogy, Emerson sired Whitman just as he sired Thoreau. In 1957 Gay Wilson Allen cited critical consensus that Emerson was "the one single greatest influence on Whitman during the years when he was planning and writing the first two or three editions of *Leaves of Grass*." And, more recently, calling theirs "the most important literary relationship in our poetic history," H. H. Waggoner showed how seriously Whitman regarded himself as "*the* Emersonian poet."[1] Their kinship was amply borne out by those striking similarities between Emerson's essay "The Poet" and Whitman's 1855 preface. No wonder Emerson so enthusiastically greeted Whitman as his long-awaited ideal American poet when he read through the twelve untitled poems in the first edition of *Leaves of Grass*. No wonder Whitman responded in kind, addressing him as "Master," and years later summed up their relationship: "I was simmering, simmering, and simmering; Emerson brought me to a boil."[2]

For this reason one might suggest that Whitman's interest in the Orient, like Thoreau's, was one of the legacies he received from Emerson. But such a suggestion, however tempting, has no supporting evidence. Whatever the case, Emerson was the first to recognize Whitman's Orientalism by describing *Leaves of Grass* as "a remarkable mixture" of the *Bhaga-vad-Gita* and the *New York Herald*.[3] Thoreau, too, found it "wonderfully like the Orientals," and in fact asked Whitman if he had read them.[4] Although on that particular occasion he responded: "No: tell me about them," Whitman himself, in "A Backward Glance O'er Travel'd Roads" (1888), admitted his reading of "the ancient Hindoo poems"—along with Homer, Dante, Shakespeare, and other classics—as "some further embryonic facts of *Leaves of Grass*." This self-contradiction on Whitman's part has not helped his students; nor has it discouraged them from venturing their own opinions on the matter.

As early as 1866 Moncure D. Conway, who also noted Thoreau's Orientalism, did suggest, in spite of Whitman's early denial, that the Orient was as vital to his thought as to that of the Transcendentalists. In 1897 William N. Guthrie was more specific in suggesting that Whitman and Emerson would be better understood in terms of Hinduism, especially

55

the *Gita*. And in 1906 Edward Carpenter, an English mystic-poet and Orientalist who had met Whitman, noted parallels between Whitman and the *Upanishads* and concluded that *Leaves of Grass* sprang from the same root, the root of all known mystical traditions the world over. These and other early commentators by and large confined themselves to enumerating Whitman's similarities and parallels to Indian thought rather than studying Indian influences on his work, thus setting a certain pattern for modern scholars to follow.

Among the first modern scholars to refine this pattern was Dorothy F. Mercer. In her doctoral dissertation, "*Leaves of Grass* and the *Bhagavad Gita*: A Comparative Study" (1933), instead of designating the *Gita* as one of Whitman's actual sources, she merely suggested that it may have been. She detected their basic similarity in the doctrine of the self.[5] More recently, Malcolm Cowley found Whitman's outlook more Oriental than Occidental—which is in his view "extraordinary" inasmuch as the poet "seems to have known little or nothing about Indian philosophy," much less to have read the *Gita* and the *Upanishads*. Using "Song of Myself" as his evidence, Cowley suggested that Whitman's mystical experience belonged to the so-called perennial philosophy, like those of Indian saints and mystics.[6]

All this reminds us of Tagore, who once said: "no American poet has caught the Oriental spirit so well as Whitman."[7] In fact, Indians have regarded him as a kindred spirit. In *Whitman in the Light of Vedantic Mysticism* (1964) V. K. Chari presented an in-depth study of the poet's Indian parallels. Calling his thought more Indian than Hegelian, Chari went on to suggest that his concept of self is best understood in terms of Vedantic mysticism, especially in terms of the Upanishadic and Sankara tradition. Whitman's concept of the self, which is central to his poetry, was in Chari's words "the dynamic, cosmic 'I' of the Upanishads, the *atman-brahman*—attained through a process of universalizing the 'ego,' by meditating on the universal nature of the self, its at-one-ness with the all."[8] Likewise, O. K. Nambiar, in his *Walt Whitman and Yoga* (1966), attempted to show how Whitman at times expressed views similar to the spirit of yoga, thus making *Leaves of Grass* a sort of modern Yoga guidebook.[9]

Unique in this sense is T. R. Rajasekharaiah's *Roots of Whitman's Grass* (1970). By scanning several hundred books and magazine articles on Oriental and related subjects available at New York libraries in the early 1850s, in the years up to the publication of *Leaves of Grass*, Rajasekharaiah hoped to identify the sources of Whitman's poetry. Not merely another study of his Indian parallels, it purported to dispose of all those myths which have clustered around *Leaves of Grass* and to deprive its author of his claim to originality. As Rajasekharaiah stated his case, the identity Whitman "celebrates in *Leaves of Grass* is neither a purely human being, nor an average individual, nor the typical man, nor the soul, nor the Spirit: it is a medley of all these; a robe pieced together from various dresses, gorgeous but incongruous."[10] He contended that *Leaves of Grass* is thoroughly Indian simply because it consists largely of those passages Whitman deliberately appropriated from various Indian sources—without any proper acknowledgment—in short, a case of outright plagiarism.

An examination of Whitman's Orientalism must begin with the role which the Orient, in this instance India,[11] played in the making of the first edition of *Leaves of Grass*, the matrix of all the subsequent editions. And yet there is hardly an Oriental reference in the first edition, despite what Emerson and Thoreau said.[12] To determine the extent of his Orientalism at that early stage of Whitman's career is no easy task, for he successfully carried out his own injunction to "make no quotations & reference to any other writers";[13] furthermore, his Orientalism is involved with his alleged mysticism, as already suggested in the foregoing survey. Although the same problem besets the study of Emerson and Thoreau, Whitman's case is more complicated and crucial; the question is not merely whether he had the same kind of mystical experience but whether such a mystical experience transformed him into the kind of poet he was and made *Leaves of Grass* the kind of book it is.

The problem can easily be dismissed if we agree with Rajasekharaiah that Whitman, no mystic in any sense, simply appropriated mystical passages from his Indian sources, or if we accept the poet's own disavowal of mystical experience. In "A Backward Glance" he described those crucial years prior to the publication of *Leaves of Grass*: "After years of those aims and pursuits, I found myself remaining possess'd, at the age of thirty-one to thirty-three, with a special desire and conviction. Or rather, to be quite exact, a desire that had been flitting through my previous life, or hovering on the flanks, mostly indefinite hitherto, had steadily advanced to the front, defined itself, and finally dominated everything else." Nothing here suggests any sort of mystical experience, an experience of a sudden, dramatic nature; instead, there is a long, perfectly natural process in which youthful dreams and ambitions crystallized into "a special desire and conviction."

Whitman's own description here still fails to explain the enormous gap that separates those twelve unnamed poems in the first edition from his earlier attempts, all quite conventional in form and spirit and often inept and imitative. While only three out of some twenty poems, those written in 1850,[14] anticipate typical Whitman in their free verse form, none seems to adumbrate the ecstatic song of self-discovery, the opening poem of the first edition, eventually titled "Song of Myself." Theories about Whitman's mystical experience have sought to account for this great creative leap.

Among the first to voice this theory was Dr. Richard Maurice Bucke, a Canadian psychiatrist, who knew the old Whitman intimately. In his *Cosmic Consciousness* (1901) Dr. Bucke designated Whitman as "the best, most perfect, example the world has so far had of the Cosmic Sense" because in him the faculty was most perfectly developed, because he wrote from the point of view of Cosmic Consciousness, and because he referred to its facts and phenomena more fully than any other writer, ancient or modern. Bucke dated the onset of Whitman's mystical experience in "June, probably in 1853, when he had just entered upon his thirty-fifth year." As one of his proofs he cited the "mystical experience" passage in the first edition, which begins "I mind how we lay in June. Such a transparent summer morning."[15] William James, too, in *The Varieties of Religious Experience* (1902), selected Whitman as a legitimate subject for his inquiry into mystical experience. Following Bucke, James quoted the same passage from the fifth section of "Song of Myself" as a classical expression of this sporadic type of mystical experience."[16] In *Mysticism* (1911) Evelyn Underhill also wrote that Whitman, though not one of those "pure mystics," was a type of mystical poet capable of what she called "illuminated consciousness." Indeed, according to her, Whitman "possessed in a supreme degree the permanent sense of this glory, the 'light rare, untellable, lighting the very light.' "[17]

Bucke, James, and Underhill, all acknowledged students of mysticism, seem to concur that Whitman not only had some kind of mystical experience but also incorporated it into his poetry. Whereas Bucke, James, and Underhill depended heavily on Western documents, many Whitman scholars, from Conway down to Cowley, Chari, and Nambiar, have branded his mysticism as Oriental, more specifically Hindu. Helpful in this regard is W. T. Stace's suggestion that the Indian terms *enlightenment* and *illumination* describe the experience more accurately than the traditional Western term *mysticism*.[18] It is this kind of enlightenment, illumination, or *release*, to use Heinrich Zimmer's term,[19] that sustains "Song of Myself" and *Leaves of Grass* as a whole. And this quality of Whitman's poetry must have made Emerson and Thoreau call the first edition Oriental, for at this stage the mystical and the Oriental resemble each other so closely that they are almost indistinguishable.

If Whitman's mysticism complicates his Orientalism, still another factor adds to our confusion, namely, his mode of artistic creation, which makes his Orientalism more elusive than that of Emerson and Thoreau.

Certain affinities between mysticism and artistic creation have long been suspected.[20] With Whitman they are intimately related to one another, and their intimacy is borne out by his repeated reference to his poetic vocation as "the impulse of the spirit"—his "greatest call."[21] The prophetic vision and evangelistic tone which characterize *Leaves of Grass* reflect no mere rhetoric on his part. In his prefaces and elsewhere Whitman time and again stressed the religious basis of his poetry. In his 1872 preface, "As a Strong Bird on Pinions Free," for instance, he declared: "When I commenced, years ago, elaborating the plan of my poems, and continued turning over that plan, and shifting it in my mind through many years, (from the age of twenty-eight to thirty-five,) experimenting much, and writing and abandoning much, one deep purpose underlay the others, and has underlain it and its execution ever since—and that has been the Religious purpose." For this reason he warned his readers, as he did in "A Backward Glance": "No one will get at my verses who insists upon viewing them as a literary performance, or attempt at such performance, or as aiming mainly toward art or aestheticism." His was a literary performance, and at the same time more than that, as he pronounced in *Democratic Vistas*: "The altitude of literature and poetry has always been religion—and always will be." Whitman's insistence on the fundamental identity of poetry and religion may disturb some modern critics, but it is traditional. Such an attitude still persists in the East, as is evident in the religious implications of the Indian dramatic doctrine of *rasa*, the Taoist spirit of Chinese painting and poetry, and the Zen background of Japanese haiku. Whitman's outlook would seem as Oriental as it is traditional.[22]

Whitman was no automatic writer. Whatever impressions one gets from his "barbaric yawp" are altogether superficial in view of the enormous energy, patience, and care he put into his composition. The entire process of poetic creation as Whitman practiced it, from inspiration to execution, was as deliberate as a religious ritual. Clifton Joseph Furness illustrated this process in terms of "inspiration," "meditation," "voice," and other esoteric concepts. And Whitman had his own method of composition. As Harrison S. Morris reported:

> He said an idea would strike him which, after mature thought, he would consider fit to be the "special theme" of a "piece." This he would revolve in his mind in all its phases, and finally adopt, setting it down crudely on a bit of paper,—the back of an envelope or any scrap,—which he would place in an envelope. Then he would lie in wait for any other material which might bear upon or lean toward that idea, and, as it came into his mind, he would put it on paper and place it in the same envelope. After he had quite exhausted the supply of suggestions, or had a sufficient

number to interpret the idea withal, he would interweave them in a "piece," as he called it. I asked him about the arrangement or succession of the slips, and he said, "They always fall properly into place."[23]

Whitman knew that the process could not be forced if he wanted the full cooperation of his own unconscious. There is little doubt that this peculiar writing habit had much to do with the growth and the resultant shape of *Leaves of Grass*.

All indications are that Whitman was familiar with the artistic value of the unconscious. In his essay "Poetry To-day in America—Shakspere—The Future" (1881) he wrote: "Only to the rapt vision does the seen become the prophecy of the unseen." In a lengthy footnote he mentioned two sets of will in nations and persons. While the one set operates from "explainable motives," the other set is "perhaps deep, hidden, unsuspected, yet often more potent than the first, refusing to be argued with, rising as it were out of abysses, resistlessly urging on speakers, doers, communities, unwitting to themselves—the poet to his fieriest words—the race to pursue its loftiest ideal." These two sets of will, he further pointed out, find themselves "sometimes conflicting, each operating in its sphere, combining in races or in persons, and producing strangest results." Whitman remained convinced that this second will alone, "the permanent and sovereign force," could guide America to her great destiny—"amid the dangers and defections of the present, and through all the processes of the conscious will." (The second will, as Whitman explained it, recalls Emerson's reference to the poet's "great public power" in contrast to "his privacy of power as an individual man," and his further comparison of the poet to the "divine animal" whose instinct could guide us through this world.[24]) The emergence of this second will Whitman described more fully in *Democratic Vistas*:

> There is, in sanest hours, a consciousness, a thought that rises, independent, lifted out from all else, calm, like the stars, shining eternal. This is the thought of identity—yours for you, whoever you are, as mine for me. Miracle of miracles, beyond statement, most spiritual and vaguest of earth's dreams, yet hardest basic fact, and only entrance to all facts. In such devout hours, in the midst of the significant wonders of heaven and earth (significant only because of the Me in the centre), creeds, conventions, fall away and become of no account before this simple idea. Under the luminousness of real vision, it alone takes possession, takes value. Like the shadowy dwarf in the fable, once liberated and

look'd upon, it expands over the whole earth, and spreads to the roof of heaven.

The whole passage has the authentic ring that only comes from one who actually did experience this "miracle of miracles"—"the mystical identity, the real I or Me or You," as he called it elsewhere.[25]

Leaves of Grass is a ceaseless dialogue between this real Me and its earthly partner, between those two sets of will. Whitman was fully convinced of their coexistence in himself when he said: "I cannot understand the mystery, but I am always conscious of myself as two—as my soul and I: and I reckon it is the same with all men and women."[26] Whether or not it is the same with all men and women, as he suggested, we know that it was the same with Emerson and Thoreau, judging from the former's double consciousness and the latter's conscious doubleness. If this was characteristic of the Transcendental mind, it was also a concept central to both the *Upanishads* and the *Gita*.[27]

Like his writing habit, Whitman's habit of addressing himself as a third person no doubt originated in this awareness of the double self. Furness noted Whitman's curious habit of conceiving "his writing or creative self as an identity separate from his ordinary self-conscious personality."[28] Moreover, Whitman devised a way of detaching one self from the other. As he wrote in one of his notes:

> To you. First of all prepare for study by the following self-teaching exercises. Abstract yourself from this book; realize where you are at present located, the point you stand that is now to you the centre of all. Look up overhead, think of space stretching out, think of all the unnumbered orbs wheeling safely there, invisible to us by day, some visible by night; think of the sun around which the earth revolves; the moon revolving round the earth, and accompanying it; think of the different planets belonging to our system. Spend some minutes faithfully in this exercise. Then again realize yourself upon the earth, at the particular point you now occupy. Which way stretches the north, and what country, seas, etc.? Which way the south? Which way the east? Which way the west? Seize these firmly with your mind, pass freely over immense distances. Turn your face a moment thither. Fix definitely the direction and the idea of the distances of separate sections of your own country, also of England, the Mediterranean Sea, Cape Horn, the North Pole, and such like distinct places.[29]

Once again we may recall Emerson's strategy of victory by disengagement and Thoreau's "conscious effort of the mind." Emerson's strategy was meant to reconcile the conflicting claims of the ideal and the real, the absolute and the relative; Thoreau's method was meant to resolve the tension ever present in his life between action and contemplation, and by turning this tension into creative fusion he strove to perfect his life as art. Now Whitman's method, likewise, clearly suggests the deep-seated psychological origins of his favorite devices and techniques—his soaring flight imagery and his cataloging. There is little doubt that Whitman cultivated his psychical experience as the source of his poetic creation.

Whitman's Orientalism prior to 1855 is, though apparent, hard to determine, not just because of his initial denial, not just because of his poetic genre, but because of the difficulty of detaching the Oriental from the shadowy depths of his psyche. We must remain content with those endless parallels until some new evidence becomes available. What can be said at this point is that Whitman apparently knew a great deal more about the Orient than he pretended, and that, whether the knowledge came through Emerson or other channels, the Orient functioned similarly in Whitman's creative life and in Emerson's. As it helped Emerson, the Orient, in all probability, helped Whitman define his own self and assured him of the authenticity and universality of his personal experience.

Take, for instance, "Out of the Cradle Endlessly Rocking" (1859). Admittedly one of Whitman's best poems, it has elicited various interpretations. Leo Spitzer, in a formalistic analysis, demonstrated how miraculously the traditional ode, the romantic theme of love and death, and the familiar nightingale are all transformed into something typically American and Whitmanesque.[30] Yet few would deny that the poem is profoundly personal. Although Emory Holloway, among others, suggested that it originated in the poet's own loss of love,[31] the poem focuses on the birth of Whitman the poet. It is important to see what motivates the poem itself, the little incident which turns this sensitive boy, "Cautiously peering, absorbing, translating" into a "chanter of pains and joys." It simply involves the boy's emotional reaction to the mockingbird grieving over its lost mate, and this awakening to life's drama of love and death marks his birth as a poet. Whether or not the incident actually happened to Whitman is of no special consequence. In dramatizing the birth of a poet, however, the episode certainly resembles the one surrounding Valmiki's composition of the *Ramayana*. Once, when the sage went out for a walk along the riverbank, he saw a loving pair of krauncha birds in a nearby tree. Suddenly, the male bird fell, shot by a hunter's arrow, and the female began lamenting piteously. No sooner had he cursed the hunter than Valmiki realized that his spontaneous utterance had a perfect rhythm and melody —a realization which eventually resulted in the great epic of Prince Rama and his consort, Sita.[32] The *Ramayana* is undoubtedly one of "the ancient Hindoo poems" Whitman read in preparation for the first edition of *Leaves of Grass*.[33] Whether or not he knew of this Valmiki episode in the opening sections of the *Ramayana*, the similarity between the two episodes is noteworthy in that they serve the same function, a sort of emotional catalyst to poetic composition.

Although Emerson and Thoreau found the first edition Oriental, *Leaves of Grass* did not contain anything ostensively Oriental—until "Facing West from California's Shores" appeared in the third, and "A Broadway Pageant" in the fourth edition. Celebrating the arrival of a Japanese diplomatic mission, "A Broadway Pageant" first appeared in the *New York Times* for June 27, 1860, under the title "The Errand-Bearers." When it was included as "A Broadway Pageant" in the *Drum-Taps* and finally in the fourth edition of 1867, the opening lines read:

> Over sea, hither from Niphon,
> Courteous, the Princes of Asia, swart-cheek'd princes,
> First-comers, guests, two-sworded princes,
> Lesson-giving princes, leaning back in their open barouches,
>   bared-head, impassive,
> This day they ride through Manhattan.

This parade down Broadway no doubt bestirred Whitman's pride as a poet of America, so much so that by dropping the phrase "Lesson-giving princes" from the fifth edition on, he shifted the emphasis from homage to the Orient to America's lofty role as champion of liberty.[34]

"A Broadway Pageant" is the most explicitly Oriental poem in *Leaves of Grass*; it is also the first poetic treatment of Japan by any major American poet.[35] As the poem progresses into the second section, however, something curious begins to happen:

> The Originatress comes,
> The nest of languages, the bequather of poems, the race of eld,
> Florid with blood, pensive, rapt with musings, hot with passion,
> Sultry with perfume, with ample and flowing garments,
> With sunburnt visage, with intense soul and glittering eyes,
> The race of Brahma comes.

In the poet's imagination the Japanese quickly cease to be Japanese, assuming symbolic identity. They are made to represent the Orient, specifically, India. Whitman's poetic imagination invariably turns toward India, his ultimate symbol of Asia.

This is exactly what happens in the other poem, which is short enough to be quoted in its entirety:

> Facing west from California's shores,
> Inquiring, tireless, seeking what is yet unfound,
> I, a child, very old, over waves, towards the house of maternity,
>   the land of migrations, look afar,
> Look off the shores of my Western sea, the circle almost circled;
> For starting westward from Hindustan, from the vales of
>   Kashmere,
> From Asia, from the north, from the God, the sage, and the hero,
> From the south, from the flowery peninsulas and the spice islands,
> Long having wander'd since, round the earth having wander'd,
> Now I face home again, very pleas'd and joyous,
> (But where is what I started for so long ago?
> And why is it yet unfound?)

Although Whitman never visited the West Coast, his imagination did much traveling and his mind's eye scanned the wide expanse of the Pacific. For this reason perhaps, he could easily assume the role of a wanderer representing the human race. Inasmuch as the poem originally appeared in the "Enfans d'Adam" group and the manuscript version carried the title "Hindustan, from the Western Sea," its theme is clear enough: having long wandered away from its cradle, the human race is now returning home full circle. Hindustan stands for Asia, "The house of maternity, the land of migrations"—a notion widely held at the time and still lingering in "Mother India." This westward course of civilization around the globe, it may be recalled, inspired the young Emerson to write "Indian Superstition," and here in Whitman's poem it has become pilgrimage, as Crèvecoeur predicted. In stressing the maternal and the pilgrim figures the poem calls for comparison with Poe's "To Helen." The line "Long having wander'd since, round the earth having wander'd" echoes Poe's line "The weary, way-worn wanderer." What is interesting, however, is that the theme of return, while common to both poets, lures them in opposite directions, one toward the Mediterranean and the other toward the Pacific, one toward Greece and the other toward India.[36]

In Whitman's imagination the Orient thus began to loom as a great mother figure, the source of the human race. He suggested this idea in his epithets, such as "primal Asia" (in *Democratic Vistas*) and "always the mystic Orient" (in "Poetry To-day in America"), and more fully in *Speci-*

men Days—significantly in connection with the dawn of a summer day:

> The East.—What a subject for a poem! Indeed, where else a more pregnant, more splendid one? Where one more idealistic-real, more subtle, more sensuous-delicate? The East, answering all lands, all ages, peoples; touching all senses, here, immediate, now—and yet so indescribably far off—such retrospect! The East —long-stretching—so losing itself—the orient, the gardens of Asia, the womb of history and song—forth-issuing all those strange, dim cavalcades—
>
> > Florid with blood, pensive, rapt with musings, hot with passion,
> > Sultry with perfume, with ample and flowing garments,
> > With sunburnt visage, intense soul and glittering eyes.
>
> Always the East—old, how incalculably old! And yet here the same—ours yet, fresh as a rose, to every morning, every life, to-day—and always will be.

In most of Whitman's poems, the Orient is not immediately apparent. Take, for example, "I Sit and Look Out" (1860):

> I sit and look out upon all the sorrows of the world, and upon all oppressions and shame,
> I hear secret convulsive sobs from young men at anguish with themselves, remorseful after deeds done,
> I see in low life the mother misused by her children, dying, neglected, gaunt, desperate,
> I see the wife misused by her husband, I see the treacherous seducer of young women,
> I mark the ranklings of jealousy and unrequited love attempted to be hid, I see these sights on the earth,
> I see the workings of battle, pestilence, tyranny, I see martyrs and prisoners,
> I observe a famine at sea, I observe the sailors casting lots who shall be kill'd to preserve the lives of the rest,
> I observe the slights and degradations cast by arrogant persons upon laborers, the poor, and upon negroes, and the like;
> All these—all the meanness and agony without end I sitting look out upon,
> See, hear, and am silent.

With its parallelism and reiteration, it is typically Whitman's, and yet critics have noted its Oriental quality. Gay Wilson Allen noted its "almost Brahman serenity''; V. K. Chari compared the poem to a certain passage of the *Upanishads*; and T. R. Rajasekhariah suspected that the source of Whitman's inspiration was the Hindu notion of God as ''the universal witness, who seated internally, beholds the good and ill of all.''[37] They concurred in the ''I'' of the poem, whose holy indifference and supreme detachment culminate in silence. While the poem is Upanishadic, the sense of cosmic perspective it reveals does recall the one suggested by Emerson's double consciousness and Thoreau's conscious doubleness. The ''I'' of the poem is Whitman's poetic realization of the Transcendental Emerson who said of the death of his beloved son: ''I seem to have lost a beautiful estate—no more,'' and also of the yogic Thoreau who spoke of the self, the ''spectator,'' detaching itself from the drama of life. ''I Sit and Look Out,'' though one of Whitman's minor poems, illustrates parallelism and reiteration which, together with his catalog method, constitute the principal technical resources of ''Song of Myself.'' ''I Sit and Look Out'' thus provides a close-up view of the transcendental self in action, without which ''Song of Myself'' would collapse at once.

What Whitman said of *Leaves of Grass*—''the absence, ostensively at least, of any thing like plot, or definite point or purpose in the poems''[38] —also applies in the central piece ''Song of Myself.'' Various attempts have been made to impose some sort of logic on the poem without much insight into the sense of expansion, liberation, and celebration it generates. Whitman, it should be pointed out, wrote only one volume of poems in the sense that one can write only one autobiography. Moreover, in his poetic autobiography Whitman did not have to invent any plot, for life knows no plot; it simply grows. *Leaves of Grass* did grow out of ''Song of Myself.'' If the one is the poetic autobiography of a soul, the other dramatizes that soul awakening to itself.

Accepting this momentous experience of self-awakening as mystical, critics have approached ''Song of Myself'' with varied emphases. James E. Miller, Jr., for instance, applying Underhill's Mystic Way, found there a seven-stage cycle of mystical experience. Malcolm Cowley, on the other hand, called the poem more Hindu than Christian and thereon based what he considered its nine-sequence narrative structure.[39] Whatever their differences, one thing is obvious: ''Song of Myself'' centers on the poet's mystical experience, and this experience provides universality for the poem. Whitman's own growing conviction of the universality of the experience informing his poem is apparent in the succession of titles he gave to it. Because he had no ready-made name for his experience, the poem bore no name in the first edition; the very specific title ''Poem of Walt Whitman, an American,'' which he chose for the next edition, became simpler and more individualized—simply ''Walt Whitman''—in the third edition;

and only in the seventh edition of 1881–82 did the poem acquire the current "Song of Myself"—a perfect title for the poet's universal and universalized experience. As he declared at the outset of the poem:

> I celebrate myself, and sing myself,
> And what I assume you shall assume,
> For every atom belonging to me as good belongs to you.

And at the mid-point:

> Walt Whitman, a kosmos, of Manhattan the son,
> Turbulent, fleshy, sensual, eating, drinking and breeding,
> No sentimentalist, no stander above men and women or apart
>   from them,
> No more modest than immodest.

And near the end:

> Do I contradict myself?
> Very well then I contradict myself,
> (I am large, I contain multitudes.)

"Song of Myself" is a mystical poem, not only because it resulted from the poet's mystical experience but because it concerns the mystical experience itself. And that mystical experience is Whitman's discovery of the double self, or what Underhill calls the twofold mystical consciousness, the kind of illumination often found among poets and artists.[40] To quote him again: "I cannot understand the mystery, but I am always conscious of myself as two—as my soul and I: and I reckon it is the same with all men and women." Note the casual tone of "I reckon it is the same with all men and women," as though he had thought nothing extraordinary of his own experience. To him the experience of the double self seemed ordinary—so ordinary that he denied having had any mystical experience, which is why he insisted that *Leaves of Grass* was meant to be "the Poem of average Identity," as he said in the 1876 preface: "To sing the Song of that law of average Identity, and of Yourself, consistently with the divine law of the universal, is a main intention of those 'Leaves.' "

"Song of Myself" unfolds the deepest mystery of identity, the drama of the double self, the emergence of the transcendental self out of the poet's personal self, thus enlarging itself to the limits of the world—as Whitman described it in *Democratic Vistas*: "Like the shadowy dwarf in the fable, once liberated and look'd upon, it expands over the whole earth, and spreads to the roof of heaven," and also in "Song of Myself": "I sound my barbaric yawp over the roofs of the world." Born out of Whitman's determination to describe this unfolding mystery of "average Identity" as well as he could were those devices of catalog and parallelism, his well-known trademarks. This intimate relationship between Whitman's mystical experience and his poetic method cannot be overemphasized, for it is the ultimate testimony to his integrity as man and as poet. Noting the physical basis of Whitman's mystical experience George R. Carpenter wrote:

> In this state of rapt contemplation the mind, rather out of itself than concentrated within itself, dwelt in rapid succession upon a multitude of outward objects, until, under this swift and dionysiac sequence of parallel, unrelated percepts, there followed the mystic experience, the illusion or the verity, of knowledge of the Whole. The most marked characteristic of Whitman's poetic method, that by which he catalogues or inventories objects, without close subordination or orderly classification, is perhaps but the same process on a small scale. The reader's attention reels under the weight of unrelated particulars until, just as the mind refuses to go further in the hopeless task of coördination, it is suddenly suffused, as it were, with a glow of comprehension, and there is born an impression of totality.[41]

As the transcendental self, once liberated, soars heavenward, the poet's vision begins to embrace panoramic dimensions, literally absorbing the earth, with all its particular details. These details, once seen in a cosmic perspective, find their proper places and gain significance. And accordingly the poet's delight in the things of the earth becomes all the greater while partaking of this supreme vision. From this joy and ecstasy of the poet capable of double vision—vision of heaven and earth—comes a tremendous sense of detachment and liberation alternating with an intense sense of attachment and involvement—something no reader of "Song of Myself" can fail to experience. Read section 4:

> Trippers and askers surround me,
> People I meet, the effect upon me of my early life or the ward and
>   city I live in, or the nation,
> The latest dates, discoveries, inventions, societies, authors old
>   and new,
> My dinner, dress, associates, looks, compliments, dues,
> The real or fancied indifference of some man or woman I love,
> The sickness of one of my folks or of myself, or ill-doing or loss
>   or lack of money, or depressions or exaltations,

Battles, the horrors of fratricidal war, the fever of doubtful news,
    the fitful events;
These come to me days and nights and go from me again,
But they are not the Me myself.

Apart from the pulling and hauling stands what I am,
Stands amused, complacent, compassionating, idle, unitary,
Looks down, is erect, or bends an arm on an impalpable certain
    rest,
Looking with side-curved head curious what will come next,
Both in and out of the game and watching and wondering at it.

Backward I see in my own days where I sweated through fog
    with linguists and contenders,
I have no mockings or arguments, I witness and wait.

"Song of Myself" is thus a poetic celebration of life itself. It is to this
celebration that Whitman invites his readers, men and women. As he said
in his 1855 preface: "A great poem is no finish to a man or woman but
rather a beginning." "Song of Myself," by Whitman's own criterion,
was just such a poem. Emerson was certainly perceptive when he saw in
the original *Leaves of Grass* both the *Bhavagad-Gita* and the *New York
Herald*. What he said would apply especially to "Song of Myself," for it
best exemplified Whitman's own version of double vision, a vision capable of accommodating both the sublime and the mundane. Interesting in
this connection is Emerson's later, more specific comment that Whitman's reiterated "I" was close kin to the "communal 'I' " of Krishna.[42]
The point was duly taken up by Mercer, as we have already noted. On this
matter Chari also concurred with Emerson. Calling the poem "a pro-
longed enactment of a single static situation, namely the paradox of Identity," Chari observed: "It is an epic of the self set in the framework of
heroic and cosmic concepts, comparable in its expansive quality to *Paradise Lost*, or better yet, the heroic Song of Krishna in the Bhagavad-
Gita."[43] This, in spite of Chari's thesis that Whitman can best be understood in terms of the *Upanishads*. In pointing out the similarity between
"Song of Myself" and the *Gita* Rajasekhariah was no exception, though
he was intent on exposing Whitman's plagiarism. "The major processes
through which he has rendered the contents of the *Gita* fit for his song are
those of verbal alteration, fanciful development, or a philosophically
reckless metamorphosis."[44] Yet Chari and Rajasekhariah agreed on the
basic similarity between "Song of Myself" and the *Gita*, understandably
enough, since the central message of the *Gita* rests on man's double
nature, at once heavenly and earthly. As it helped to reinforce Emerson's
doctrine of double consciousness and to restate Thoreau's problem of

action versus contemplation, so may the *Gita* now help to define the animating principle of "Song of Myself."

If "Song of Myself" is the matrix of *Leaves of Grass*, "Passage to India" constitutes a most fitting symbol of Whitman's poetic career. The poem was originally meant to be the nucleus of a new volume, "special chants of Death and Immortality," a volume which Whitman said was to give "freer vent and fuller expression to what, from the first, and so on throughout, more or less lurks in my writings, underneath every page, every line, every where."[45] Even after giving up on this projected sequel to *Leaves of Grass*, he had every reason to say about "Passage to India": There's more of me, the essential ultimate me, in that than in any of the poems."[46]

More than an occasional poem, more than an international poem, "Passage to India" articulates the poet's final conviction. It is a metaphysical poem. Critics, though agreeing over its special significance, have contradicted one another as to its Oriental dimensions. According to Cowley, Whitman, in his post–Civil War years, was turning back toward the Eastern beliefs expressed in "Song of Myself," perhaps because of another mystical experience. In any case, Cowley suggested that "Passage to India" indicates this return.[47] Chari, however, while calling it "one of the finest of Whitman's poems," admitted that the poem, "which might have been the only direct evidence of Whitman's enthusiasm for India, reveals no precise knowledge about India and is the least Indian of his poems."[48] Even Rajasekharaiah had little to say about this poem, thereby lending implicit support to Chari. Allen, who regards it as "the capstone of Whitman's poetic mythology," also believed that as the poem moves forward the poet's spiritual self begins to come closer to the Christian concept of soul.[49] Strangely enough, these critics all failed to heed the obvious, the poem's title; they failed to ask what made Whitman originally choose this particular title and adhere to it to the last. To put it simply, why India, of all places in the world?

The title "Passage to India" was a deliberate choice on Whitman's part, as the following notebook entry indicates:

> Passage to India. Completion Pacific R. R. 1869? quite a long piece—The spinal Idea: That the divine efforts of heroes, & their ideas, faithfully lived up to will finally prevail, and be accomplished however long deferred. Every great problem is *The passage to India* (put this in literally). Columbus, type of faith? perseverence. O for the free, clear O the way! the free, clear passage! At outset draw a simple picture of the setting out of the

Columbus expedition of discovery—?the voyage—In course of the piece, a geographical & other description of the country through which the continental Road passes—the states, (their names,) the fauna, mountains, rivers, &.—Bring in the discovery of the route by Cape of Good Hope—who was it? Vasca de Gama? And I saw the lesson. ?A main idea is to be that a brave heroic thought or religious idea faithfully pursued, justifies itself in time, not perhaps in its own way, but often in grander ways. ?then at end—What else remains? [Here follows a page of incoherent and almost illegible phrases] what other passage to India? A religious sentiment is in all these heroic ideas & underneath them. What Thou too O my Soul, (what is thy) takest thou passage to India? To The mystic wisdom—the lore of all old philosophy To All the linked transcendental streams, their sources, To vast and mighty poems the Ramayana, the Mahabarata, The Vedas with all their hymns & sacred odes. And you O my Soul? Have not you & I long sought the passage to India Sought the Source, sought some fond and ?strait Some Suez or some Darien Panama?(What are the straits) O Love! passage to India—Pride of man! passage to India. Other after the rest: Passage to India, O, my Soul. Make a fine, full gorgeous picture of the starting point/((?) or landing?) of Columbus— Also about Vasca de Gama—also of the Pacific R. R. route—its features— geography & & I see Columbus sailing out of port at ?I see— (then ?the voyage in brief). ?open the piece with a lofty declamatory passage declaiming the phrase "passage to India." set forth? Columbus from Palos Aug. 3, 1492 he landed and with his great footstep imprest a New World (12th October 1492 he landed in America at daybreak) Not to Castile & Leon but to all the old world, Columbus gave a Newer World see p. 158 vol. vii *Enc. Amer* In old age poverty dejection, humiliated & in prison He was of deepest piety . . . *portraiture of Columbus.*[50]

Whitman chose the poem's title because he was convinced that India as the goal of Columbus's voyages, represented all great human endeavors, and that as the cradle of mystic wisdom, India represented all religious aspirations. In Columbus's passage to India Whitman saw the twofold symbol, a supreme symbol of man's quest, both physical and spiritual.

In a way the poem extended his earlier attempts, "A Broadway Pageant" and "Facing West from California's Shores." In both poems Whitman turned toward India, "the house of maternity," and in the latter he concluded his gnawing question: "But where is what I started for so long ago? / And why is it yet unfound?" To this question Whitman now returned in "Passage to India":

> Down from the gardens of Asia descending radiating,
> Adam and Eve appear, then their myriad progeny after them,
> Wandering, yearning, curious, with restless explorations,
> With questionings, baffled, formless, feverish, with never-happy
>   hearts,
> With that sad incessant refrain, *Wherefore unsatisfied soul?* and
>   *Whither O mocking life?*

In Whitman's scheme the poet is the answerer, the one who answers such a question by reintegrating nature and man in the name of God. The moment signifies a paradise regained, man's ultimate return to his source.

> Passage indeed O soul to primal thought,
> Not lands and seas alone, thy own clear freshness,
> The young maturity of brood and bloom,
> To realms of budding bibles.
>
> O soul, repressless, I with thee and thou with me,
> Thy circumnavigation of the world begin,
> Of man, the voyage of his mind's return,
> To reason's early paradise,
> Back, back to wisdom's birth, to innocent intuitions,
> Again with fair creation.

The passage to India expresses what Mircea Eliade calls man's nostalgia for the origins.[51] And Whitman, like Emerson and Thoreau, also reaffirms the Transcendental conviction of man's capacity for recovering original innocence. The passage to India thus ends in this return to more than India.

Registering the soul's return to its divine source, the passage to India is a mystical way, a process of absorption as Whitman describes this point[52] —far beyond time, space, and death:

> O Thou transcendent,
> Nameless, the fibre and the breath,
> Light of the light, shedding forth universes, thou centre of them,
> Thou mightier centre of the true, the good, the loving,
> Thou moral, spiritual fountain—affection's source—thou
>   reservoir.

The moment of divine vision as it concentrates on this "Light of the light" recalls Dante's final vision of God in the *Paradiso*. (Perhaps that is why Allen stresses the Christian dimensions of the poem as it progresses toward the climax, and Chari finds it the least Indian of Whitman's poems.) Whether this vision is Christian or not, the fact remains that Whitman found his ultimate symbol in the passage to India. In order to convey his primal vision, he turned to India, much as Emerson and Thoreau had done before him.

Columbus, whose name is repeatedly invoked in Whitman's notebook entry as a supreme symbol of all heroic explorations, finds his rightful place in "Passage to India":

> (Ah Genoese thy dream! thy dream!
> Centuries after thou are laid in thy grave,
> The shore thou foundest verifies thy dream.)

Whitman's identification with Columbus becomes increasingly evident as the poem moves forward. The process of identification was completed in "Prayer of Columbus." In Columbus, "A batter'd, wreck'd old man," Whitman found his own image, as a man whose life was all but wrecked by a paralytic stroke, the loss of his mother, and continuing public neglect. But at the same time, in Columbus's vision he also found his own:

> One effort more, my altar this bleak sand;
> That Thou O God my life has lighted,
> With ray of light, steady, ineffable, vouchsafed of Thee,
> Light rare untellable, lighting the very light,
> Beyond all signs, descriptions, languages;
> For that O God, be it my latest word, here on my knees,
> Old, poor, and paralyzed, I thank Thee.

Whitman's acceptance of Columbus as a personal symbol of his own career is borne out in the fact that "Prayer of Columbus" and "Passage to India" found their final forms in 1881, and that in *Leaves of Grass* the former appears immediately after the latter. Whitman himself acknowledged the autobiographical nature of "Prayer of Columbus."[53] As Mrs. Anne Gilchrist called him "our Columbus,"[54] Whitman, in his own way, was a Columbus, an explorer in the realm of human art and thought.

And yet Columbus was also more than a personal symbol, as Whitman wrote in "Passage to India": "The shore thou foundest verifies thy dream." In the sense that America was discovered on Columbus's passage to India, it had also to be America's passage; it would therefore be America's noble role, mission, and privilege to complete Columbus's unfulfilled dream by finding a passage to India. More than any other of his contemporaries, Whitman was convinced of America's unique role as a bridge connecting the two worlds, a unifier of East and West, when he wrote in "Poetry To-day in America":

Years ago I thought Americans ought to strike out separate, and have expressions of their own in highest literature. I think so still and more decidedly than ever. But those convictions are now strongly temper'd by some additional points, (perhaps the results of advancing age, or the reflections of invalidism.) I see that this world of the West, as part of all, fuses inseparably with the East, with all, as time does—the ever new, yet old, old human race—"the same subject continued," as the novels of our grandfathers had it for chapter-heads. If we are not to hospitably receive and complete the inaugurations of the old civilizations, and change their small scale to the largest, broadest scale, what on earth are we for?

PART TWO

FOUR

Yankee Pilgrims
in Japan

Ever since Marco Polo's account of Zipangu as a veritable El Dorado,[1] Japan had been the ultima Thule as far as Western consciousness was concerned. Although Saint Francis Xavier, setting foot in Japan in 1549, called it "the delight of my soul," its two-century-long isolation kept it remote, remote enough for Swift to have his Gulliver visit there on one of his fantastic voyages. But these scattered impressions began to crystallize into an alluring image as Orientalism, passing beyond India and China, at last touched the island kingdom. It was in the second half of the nineteenth century that Japan emerged, bearing its ancient gift to the West. Unlike those previous gifts from India and China, Japan's was never claimed to be wisdom, either religious or philosophical. Rather, it was beauty itself, a gift worthy of its reputation as a kingdom of beauty. No gift arrived at a more opportune time inasmuch as the West was entering one of the most aesthetic periods of its history.

What resulted was *japonisme*, reminiscent of *chinoiserie* in the eighteenth century. This Japanese vogue kept raging through the period 1865–95 as it quickly spread from France to England, from small circles of artists and writers to the curious public. Jules de Goncourt knew what he was saying when he wrote: "The search after *reality* in literature, the resurrection of eighteeth-century art, the triumph of *Japonisme*—are not these the three great literary and artistic movements of the second one-half of the nineteenth century?" So did Oscar Wilde: "And this indeed is the reason of the influence which Eastern art is having on us in Europe, and the fascination of all Japanese work. While the Western world has been laying on art an intolerable burden of its own intellectual doubts and the spiritual tragedy of its own sorrows, the East has always kept true to art's primary and pictorial conditions."[2] By the end of the century, when the Japanese vogue had run its course, it left an image of Japan still alluring but far more familiar in the Victorian mind.

America was no exception to this general trend, but at the same time its distinct pattern manifested itself as the country became aware of its own historical destiny. Japan, as a place name, was not unknown to some curious Puritans. Cotton Mather, in his *Christian Philosopher* (1721), mentioned Japan with reference to Halley's theory of the variation of the magnetic compass: "To this the Needle pays its chief respect in all North *America*, and in the two Oceans on either side, even from the *Azores* Westward, unto *Japan*, and further."[3] Japan attained no prominence in Franklin's writings, although as a man of the Enlightenment he took a keen interest in China. More or less the same was true of the Transcendentalists who looked beyond Japan—to China and especially to India.

Once the nineteenth century had entered into its second half, Japan became increasingly visible. When Melville wrote of "low-lying, endless, unknown Archipelagoes and impenetrable Japan,"[4] he may well have remembered its shoreline seen from his whaling ship. And Hawthorne, if only he had wanted, could have written the narrative of Commodore Matthew C. Perry's historic expedition to Japan.[5] All of a sudden Japan was bursting on American literary horizons, no longer as a faraway fairyland but as a physical reality. This sense of immediacy, this sense of urgency, was both geographical and historical. After all, America and Japan faced each other across the Pacific which they shared, and this geographical intimacy was further enhanced by the historical fact that America had forced Japan to open its door to the West. All this Whitman must have had in mind when he wrote: "Over the Western sea hither from Niphon come," the first line of "A Broadway Pageant."

Although the American response to Japan inevitably lagged behind the European, it was, for this very reason, all the more eager, concentrated, and intense. Even in the middle 1870s Japanese art was hardly known to most Americans. The Japanese exhibit at the Philadelphia Centennial Exposition of 1876 thus came as "a revelation to most people," according to one contemporary account. The following year Tiffany and Company of New York, for instance, offered for sale 1,900 lots of Japanese curios, an indication of the instantaneous public interest in things Japanese, an American version of *japonisme*.[6] In their basically aesthetic excitement over Japan Americans in no way differed from Europeans, but the American response to Japan was peculiar in that it involved something more than the aesthetic—something more urgent and immediate, something personal, since many Americans actually crossed the Pacific to Japan, and this made all the difference.

To the great majority of the Americans who did cross the Pacific, Japan remained just another exotic land where they could hunt treasures and satiate their curiosity. Unlike these transient travelers and tourists, there were some chosen few who became involved with Japan as it engaged their inquisitive minds. One of them was Edward Morse (1838–1925),[7] a noted New England zoologist who studied conchology under Louis

Agassiz. Having established himself as an authority on the brachiopods along the Atlantic seacoast, Morse went to Japan in 1877, hoping to continue his research in Japanese waters. During this expedition he was invited to take the chair of zoology at Tokyo University, and he introduced to the Japanese modern methods of scientific collection and classification. Furthermore, his discovery and subsequent excavation of shell heaps opened a new chapter in Japanese anthropology, and his discovery of the earliest Japanese potteries led to his attempting a complete collection of Japanese ceramics.

Upon returning from this first Japanese residence (1877–80), Morse made himself a popularizer of Japan—its land, people, and culture. A born lecturer, spontaneous, dramatic, witty, and well-informed, he helped bring Japan closer to his American audiences. His Lowell Institute lecture series of 1881–82, for example, was duly noted by Henry Adams, Percival Lowell, and others. Indeed, it was Morse who helped the young Ernest Fenollosa secure a teaching position at Tokyo University in 1878, enticed a Boston Brahmin named William Sturgis Bigelow to Japan in 1882, and introduced another, Percival Lowell, to Japan. Bigelow in turn induced Henry Adams to follow, along with John La Farge, in 1886; likewise, Lowell, through his *Soul of the Far East*, lured Lafcadio Hearn into this distinguished company of Yankees in Japan. Directly and indirectly, Morse paved the way for his more famous followers—all eager to explore Japan, the gateway of Asia.[8]

Best known of Morse's Oriental studies is *Japan Day by Day* (1917). Based on extensive notes taken during his two Japanese sojourns, this study of Japanese life records the daily details of an enterprising, energetic fieldworker with an encyclopedic curiosity. Generously provided with illustrative drawings, it contains a wealth of information on a wide range of Japanese subjects, from geography to architecture, from anthropology to ethnography. Morse makes clear his growing conviction that the Japanese are civilized, and even more refined than Westerners in certain areas: love of animals, love of nature, religious tolerance, and sentiment of life. In his conclusion he declares: "I believe that we have much to learn from Japanese life, and that we may to advantage frankly recognize some of our weaknesses."

Although he praised the Japanese for their religious tolerance, Morse showed little interest in Japanese Buddhism and Shintoism, an omission to be expected from such a staunch Darwinian.[9] But this sin of omission was amply compensated for by those who followed him across the Pacific. Among them was Dr. William Sturgis Bigelow (1850–1926), who became a Buddhist, despite his scientific background.[10] Born into Boston's prominent medical family, Bigelow went through the routine: Harvard

College and its Medical School, completed by further training in Europe. In 1882, for diversion, he sailed to Japan, where he remained for seven uninterrupted years. As he later wrote to Morse: "Well, for good or ill, the cruise to Japan was the turning point of my life."[11] Here Bigelow referred not so much to his collection of Japanese art works, especially prints and swordguards, as to his conversion to Buddhism. For the rest of his life he continued his study of Buddhism, and in 1908 gave his Ingersoll lecture, "Buddhism and Immortality."[12]

In the lecture, after a technical discussion of the body and the soul, Bigelow addresses himself to the question: What is a man? Much to his delight, he finds Dr. Holmes's definition—"a series of states of consciousness"—to be identical with that of Buddhism—"A man consists of states of consciousness." Pursuing various ways in which states of consciousness originate, Bigelow points out that unlike matter, these states of consciousness are quite independent of time and space. "Consciousness is continuous and universal. Matter is separate and particular. But we habitually think in terms of matter. In short, we live in terms of matter. It is only on those terms that we live at all." Only when purified of matter, which is finite, can we realize this universal consciousness, the origin and end of all existence, where alone peace reigns—in Bigelow's words, "that peace that the material world cannot give,—the peace that passeth understanding trained on material things,—infinite and eternal peace,— the peace of limitless consciousness unified with limitless will. That peace is NIRVANA."[13]

All the while speaking as a Mahayana Buddhist, Bigelow remains analytical, logical, and scientific—true to his medical training. He accepts evolutionism as a matter of course, often invoking Darwin as his authority. Well aware of the barrier between East and West in the realm of thought, he eschews traditional categories in the interest of facts. Juxtaposing heredity and reincarnation, he states: "The fact of the resemblance of offspring to parents is a matter of everyday knowledge all over the world. In the West we call it an illustration of heredity or atavism, the persistence of a parental or ancestral type. In the East it is regarded as an illustration of rebirth or reincarnation. There is no mystery about it. There is no disagreement in regard to the facts." Bigelow dismisses the common anthropomorphic notions of religious paradises and goes on to observe: "Such glorified celestial existence is the final goal of most religions. In Northern Buddhism it is not the goal, but an intermediate step in normal evolution between the human consciousness and the infinite consciousness, and the difference between these is as great as that between the dimensions of the material physical body and the whole physical universe." It is as though Bigelow the scientist were verbalizing the Tran-

scendental doctrine of the Over-Soul. As a matter of fact, he does familiarly mention Emerson. To formulate his doctrine, however, Emerson did
not have to journey to India, whereas Bigelow spent seven long years in
Japan studying Buddhism. Theirs were not only the differences between
two separate individuals but also the differences between generations,
though they both came from the same Puritan New England.

In July 1886 Henry Adams arrived in Japan with his painter-friend John
La Farge for a three-month stay—a trip which Adams and his late wife,
Marian, had thought of taking together at the urging of her cousin Bigelow. Although it was their first trip to Japan, both Adams and La Farge
had already had some contact with the country. While back in Washington, D.C., Adams had befriended a Japanese diplomat; something of a
connoisseur of Oriental art, he had filled his residence with Chinese and
Japanese vases, bronzes, porcelains. La Farge had long before contributed an essay on Japanese art to Raphael Pumpelly's *Across America and
Asia* (1870).

Once in Japan, Adams and La Farge were able to enlist the eager
assistance of Bigelow, their "courier and master of ceremonies,"[14] as
well as of Fenollosa, both by then acknowledged experts on Japanese art.
Adams apparently used their assistance well. When he returned to America in October he brought with him a houseful of curios, worth two
thousand dollars, for himself and his friends. As far as Adams the curio-
hunter was concerned, the whole venture turned out to be a success.

Undertaken in a holiday mood, it was a pleasure trip, a sort of prelude
to his period as a world traveler. *The Education of Henry Adams* makes no
mention of this Japanese trip, but since it makes no mention either of his
wife's suicide or of his longer and more fruitful sojourn in the South Seas,
the omission may not mean much.

Yet Ernest Samuels has suggested that Adams's Japanese trip was
motivated by his intellectual curiosity as much as by his love of the
picturesque. In particular, Adams had long been interested in Japan as a
case of an archaic society.[15] If these, among other factors, had motivated
his Japanese trip, it was a failure, judging from his Japanese letters, the
principal documents it yielded.

The letters he wrote home to his friends—John Hay and Elizabeth
Cameron, for instance—reveal nothing of Adams the historian. The politics of contemporary Japan was perhaps too complicated for him to grasp,
even if he had wanted to. But he must certainly have known what desperate efforts Japan was making to survive in the arena of international power
politics; he must at least have seen the ever-widening gulf between Old
and New Japan. If so, he must have determined to turn away from the

drama of modern Japan in the making. It is as though he had determined to make a holiday of the whole affair,[16] often indulging in a tone of levity, something not to be expected from a man of Adams's intellectual stature —even if he was but a sojourner.

True, Nikko, the highlight of his Japanese trip, elicited the grudging praise of Adams as being "one of the sights of the world" beside which Louis Quatorze and Versailles were "not much of a show."[17] This was rather an exception, however. A week after his arrival in Yokohama, Adams wrote to Hay, touching on his first impressions—Japanese laughter, Japanese smells, and Japanese smallness[18]—all of which Morse and fellow Americans duly noted at one time or another. Adams's lighthearted tone was not out of place, considering his bantering familiarity with Hay. But what was curious was his unwillingness or inability to go beyond his first impressions. The case in point was his view of Japanese women. Whie speaking of Japanese laughter, Adams described Japanese women in these terms: "I have not yet seen a woman with any better mechanism than that of a five-dollar wax doll; but the amount of oil used in fixing and oiling and arranging their hair is worth the money alone."[19] Six weeks later, he wrote to Elizabeth Cameron about the same subject: "The Japanese women seem to be impossible. After careful inquiry I can hear of no specimen of your sex, in any class in society, whom I ought to look upon as other than a *curio*. They are all badly made, awkward in movement, and suggestive of monkeys."[20] That he was not saying this out of deference to the addressee is clear in view of what he wrote to Hay nine days later, that is, past the midpoint of his Japanese sojourn. On that occasion Adams had this to say about the sexual mores of the Japanese: "I cannot conquer a feeling that Japs are monkeys and the women very badly made monkeys; but from others I hear much on the subject, and what I hear is very far from appetising. In such an atmosphere one talks freely. I was a bit aghast when one young woman called my attention to a temple as a remains of phallic worship." In the same letter Adams finally summed up his observations: "Sex begins with the Aryan race. I have seen a Japanese beauty, which has a husband, *Nabeshame*, if I hear right—a live Japanese Marquis, late Daimio of Hizo, or some other place; but though he owns potteries, he has, I am sure, no more successful bit of bric-à-brac than his wife is; but as for being a woman, she is hardly the best Satsuma."[21]

Adams's reaction to Japanese women is puzzling, to say the least, when one thinks of his later response to Polynesian women, which was surprisingly open, natural, and warm, and also of his final attempt to enshrine women in the image of the Virgin Mary. It is as though Adams, from the outset, had made up his mind about Japanese women, and about Japan for that matter. His reaction to the women more or less indicated his response to the country. In a word, Adams remained superficial. As Motoshi Karita said, "The trip to Japan did not enable Adams to penetrate the inside of the country."[22]

In this Adams stood in sharp contrast to his companion, La Farge, who responded to the country freely and fully, as is evident in *An Artist's Letters from Japan* (1897). An original artist capable of seeing the world afresh, he was at the same time an accomplished writer capable of articulating his reactions. This combination made his account vivid, lively, and highly readable.

Time and again La Farge was impressed with the primal harmony between man and nature still existing in Japan, especially with the natives' aesthetic sense, which was "something much more delicate and complex and contemplative, and at the same time more natural, than ours has ever been." In like vein he approached the tomb of Tokugawa Iyeyasu, the center of Nikko: "But the solemnity of the resting-place cannot be broken. It lies apart from all associations of history, in this extreme of cost and of refined simplicity, in face of the surrounding powers of nature. There is here no defiance of time, no apparent attempt at an equal permanency; it is like a courteous acceptance of the eternal peace, the eternal nothingness of the tomb." (Speaking of Japanese laughter, Adams wrote: "Everything laughs, until I expect to see even the severe bronze doors of the tombs, the finest work I know, open themselves with the same eternal and meaningless laughter, as though death were the pleasantest jest of all."[23])

"Everything here exists for a painter's delight," wrote La Farge with the delight of recognizing familiar things. As a creative artist he took a special interest in art and those who created it. He took due note of the Japanese artist still following "the law of *Tao*"—"of an old obedience to an unwritten law common to all art." And in the chapter "Tao: The Way" La Farge pondered on this law of laws underlying all artistic activities. Fully aware that art and religion merge into one, he concluded in an Emersonian vein: "The radiance of the landscape illuminates my room; the landscape does not come within. I have become as a blank to be filled. I employ my mind as a mirror; it grasps nothing, it refuses nothing; it receives, but does not keep. And thus I can triumph over things without injury to myself—I am safe in Tao."[24]

The difference between Adams's letters and La Farge's *Letters* is that between a philosopher and an artist, and ultimately that between their authors, two distinct individuals. Adams recognized this difference better than anyone else. In his *Education* he spoke of his friend's mind as capable of equanimity, whether he was in Japan, Samoa, or Ceylon—a mind capable of "carrying different shades of contradiction." "Constantly," continued Adams, "he repulsed argument: 'Adams, you reason too much!' was one of his standing reproaches even in the mild discussion of rice and mangoes in the warm night of Tahiti dinners. He should have blamed Adams for being born in Boston. The mind resorts to reason for want of training, and Adams had never met a perfectly trained mind."[25]

An Artist's Letters from Japan suggests that La Farge found there what he had originally hoped for, and perhaps more. In Japan he finally found what would serve as the background for *The Ascension*, which was, according to a critic, "undoubtedly the greatest mural painting of a religious subject produced anywhere" in his time.[26] Adams also came home with his inspiration, an inspiration for the monument which would mark the grave of his wife, Marian, and eventually his own in Rock Creek Cemetery, Washington, D.C. Conceived by Adams, designed by La Farge, and executed by Homer Saint-Gaudens, the statue stands as a symbol of rare artistic collaborations, and also of the meeting of East and West, much like La Farge's *Ascension*.[27]

Theirs was more than a summer pleasure trip, after all, as was evident in the incident at Omaha while they were on their way to Japan. To a young local reporter curious about their trip, La Farge blurted out that they were "in search of Nirvana." (The young man rejoined: "It's out of season!")[28] Although determined to make the trip as innocent as possible, Adams kept reading about Buddhism on the train while his companion grew excited about the unfolding scenery outside. Three weeks after their arrival in Japan, Adams wrote to Hay, calling Fenollosa "a kind of St. Dominic": "He has joined a Buddhist sect; I was myself a Buddhist when I left America, but he has converted me to Calvinism with leanings towards the Methodists."[29] Once again it was La Farge who wrote about nirvana in his book. In a brief chapter entitled "Nirvana" he related the Omaha incident and then proceeded to the subject: "Of all the images that I see so often, the one that touches me most—partly, perhaps, because of the Eternal Feminine—is that of the incarnation that is called Kuwanon, when shown absorbed in the meditations of Nirvana." Noting the transformation this Buddhist deity underwent from the ideal of contemplation to the ideal of compassion, La Farge concluded: "In its [Buddhist] full ideal here below civil and religious society would be the same; the continual rest of Nirvana becoming finally inseparable from our transmigrations—our passions living together with complete wisdom, and our further existence not demanding, then, another world. And if civilization shall have finally perfected the world of mind and the world of matter, we shall have here below Nirvana, and we shall dwell in it as Buddhas." Years later, in his dedicatory note to *An Artist's Letters from Japan*, La Farge reminded his friend of the Omaha incident: "If only we had found

84

Nirvana—but he was right who warned us that we were late in this season of the world." As La Farge admitted, they were no mere pleasure-seekers, no mere curio-hunters. They were pilgrims in search of nirvana.

Whether or not, as that young reporter had warned, nirvana was "out of season," Adams continued his search for it. Five years later, on his way to Europe from his longer sojourn in the South Seas, he stopped at Ceylon, and during his brief stay undertook an arduous oxcart trip through the tropical jungles to visit the sacred bo tree in the ruined city of Anu-radhpura—the original shoot having been brought there more than two thousand years earlier from the bo tree under which Buddha had attained enlightenment. Under this bo tree, "now only a sickly shoot or two from the original trunk," Adams sat "for half an hour, hoping to attain Nir-vana" and left it "without attaining Buddhaship."[30] The trip was "the last aesthetic ritual of his sentimental pilgrimage," as Ernest Samuels pointed out.[31] In a meditative mood while crossing the Indian Ocean, Adams wrote a long blank verse poem, "Buddha and Brahma," whose existence he shared with only a few intimates until its publication twenty years later.

Based partly on an anecdote in *Questions of King Milinda*,[32] the poem attempts to resolve the ever-present conflict between two ways of life: the way of thought and the way of action—the problem close to Adams's heart. Malunka, one of Buddha's disciples, asks in earnest whether or not the world exists eternally. To this ultimate question Buddha, as usual, makes no answer, sitting still, contemplating the pure white lotus in his hand. Dissatisfied with this answer of silence, the youth turns to his father, Rajah of Mogadha. Although the old wise man reminds his questioning son of his duty to act, the youth persists: "Life for me is thought, / But, were it action, how, in youth or age, / Can man act wisely, leaving thought aside?" The Rajah finally responds by recalling the two separate paths Gautama and he had taken in their youthful rebelliousness, even though both were of the same warrior caste—one following the way of thought and the other the way of action:

> Your Master, you, and I, and all wise men,
> Have one sole purpose which we never lose:
> Through different paths we each seek to attain,
> Sooner or later, as our paths allow,
> A perfect union with the single Spirit.
> Gautama's way is best, but all are good,
> He breaks a path at once to what he seeks.
> By silence and absorption he unites
> His soul with the great soul from which it started.
> But we, who cannot fly the world, must seek

> To live two separate lives; one, in the world
> Which we must ever seem to treat as real;
> The other in ourselves, behind a veil
> Not to be raised without disturbing both.

Both the way of thought and the way of action culminate in Buddha's silence. No mere emptiness, it synthesizes both; it is full, as full as nirvana, the highest wisdom of Buddhism. It is this Peace of God, the mystic moment Adams hoped to envision in the hooded figure guarding the graves of his wife and himself.

If Adams the man of emotion was in search of nirvana, then Adams the man of reason was in search of what he called "the Asiatic mystery." No sooner had he returned from Japan in October 1886 than he wrote to Hay:

> Japan and its art are only a sort of antechamber to China and . . . China is the only mystery left to penetrate. I have henceforward a future. As soon as I can get rid of history, and the present, I mean to start for China, stay there. In China I will find bronzes or break all the crockery; . . . Five years hence I expect to enter the celestial kingdom by that road, if not sooner by a shorter one as seems most likely to judge from the ways of most of my acquaintances at home.[33]

At the end of the same year he wrote to another friend: "The only practical result of the trip has been to make one earnest to close up everything here, finish history, cut society, foreswear strong drink and politics, and start in about three years for China, never to return. China is the great unknown country of the world."[34] Visualizing himself setting out "after the manner of Ulysses, in search of that new world which is the old," Adams began to study Chinese for two hours daily—after having spent six on his historical writing.[35]

"He is up to his eyes in Chinese art, history, and geography, and proposes to leave Marco Polo out of sight in his travels and explorations," Hay reported on Adams to their mutual friend.[36] Adams himself, after calling on the Russian chargé to express his intent to visit Central Asia, reported: "Luckily he offers no objection to our Asiatic mystery, and I expect to make a sort of Marco Polo caravan."[37] In the meantime he kept his "Central Asian talk" alive with Clarence King and other friends. According to his plans, Adams would approach the mystery by way of the South Seas and India, and therefrom trace out the medieval trade route explored by Marco Polo from the upper reaches of the Oxus across Sinkiang and the Gobi to Peking. In so doing he would see for himself the elements of the problems that were then exciting ethnologists and anthro-

pologists in Washington and elsewhere. If he were lucky, he would be the
first to deduce the true laws of the origin and transit of civilizations.[38]
With this ambitious scheme in mind, Adams, once again accompanied by
La Farge, sailed for the South Seas from San Francisco in August 1890,
and, as we know, Ceylon was as far as he progressed in his attempt to
unveil the Asiatic mystery.

This scheme, too, ended in failure, a familiar pattern in Adams's
career. If this failure stemmed from the dichotomy between Adams the
man of emotion and Adams the man of reason, it also anticipated his
dilemma between the Virgin Mary and the Dynamo. Caught in his self-
made dilemma, Adams was unable to see that the Virgin Mary and the
Dynamo, despite their categorical difference, are but twin symbols sprung
from the same life force. His historicism, which was no doubt responsible
for this dilemma, resulted from his Cartesian dualism.[39] In personal terms
this dualism accounted for his failure to reconcile his emotion and his
reason—always in mutual distrust and suspicion. His only defense mechanism was a sense of irony, a gift he was blessed with, but irony was of no
help in his search for unity. As Adams himself admitted, La Farge was
right when he chided: "Adams, you reason too much!" Reason could not
help him penetrate Japan. But he did try, even though he failed; herein lay
the significance of Adams's pilgrimage to the Orient.

Another Boston Brahmin who responded to the call of the Far East was
Percival Lowell (1855–1916),[40] brother of the poet Amy Lowell. Having
already made his name in the business world, the young Lowell visited
Japan in 1883, where he spent the next ten years. (Upon his return home,
Lowell took up his old interests, mathematics and astronomy, and soon,
as the leading spirit of the Lowell Observatory in Flagstaff, Arizona,
studied the solar system, speculating about the so-called Martian civilization, among other things.) Based on his Far Eastern experience, he wrote
a series of books: *Chosön: The Land of the Morning Calm* (1886); *The
Soul of the Far East* (1888); *Noto* (1891); and *Occult Japan* (1895)—a
fascinating chronicle of the author's progress toward the Asiatic mystery.

Shortly after his arrival in Japan Lowell was, through Morse or someone else, appointed foreign secretary and counselor to the Korean special
mission to the United States, the first diplomatic overture from the hermit
kingdom to the West. In appreciation of his service the Korean government invited Lowell as an official guest, and his half-year stay, from 1883
to 1884, resulted in *Chosön*.

In accord with its subtitle, "A Sketch of Korea," *Chosön* relates
Lowell's experiences during his stay, from his arrival in Inchon to his
departure from Pusan. Although his social contact was limited to the

upper class of Korean society and some of his acquaintances were to play important roles in one of the most turbulent periods of modern Korean history, *Chosön* has little to do with political reality in Korea. Still, it offers a great deal more than we could expect from such a brief period of residence in a foreign city and covers a wide range of subjects: geography, climate, transportation, government, entertainment, religion, architecture, gardening, costume, history, language, and the like. As a photo-illustrated account of what one of the nine Western residents in Seoul at the time saw, heard, and learned, *Chosön* has remained a valuable item in the Koreana. This is rather remarkable considering that Lowell, not knowing Korean, depended on interpreters in order to communicate with the natives. He had other necessary qualities to compensate for this handicap; besides being curious, inquisitive, humorous, and often ironic, he had a mind capable of observation and speculation.

In *Chosön* Lowell is not without his prejudices, one being a boundless faith in science. Always interested in mathematics, he is delighted to discover a Korean mathematician and speak of the blood kindship of mathematics and poetry, twin sisters born to their mother, imagination. His scientific outlook makes him dismiss as superstition the tradition of geomancy, which often dictated the Korean system of agriculture. This same outlook also makes Lowell call Korea "a land without a religion," ignoring shamanism, Confucianism, Taoism, and Buddhism, which together have shaped Korean culture.

Lowell's generalizations and speculations culminate in what he calls "the triad of principles"—the quality of impersonality, the patriarchal system, and the position of women. As he points out in *Chosön*, it is essential to know fully these racial characteristics now developed into institutions if one is to understand the myriad details of Far Eastern life and the still more interesting modes of Far Eastern thought.

Lowell sees Koreans as a race which "has the semblance of being grown up while it has kept the mind of its childhood"—"a living anachronism." In Korea the patriarchal system, having survived from the earliest ages, was reinforced with the arrival of Confucianism from China. This still-powerful patriarchal system accounts for the humble position of women in that part of the world. Not only are these two traits related to each other, but they are subordinate to the third, that of impersonality. Although, Lowell continues, most peoples outgrow the primitive stage of impersonality and move on to the second stage, the Korean and Japanese peoples have remained at the first stage, as is evident in their languages, which show no sense of distinction in gender, number, or person.

While examining Korea, Lowell often refers to Japan and China for comparison and contrast. When he brings these three together, a new perspective of East versus West emerges. In formulating his triad of principles Lowell writes revealingly: ''It is because the far-East holds up the mirror to our own civilization,—a mirror that like all mirrors gives us back left for right,—because by her very oddities, as they strike us at first, we learn truly to criticise, examine, and realize our own way of doing things, that she is so very interesting. It is this that her great attraction lies. It is for this that men have gone to Japan intending to stay weeks, and have tarried years.''

In his next book, *The Soul of the Far East*, Lowell continues this mirror metaphor by emphasizing ''the possibility of using it [the Far Oriental's point of view] stereoptically,'' even the need of doing so, because neither East nor West is ''perfect enough to serve in all things as standard for the other.'' While *Chosön* remains more or less a travel book, *The Soul of the Far East* is not. As the title suggests, it is Lowell's full-scale attempt to interpret Japan in particular and the Far East in general from a world-wide perspective. Here Lowell more confidently marshals his array of illustrations, and with his triad of principles rolled into one theme of Oriental impersonality, his focus becomes sharper and more penetrating; in short, Lowell at his best.

Manifest in various aspects of Japanese culture—family, language, nature, art, religion—is the theme of impersonality. As Lowell develops this central theme, it gradually turns into the theme of Western personality versus Eastern impersonality. As he puts it, ''We stand at the nearer end of the scale, the Far Orientals at the other. If with us the *I* seems to be of the very essence of the soul, then the soul of the Far East may be said to be Impersonality.'' Since humanity evolves from the simplicity of nature toward the complexity of individuation, he contends that the West represents the adulthood of self-consciousness and the East its undifferentiated childhood.

Lowell attributes this apparent difference between East and West primarily to the soul itself, which possesses ''the germ of its own evolution,'' though environment has contributed to the total process, the cosmic evolution from a state of simple homogeneity to a state of complex heterogeneity. From this analysis of the general cause he then deduces its threefold effects: first, Eastern civilization is not as advanced as Western; second, the rate of Oriental progress has been and will be less rapid; and third, the remarkable homogeneity of the Orientals is the result of their lack of divergence or their comparative lack of genius. Lowell declares: ''*The degree of individualization of a people is the self-recorded measure of its place in the great march of mind.*'' In this great march of mind, he warns, these Far Eastern peoples will disappear from the face of the earth—before the advancing nations of the West—unless their newly imported ideas really take root.

Noto, the third of Lowell's Oriental series, is a travelog, a delightful, relaxed, thesis-free account of his exploration of the Noto peninsula. In his next book, *Occult Japan*, however, Lowell returns to his theme of Japanese impersonality. In this study of the Japanese psyche, an exploration of the inner core of Japanese culture, Lowell relentlessly pursues his obsession, his *idée fixe*, to use B. H. Chamberlain's designation, to its logical limits.[41]

Here for the first time Lowell takes up Shintoism. This change of heart occurred during his climb of Ontake, foremost among the sacred Shinto mountains, when he witnessed a strange scene of three pilgrims falling into a trance. Pressing his inquiry, he learned that the trance was part of the time-honored system of divine possession, a cult of esoteric Shintoism. Now it dawned on him what it was that animated those thousands and thousands of pilgrims in groups visiting various sacred places throughout Japan. After some intensive fieldwork Lowell finally became convinced of the significance of these divine possessions. "For," he points out, "they are as essentially Japanese as they are essentially genuine. That is, they are neither shams nor importations from China or India, but aboriginal originalities of the Japanese people. They are the hitherto unsuspected esoteric side of Shinto, the old native faith."

In tracing Japanese religious history Lowell takes pains to distinguish the Shinto from the Buddhist element. (At this point he speaks of Japanese Buddhism: "Emotionally its tenets do not at bottom satisfy us Occidentals, flirt with them as we may.") He goes on to discuss three Shinto rites: ordeal by boiling water; walking barefoot over a bed of live coals; and climbing the ladder of sword blades. In identifying, classifying, and describing these forms of divine possession Lowell is thoroughly scientific. When he begins to explain their essence, however, his *idée fixe* takes over the stage. The Japanese, in Lowell's opinion, all too easily fall victim to these divine possessions because of their impersonality, or their lack of personality. Their impersonality also accounts for their "marvelous faculty of being influenced by other people." "Fundamentally unoriginal, they have always shown a genius for self-adaptation. They are at present engaged in exemplifying their capacity upon a wholesale national scale." "It is," Lowell concludes, "hardly exaggeration to say that Japan at this moment is affording the rest of the world the spectacle of the most stupendous hypnotic act ever seen, nothing less than the hypnotization of a whole nation, with its eyes open."

After his initial glance at *Occult Japan*, Hearn remarked: "It is a very clever book—though disfigured by absolutely shameless puns. It touches truths to the quick,—with a light sharp sting peculiar to Lowell's art. It is painfully unsympathetic—Mephistophelian in a way that chills me. It is scientific. . . . Still it is a wonderful book.'' After another glance, however, Hearn found himself less favorably disposed: ''It strikes me only as a mood of the man, an ugly, supercilious one, verging on the wickedness of a wish to hurt. . . . But there was in the *Soul of the Far East* an exquisite approach to playful tenderness—utterly banished from *Occult Japan*.'' Chamberlain was far more objective in his judgment. Referring to it as ''a curious book,'' he nonetheless rendered credit where it was due: ''Lowell . . . discovers to us Japanese possession, exorcism, and miracle-working, whose very existence had scarcely been suspected.''[42]

What is curious about *Occult Japan*, and all of Lowell's Far Eastern studies for that matter, is that his tone grew negative as his findings turned into themes and his themes turned into obsessions. But this should not blind us to the genuine significance of his contributions in comparative culture. Even his *idée fixe*, the theme of Western personality versus Eastern impersonality, however schematic and simplistic, cannot be dismissed merely as his personal obsession, for Lowell, in his own way, extended what Emerson had tried to formulate in his essay ''Plato.'' And his Far Eastern studies, taken together, register American Orientalism in its second phase as it tried to penetrate the Asiatic mystery.

FIVE

Fenollosa

Like Morse, Bigelow, Adams, and Lowell, Ernest Fenollosa (1853–1908) was a New Englander, but unlike the last three he was not a Boston Brahmin. A native of Salem, he was half-Spanish through his father, a musician. By birth, he was destined to be a cosmopolitan.[1]

At Harvard, steeping himself in Emerson, Hegel, and Spencer, Fenollosa studied philosophy, a subject which became a lifelong interest. After two years' postgraduate study of philosophy and additional study of theology, he turned, however, to art training—working on mechanical drawing, perspective, and historical ornament at the new Massachusetts Normal Art School and studying painting at the Boston Museum of Fine Arts. He was thus groping for a vocation when the call came from the Orient through his Salem neighbor Edward Morse, who, while getting ready for his second Japanese sojourn, was looking for someone to teach philosophy at Tokyo University. All things considered, Fenollosa was the man for the position, just as it was the opportunity for him. The offer was made and accepted. He married the girl he had long courted, and they, bride and bridegroom, sailed for Japan in 1878.

When the young Fenollosa arrived, Meiji Japan, New Japan, then only ten years old, was plunging headlong into all-out modernization for survival. To the Japanese, modernization meant Westernization, and vice versa—one and the same thing. The Japanese accepted modernization as a mandate of history, as a matter of national policy, and in implementing it they were deliberate and thoroughgoing.[2] What they did—the best course under the circumstances—was to put foreigners in charge of modernizing various branches and departments of the government: Englishmen in the navy and the mint, Frenchmen and later Germans in the army and law, Germans in medicine, Americans in education, and so on. As B. H. Chamberlain put it, these foreign employees were physicians applying their marvelous cure to the Japanese, their willing patients, and were "the creator[s] of New Japan." And as the same eye-witness noted further, "No less a feat than the reform of the entire educational system was chiefly the work of a handful of Americans."[3] At the time of Fenollosa's arrival, Tokyo University, for instance, had more than a score of foreign professors lecturing in their special fields, including, at one time or another, Morse in zoology, Thomas C. Mendenhall in physics, and Chamberlain in Japanese philology.[4] All these foreign teachers praised their students—in Chamberlain's words again, "that class of youths who are the schoolmaster's delight,—quiet, intelligent, deferential, studious almost to excess."[5] They were all eager, perhaps too eager, knowing full well that they would soon replace their foreign professors—after their further study abroad at the government's expense. Whether in academic disciplines or in more practical fields, they would be the leaders of New Japan.

Fenollosa's first Japanese sojourn (1878–90) coincided, then, with the heyday of this Western craze that giddied the island empire, a period of violent iconoclasm directed toward the destruction of all that Old Japan symbolized. The classical Noh theater, having lost the patronage of the shogunate, was all but forgotten; classical painting was so neglected that even masters were now reduced to starvation; Buddhism lost the government protection it had long enjoyed, and temples dumped their ancient art treasures into the market for a mere pittance—much to the delight of foreign curio-hunters.

Stimulated no doubt by Morse's interest in Japanese potteries, Fenollosa began to collect old paintings. In no time he became a connoisseur of native art. After all, he was no stranger to the mystery of art. Once initiated, Fenollosa pursued this new interest with his characteristic zeal, undertaking several summer trips to the Kyoto-Nara area, the center of Old Japan, which had long had a concentration of temples and shrines with ancient art collections. Equipped with a scientific bent for analysis and classification as well as a philosophical penchant for speculation and synthesis, he went beyond collectorship and connoisseurship, establishing himself as a critic, a judge, and an authority on Japanese art. In 1882, only four years after his arrival in Japan, Fenollosa spoke to the Ryuchi-kai, a club of aristocrats:

> Japanese art is really far superior to modern cheap western art that describes any object at hand mechanically, forgetting the most important point, expression of Idea. Despite such superiority the Japanese despise their classical paintings, and with adoration for western civilization admire its artistically worthless modern paintings and imitate them for nothing. What a sad sight it is! The Japanese should return to their nature and its old racial traditions, and then take, if there are any, the good points of western painting.[6]

This timely message, coming from an American professor, made an enormous impact on the audience. In fact, Fenollosa's speech, "Truth of Fine

Arts," is said to have revived interest in traditional Japanese art, marking a new epoch in the history of Meiji art. [7]

With a new sense of mission Fenollosa continued lending his prestige to the national art revival which was rapidly gaining ground. In 1884 he founded the Kangwakai, a club devoted to the appreciation and certification of ancient paintings; he also regularly lectured on art and sponsored exhibits by Hogai Kano and other artists in the hope of promoting their cause and providing much-needed financial relief. (Having been apprenticed to Kano for some time, Fenollosa was formally accepted by the Kano family—the famous academy with a long tradition—under the name Kano Eitan.) In 1886 the Japanese government, in recognition of his contributions, appointed him Imperial Commissioner of Fine Arts in charge of both the Imperial Museum and the Tokyo Fine Arts Academy, which were scheduled to open in two years. Considering what he had accomplished in the past eight years (and what he was yet to accomplish in the ensuing four), there was no doubt that Fenollosa richly deserved the honour. By earning it he proved that he was the right man for Japan—in the poet Yone Noguchi's words, "the very discoverer of Japanese art for Japan." [8]

When he returned to America in 1890, Fenollosa remembered the emperor's parting words: "We request you now to teach the significance of Japanese art to the West as you have already taught it to the Japanese." [9] And that was exactly what he did in the second phase of his career, at the Boston Museum of Fine Arts. As curator of its new department of Japanese art he inaugurated a series of special exhibitions and interpreted Japanese art and culture to an interested public. Largely through his efforts to bring together the private collections of Morse, Bigelow, and his own, the Boston Museum came to possess the best Japanese art collection in the West. [10] As his reputation spread, his eloquent voice also began to go beyond the museum walls and to reach a widening audience across the country. Appointed a member of the fine arts jury at the Chicago World's Fair of 1893, Fenollosa saw to it that Japan appeared in two categories, "Fine Arts" and "Industries," for the first time at an international exposition. In a review for the *Century Magazine* he hailed contemporary Japanese work as a sure sign of what the native tradition could absorb in its openness toward the outside world. Also in his lecture series "History of Japanese Art," Fenollosa, with the aid of slides, presented Japanese culture and envisioned the future union of Eastern and Western civilizations. [11]

In the years following his resignation from the museum in 1896, Fenollosa remained active, ever more convinced of the significance of his expanding perspective. Fenollosa carried this sense of mission, redoubled after his second Japanese sojourn (1896–1901), into his second American phase (1901–8), upholding his gospel of the new aesthetics wherever and whenever he lectured—even at the White House as the guest of President Theodore Roosevelt. (That his lectures were kept at a level as high as his topics were varied is evident in his Detroit series of 1901, for instance: "A Comparison of European and Asiatic Art," "Japanese and Chinese Poetry," and "Problems of Art Education.") While bringing the Orient closer to America, Fenollosa was equally active in art education. His basic principles of art—line, color, and *notan*—in due course came to revolutionize American art education through the efforts of Arthur Dow, his one-time assistant at the Boston Museum and later a professor at Columbia University. When Fenollosa met his untimely death in London in 1908, he was there to attend the International Congress for the Advancement of Drawing and Art Teaching, as an honorary vice-president of the American Committee, and also to continue his research at the British Museum.[12]

While working at the British Museum, Fenollosa became excited over the Alaskan walrus tusk carvings which seemed to confirm his theory that East and West had already met at the dawn of history through his so-called Pacific School of Art, a wide-spread school of design extending along the rim of the Pacific.[13] He had every reason to get excited because it was the theory he had set forth in his *Epochs of Chinese and Japanese Art*, completed two years before and still in manuscript awaiting his thorough revision. When the work finally appeared in 1912, it was hailed as the first significant study in the history and aesthetics of Far Eastern art. As Langdon Warner said years later: "Nevertheless, though Western knowledge of Oriental art has progressed since his death, it has followed the path blazed by him. While his information was derived from his Japanese friends, his conclusions were his own and they were formed at a time when there was no background of Western appreciation."[14]

Epochs of Chinese and Japanese Art abounds in personal references. Speaking of Japanese culture, he mentions his old friend Hearn's "deep studies of Shinto and family cult." Again applying Hearn's notion of the eternal feminine to East and West, the Kwannon and the Madonna, Fenollosa describes La Farge's reaction to Mokkei's Kwannon: "Mr. La Farge, devout Catholic as he is, could hardly restrain a bending of the head as he muttered, 'Raphael.' " Pointing out that "an extremely inspired type of art" exists in Japan, too, Fenollosa notes his wife Mary's novel *The Dragon Painter*.[15] Also, he familiarly calls attention to Morse's, Bigelow's, and his own collections housed at the Boston Museum, as he does to the Freer Collection, which he himself helped organize.

Not without a sense of pride he details the long tradition of his adoptive family, the Kano school of Japanese painting. Perhaps his proudest moment is when he relates his own discovery of the Korean Buddhist statue in the Yumedono Pavilion at the Horyuji Temple: "But at last the final folds of the covering fell away, and this marvellous statue, unique in the world, came forth to human sight for the first time in centuries." This 1884 discovery of what he calls "the greatest perfect monument" of Korean art may well serve as the most eloquent symbol of his discovery of Japanese and Oriental art as a whole.

Fenollosa is quite candid about his anti-Confucian bias, which obviously stemmed from his personal dislike of formalism. At the outset he declares that "almost all the great imaginative art work of the Chinese mind has sprung from those elements in Chinese genius, which, if not anti, were at least non-Confucian." What he is saying here is that Chinese art is basically Taoistic, a view now universally held. Fenollosa does not stop here, however. Time and again he returns to this point. While discussing modern Chinese art, he can hardly restrain himself: "The modern Confucian government of China is a government of corrupt Puritans." And finally this wholesale denunciation: "We can see well what would have happened to all ancient Japanese art if these Confucians had got in their deadly work a century earlier. They would have destroyed in Japan all evidences of ancient Chinese art as well, as they had already destroyed it in China. It was the institution of the samurai alone, and the genius of Tanyu and his Kano followers in particular, that stood out as a great promontory against the mad storm of Confucianism that now beat upon the past."

In yet another sense *Epochs* is a personal book. What animates it comes directly from Fenollosa's conviction as an art historian, as a thinker, and as a man. In the introduction he sets forth his guiding principle:

> After all, I am not necessarily writing this book for scholars, but for those who would try to form a clear conception of the essential humanity of these peoples. The idea may be a grand hypothesis; it surely would never be promulgated by the scholars, but I believe it to be necessary that someone should attempt it. Once granting this point of view it revivifies for us all Chinese institutions, philosophy, art, prose-literature, and poetry. It is sound evolutionary doctrine. I fully confess that my personal contribution to the evidence is a digest of the art itself, the primary document. Art is a sensitive barometer to measure the buoyancy of spirit.

Standing by this conviction he clarifies his approach: "The present volume is written from the point of view of principles of criticism which could be applied to the history of European art as well. Qualities of line, *notan*, and colour, and the use of these in expressing great ideas, are made the basis of classification and of appreciation.''

Fenollosa chose the title *Epochs of Chinese and Japanese Art*, because, as he states in the same introduction, he conceived of the art of each epoch as ''a peculiar beauty of line, spacing, and color which could have been produced at no other time, and which permeates all the industries of its day.'' Or as he further elaborates, ''If art were a Vasarish chronicling of names and popular stories, one artist-life might seem to be as good a fact to record as another, and so down to the end. But that is not a history of *Art*. Art is supreme beauty, and thus is essentially epochal.'' Based on his hypothesis of two primary centers, Eastern and Western, Fenollosa then places Chinese and Japanese art in the Eastern, his so-called Pacific School of Art, which extended along the rim of the Pacific. Applying his concept of ''epoch'' to Chinese art, he emphasizes three great epochs that crystallized the creative imagination of the Chinese people—namely, the Han, the T'ang, and the Sung period. It was, according to Fenollosa, the last of the three, the Sung period, both Northern and Southern, that successfully fused Confucianism, Taoism, and Zen Buddhism into ''a single working system''—''the greatest intellectual feat accomplished by Chinese thought during the five millennia of its existence.'' (That the idealistic art of China reached its zenith in this great age of synthesis implies that the history of Chinese art in the succeeding periods was more or less the record of its decline.) Against this background Fenollosa also presents the evolution of Japanese art. For instance, he enthusiastically discusses the art of Nara Japan as the Buddhist art that resulted from multiple influences, Korean, Chinese, Indian, and Greek. He discusses even more enthusiastically the art of Ashikaga Japan, matured in the pervading spirit of Zen Buddhism, and regards it as comparable to Sung art in China.[16] Fenollosa is thoroughly delighted that this great flowering of Japanese art was contemporaneous with Medici Florence.

What makes *Epochs of Chinese and Japanese Art* unique among studies of its kind is, in the last analysis, Fenollosa's conviction of the essential oneness of humanity. This universal vision enabled him to bring together China and Japan, East and West, without ignoring their rich variations. Countering Kipling's dictum: ''East is East, and West is West, / And never the twain shall meet,'' Fenollosa declares: ''But the truth is that they have met, and they are meeting again now; and history is a thousand times richer for the contact. They have contributed a great deal to each other, and must contribute still more; they interchange views from the basis of a common humanity; and humanity is thus enabled to perceive what is stupid in its insularity. I say firmly, that in Art, as in civilization generally, the best in both East and West is that which is common to the two, and eloquent of universal social construction.'' *Epochs of Chinese and Japanese Art* reflects Fenollosa's new aesthetics which took shape as he became aware of his own historic role in this renewed contact of East and West.

Fenollosa's second Japanese period (1896–1901) was no repetition of his first. Under the changed circumstances a repetition of the past was out of the question, even if he had wished it. And the change was mutual. Japan was no longer the same. Out of its earlier Western craze, the country was fast becoming nationalistic, chauvinistic. Having won the war with China (1894–95), Japan was marching toward another larger victory over Russia (1904–5). More self-confident, it showed little of its old anxiety to win foreign approval. Adequately manned with Japanese who had been trained abroad, it had little need of foreign teachers, even Fenollosa, much as his past services were appreciated. The best he could obtain under the circumstances was a position at the Tokyo Higher Normal School—quite a comedown from his former status. But Fenollosa was willing to accept his new position.[17]

While teaching English at school and carrying on his daily study program, Fenollosa also began to explore Chinese—Chinese philosophy with Michiaki Nemoto, an authority on the *I Ching*, and Chinese poetry with his former student Nagao Ariga and with Kainan Mori, an eminent scholar in the field. Fenollosa's interest was now extending beyond art toward philosophy and literature, beyond Japan toward China.[18]

His expanded explorations of the Orient continued after his return to America. In fact, they began to bear fruit in his second American period, the last phase of his career. Judging from those manuscripts he left at the time of his death, his second Japanese sojourn, though not as long or as glamorous as his first, yielded a harvest far richer and more lasting than he could have suspected. *Epochs of Chinese and Japanese Art* was a part of his legacy. The rest of it, luckily enough, fell into the hands of Ezra Pound, thereby making a chapter of modern literary history. The story about this historic transmission has been told in various versions,[19] but they all agree that Mrs. Fenollosa, impressed with the young Pound's recent work, entrusted him with her late husband's manuscripts, and that this Fenollosa-Pound contact signaled one of the most exciting moments in the development of twentieth-century poetry. In 1918, after having edited the Fenollosa manuscripts, his study of Noh drama, his translations of Chinese poetry, and his essay on poetics, Pound declared that in these pioneering efforts Fenollosa was clearly looking to "an American renaissance."[20]

Although Fenollosa's study of Chinese poetry was extensive (some 150 poems in his notebooks),[21] it yielded only *Cathay* (1915), a slim volume of fourteen Chinese poems. Since these poems were what Pound created out of Fenollosa's notes, *Cathay* is undoubtedly Pound's, although he could not have written it without those notes; therefore it would be best to discuss *Cathay* and its significance later, in the chapter on Pound.

Certain Noble Plays of Japan (1916), however, is Fenollosa's work. In a prefatory note to this volume which combined translations and commentaries, Pound clarified what he did and what he did not do to the original manuscript. His part in the prose was that of literary executor, and his part in the plays, "that of translator who has found all the heavy work done for him and who has had the pleasure of arranging beauty into the words." In its vision and plan, the book was altogether Fenollosa's.

In this attempt to introduce the classical Japanese drama to the West, Fenollosa was once again a pioneer. Since then, a good number of studies of this ancient dramatic form have appeared, all the products of better-equipped researchers than Fenollosa, and based on more up-to-date scholarship than was available in his time. And yet none of these studies has been able to supersede his *Certain Noble Plays of Japan*, even though it often suffers from Fenollosa's inadequate knowledge and Pound's sheer ignorance. What has kept the work alive is not only Pound's poetic magic as its translator but also Fenollosa's conviction of the significance Noh drama could have in modern literature.

Fenollosa first became interested in Noh drama in the early 1880s, during his first Japanese sojourn, probably through Morse, who was then taking lessons in Noh singing.[22] During his second sojourn Fenollosa's interest grew into a passion for the Noh as he took lessons in singing and acting, attended actual stage performances, and investigated various aspects of the Noh theater. As it happened, his mentor was Minoru Umewaka, head of a distinguished Noh theater family, who had single-handedly kept its ancient tradition alive throughout the uncertain years of the early Meiji period. This mentor, praising his American disciple's progress, declared that he was "advanced enough to sing in a Japanese company."[23] As Fenollosa himself noted with a measure of pride and confidence: "For the last twenty years I have been studying the Noh, under the personal tuition of Umewaka Minoru and his sons, learning by actual practice the method of the singing and something of the acting; I have taken from Umewaka's lips invaluable oral traditions of the stage as it was before 1868; and I have prepared, with his assistance and that of native scholars, translations of some fifty of the texts."

As a result of his two decade long study, practical and theoretical, Fenollosa became convinced of the significance of the Noh theater. "A form of drama," said Fenollosa, "as primitive, as intense, and almost as beautiful as the ancient Greek drama at Athens, still exists in the world. Yet few care for it, or see it." As usual, his sense of discovery went hand in hand with his sense of mission. In his opinion this drama, representing Oriental poetic literature, had "practical significance and even inspiration for us in this weak, transitional period of our Western poetic life." Indeed, the Noh has inspired numerous Western writers. Foremost among those who responded to Fenollosa's challenge were Pound and Yeats. In the Noh Pound discovered the needed rationale for his concern at the time, his concept of the unified image. Right or wrong, he saw that the better Noh plays were "all built into the intensification of a single Image." And as the leader of the Imagists he was especially heartened by what these Japanese plays suggested, the possibility of "a long Imagiste poem, or even a long poem in vers libre."[24] No less enthusiastically did Yeats write of this symbolic and ritualistic drama: "Therefore it is natural that I go to Asia for a stage-convention, for more formal faces, for a chorus that has no part in the action and perhaps for those movements of the body copied from the marionette shows of the fourteenth century."[25] What these moments of discovery meant to Pound and Yeats in the course of modern poetry has been well documented and needs no further comment. Suffice to say that through Pound and Yeats, Fenollosa became part of our literary history.

On the other hand, "The Chinese Written Character as a Medium for Poetry" (1919), another product of Fenollosa's Chinese study, does not pose the problem we have had with *Cathay* and *Certain Noble Plays of Japan*—the problem of distinguishing Fenollosa from Pound. This essay, according to Pound, was "practically finished" by Fenollosa at the time of his death, and all Pound did was "little more than remove a few repetitions and shape a few sentences."[26] Yet it poses another kind of problem. Ever since its appearance, the essay has been attacked or ridiculed by professional students of the Chinese language. George Kennedy, for one, called it "a small mass of confusion"—in regard to what Fenollosa had to say about the ideogrammic origin of Chinese.[27] All this is puzzling in view of his expressed intentions.

At the outset Fenollosa, while disclaiming his qualifications as a professional linguist or a Sinologue, makes it amply clear that he is speaking as "an enthusiastic student of beauty in Oriental culture." In this Pound was neither deceived nor misled, for he himself said in an introductory note: "We have here not a bare philological discussion, but a study of the fundamentals of all aesthetics." "The Chinese Written Character" was

100

intended to present Fenollosa's aesthetics, more specifically his poetics, and must be read as such. When approached in this spirit, the essay will reveal Fenollosa at the culmination of his lonely explorations of the Orient.

"My subject is poetry, not language, yet the roots of poetry are in language." With this statement Fenollosa goes directly to the nutrimental sources of "those universal elements of form which constitute poetics." Whether in Chinese or English, "all that poetic form requires is a regular and flexible sequence"—namely, syntax or sentence form. Syntax, Fenollosa argues, "ought to correspond to some primary law of nature." As he puts it, "the sentence form was forced upon primitive men by nature itself. It was not we who made it; it was a reflection of the temporal order in causation. All truth has to be expressed in sentences because all truth is the *transference of power.*" As is apparent in the agent-act-object sequence, "the act is the very substance of the fact denoted," both the agent and the object being merely limiting terms. And the normal and typical sentence, in English and Chinese, expresses just this unit of natural process. Hence Fenollosa's stress on the primacy of the transitive form, which corresponds to this universal form of action.

From this it should be clear that Fenollosa is attempting to relate language back to its origin, nature, and thereby restore its primary virtue, its primitive power. His is a theory of language based on nature, anticipated by Emerson in his essay *Nature.*[28] As Fenollosa further points out, metaphor represents the process in which material images suggest immaterial relations. No mere ornament, metaphor is a vital part of language, having evolved from the primitive stage of language which had to go beyond the seen, the concrete, and the material in order to express the unseen, the abstract, and the immaterial. Relating metaphor to poetry, Fenollosa declares:

> Metaphor, the revealer of nature, is the very substance of poetry. The known interprets the obscure, the universe is alive with matter. The beauty and freedom of the observed world furnish a model, and life is pregnant with art. It is a mistake to suppose, with some philosophers of aesthetics, that art and poetry aim to deal with the general and the abstract. This misconception has been foisted upon us by medieval logic. Art and poetry deal with the concrete of nature, not with rows of separate "particulars," for such rows do not exist. Poetry is finer than prose because it gives us more concrete truth in the same compass of words. Metaphor, its chief device, is at once substance of nature and of language. Poetry only does consciously what the primitive races did unconsciously. The chief work of literary men in dealing

with language, and of poets especially, lies in feeling back along the ancient lines of advance. He must do this so that he may keep his words enriched by all their subtle undertones of meaning. The original metaphors stand as a kind of luminous background, giving color and vitality, forcing them closer to the concreteness of natural process. Shakespeare everywhere teems with examples. For these reasons poetry was the earliest of the world arts; poetry, language and the core of myth grew up together.

The title of this essay, one may concede, is somewhat misleading since it deals with poetics, not philology. If Fenollosa at every turn refers to Chinese, it is because he believes that of all extant languages, Chinese best illustrates what he conceives of as an ideal poetic medium. (Or rather in his process of studying Chinese he came to conceive of this ideal language.) Chinese, he points out, is a language whose verbs are "all transitive or intransitive at pleasure," whose negatives still retain their root force, and whose infinitives require no weakening copulas. If this is what makes its syntax so poetical, this virtue derives from its proximity to nature.

In Fenollosa's opinion what is remarkable about Chinese is that while remaining concrete, particular, and strong, it is also capable of expressing the unseen, such as lofty thoughts, spiritual suggestions, and obscure relations, qualities which the best poetry must possess. All this, he believes, is because Chinese, unlike phonetic languages, still retains its primitive roots in its ideograms. After examining this and other obvious advantages Chinese has over phonetic languages, Fenollosa concludes that "such a pictorial method, whether the Chinese exemplifies it or not, would be the ideal language of the world."[29]

In "The Chinese Written Character" Fenollosa, by using Chinese as an actual model, attempted to delineate what he conceived of as an ideal poetic language, so that every language might realize its rich potentials. Although he dealt with Chinese, his real concern was with English. When he called attention to the lack of inflections and other similarities between Chinese and English, he remained convinced that more than any other Aryan language, English, though phonetic, approximates his ideal poetic language, and Shakespeare is the best living proof. As one who believed in the unity of humanity, Fenollosa reiterated the task the modern poet should perform. "With us," declared Fenollosa, "the poet is the only one for whom the accumulated treasures of the race-words are real and active." Whether in East or West, it is the poet, only the poet, who has kept, does keep, and will keep his language resilient, flexible, and fresh—in short, alive. Whether his language is ideogrammic really does not

102

matter, so long as the poet exploits all its potentials. In stressing the primary source of poetry Fenollosa clearly looked to the kind of poetics which has guided modern poetry and may well outlive it. As Donald Davie wrote:

> In its massive conciseness, Fenollosa's little treatise is perhaps the only English document of our time fit to rank with Sidney's *Apologie*, and the Preface to *Lyrical Ballads*, and Shelley's *Defense*, the great poetic manifestos of the past. For while the essay has already been influential (chiefly through the agency of Pound), it has not yet exerted the influence it deserves. We know as we read, in default of any historical evidence, that this is a great seminal work, speaking with the authority of a devoted and passionate solitary thinker.[30]

Along with all these projects Fenollosa continued to try his hand at poetry, fiction, and drama, as might be expected of Harvard Class Poet of 1874,[31] but the only fulfillment of his literary ambitions was a slim volume of poems entitled *East and West* (1893), which consisted of some thirty short poems and two long ones, "The Discovery of America" and "East and West." When the volume came out, one reviewer praised especially "The Discovery of America" as "the culmination of the great spontaneous and exuberant genius."[32] Although Fenollosa's poetry, by and large, reveals no great distinction, his lofty, prophetic vision commands attention, as in those two long poems which were inspired by Chicago's World Columbian Exposition in celebration of the 400th anniversary of the discovery of America.

True to its subtitle, "A Symphonic Poem," "The Discovery of America" has four movements: "The Fire and the Sky," "Dreams," "Wedding Music," and "Triumph," all centering on Columbus, "this second Ulysses," in his search for America. As Fenollosa states in his preface to the volume, the poem attempts to "exhibit the steadfast idealism of Columbus as the medium through which overshadowing Spirit arched its sublime purpose of uniting the East and the West" in the figures of Christ and Bodhisattva:

> . . . The Easts and Wests
> Are held in their two hands; and on their breasts
>   Lie child-eyed prophecies of faiths and creeds;
> And new-born worlds are twined like crystal symphonies of
>   beads.

What prophesied Columbus's discovery of America is once again to prophesy the meeting of East and West. "To-day his triumphant caravels have met the ambassadors of Xipangu on the shores of Lake Michigan," notes Fenollosa in the same preface, no doubt alluding to the World's Parliament of Religions, which met in conjunction with the Chicago Fair.

Fenollosa carries this global vision into the title poem, "East and West." In its five-part sequence ("The First Meeting of East and West," "The Separate East," "The Separate West," "The Present Meeting of East and West," and "The Future Union of East and West") Fenollosa starts with Alexander's dream of uniting East and West, traces the separate ways both have since followed, dwells on their current meeting, and concludes with their anticipated union which promises the birth of his "millennial man." East and West first met face to face under Alexander, mingling the arts of Greece and the mystical thought of India. Since their parting, the East slowly cultivated ideals which were feminine in their emphasis on social harmony, whereas the West has pursued ideals which were masculine in their emphasis on conquest, science, and industry. Eastern culture has evolved around brotherhood and Western culture has shown excessive personality. But this one-sidedness has been partly compensated for by the religion of each. The violence of the West has been softened by the feminine faith of love, renunciation, obedience, salvation from without, whereas the inertia of the East has been spurred by the martial faith of spiritual knighthood, self-reliance, salvation from within. "This stupendous double synthesis," writes Fenollosa, "seems to me the most significant fact in all history." The future union of East and West is therefore a twofold marriage. Although their attempted union has so far caused much confusion, Fenollosa stands convinced that our genuine interest in music predicts our native power to effect a greater integration. "Within the coming century," he concludes, "the blended strength of Scientific Analysis and Spiritual Wisdom should wed for eternity the blended grace of Aesthetic Synthesis and Spiritual Love."

Fenollosa's prophetic vision gradually achieves a sense of urgency toward the climax of "East and West," where he hails the birth of a new type of humanity in the marriage of East and West:

> Petals of infolded plan,
> Model of millennial man,
> Thine the vows of bride and spouse
> Plighted since the world began.

And finally:

There for a moment brief
It sits like God upon a lotus leaf;
The still unspoken Word
Before Creation stirred,
Or the transcendant Dove
Fell like a ray of love;—
Then fades in formless light
Too exquisite for human sight;
As when some saint is lifted up and hurled
Out of this mortal world,
This temple transitory
For Nature's unemancipated priest,
Into the silence of Nirwana's glory,
Where there is no more West and no more East.

Fenollosa also attempted to translate this prophetic vision into a series of more sober observations and statements. In his "Chinese and Japanese Traits," which appeared in the *Atlantic Monthly* for June 1892, he argued, while still fresh from his first Japanese sojourn, for the island empire and its people he had known personally. Objecting to the popular contrast of China's "prudent conservatism" with Japan's "hasty radicalism," he cited history to illustrate their remarkable affinities within the entire Far Eastern culture. Moreover, Japan has been deeply indebted to China, which was to the Far East what Greece was to Europe. With the situation reversed, Japan seems to have taken over the role China had played. All indications are that Japan will have much to offer to humanity as the world is once again in a position to realize Alexander's dream of fusing East and West into one. This plea finally turned into an eloquent prophecy as Fenollosa concluded: "Through her temperament, her individuality, her deeper insight into the secrets of the East, her ready divining of the powers of the West, and, more than all, through the fact that hers, the spiritual factor of the problem, must hold the master key to its solution, it may be decreed in the secret council chambers of Destiny that on her shores shall be first created that new latter-day type of civilized man which shall prevail throughout the world for the next thousand years."

This view of Japan as "the custodian of the sacred fire" was once more stressed in "The Relations of China and Japan and Their Bearing on Western Civilization," a speech Fenollosa delivered in Buffalo before sailing for his second Japanese sojourn. Japan's recent victory over China seemed not only to reinforce Fenollosa's earlier plea and prophecy but also to make him aware of the political situation that had resulted from the war. Pointing out that China, rather than accept Japanese assistance for reform, was turning to Russia, and that England, in her arrogant ignorance of Oriental civilization, refused to offer assistance, Fenollosa urged the West to respect the Japanese ambition to develop "from within" and help the entire East develop itself—an ambition which would contribute to future world civilization. Based on this analysis, Fenollosa suggested that "Japan, in alliance with England, would be able to incorporate a distinctive Oriental element in the world's future civilization by reorganizing China with her own ideas providentially preserved, unless prevented by the ultimate triumph of Russian semi-barbarism." That this suggestion was not simply politically motivated, Fenollosa made clear by stressing once again the Oriental ideal of social harmony, already mentioned in his preface to *East and West*, and also by taking issue with Lowell's thesis of Oriental impersonality versus Western personality. Branding Lowell's Western personality as excessive personality, Fenollosa explained Oriental impersonality in terms of the Oriental ideal of harmony, the kind of ideal which would encourage individuality. Expanding on what in the *Atlantic* article he had called "the last hope of a race," he stated: "The Eastern conception is to establish harmony and further the full expression of every tendency comformably with every other."[33]

His excessive enthusiasm, which perhaps blinded Fenollosa to the eventual consequences of Japanese ambition, must have sobered during his second Japanese sojourn as he witnessed the harsh political reality of Japan and also explored Chinese poetry and philosophy. He was now able to command a more balanced view of the whole question, as in his article "The Coming Fusion of East and West," written for the December 1898 issue of *Harper's*. Although he still trusted Japan's sincerity in pressuring China into action, Fenollosa made it clear in the article that once awakened by Japan, China would eventually be the "worthiest candidate" for the coming fusion of East and West. Returning to what he had suggested in the preface to *East and West*, "the blended strength of Scientific Analysis and Spiritual Wisdom," Fenollosa now rephrased it: "While the strength of the Western has tended to lie in a knowledge of *means*, the strength of the Eastern has tended to lie in a knowledge of *ends*." As he further pointed out: "If this be true, it is necessary to regard the fusion of East and West as indeed a sacred issue for which Time has waited. Each was doomed to failure in its isolation. Means without ends are blind; ends without means paralyzed. But each has the privilege to supply what the other lacks. The union of means and ends must vitalize every seed that man has sown."

As the title of this article indicates, Fenollosa was still pursuing his prophetic vision—with greater intensity now, as if it were within reach.

This sense of immediacy, doubtless, resulted from America's victory over Spain, which signaled the arrival of the new century and stirred Fenollosa's inspiration. At last America had found its proper role to play in the coming fusion of East and West. America, he believed, needed Eastern spiritual wisdom just as China needed Western scientific analysis. Envisioning what he called "a new world," Fenollosa concluded: "Columbus and his discovery are but a four-century-old stepping-stone to it, for we were obstacles in his western path that had to be first mastered. Today we enter literally into his dream and carry the Aryan banner of his caravels where he aimed to plant it—on the heights of an awakened East."

With "The Coming Fusion of East and West" Fenollosa finally succeeded in finding the missing link between "The Discovery of America" and "East and West" by defining the future role of America in his visionary scheme. In this role which she seemed to owe to history, America was destined to carry on Columbus's quest for the Orient. Invoking Columbus, whose steadfast idealism might serve to unite the world once again, Fenollosa wrote in the preface to *East and West*: "Steadfast as he, I cling to the faith that a frank recognition of the great, illuminating, spiritual verities, realized by the vivid flash of the imagination, is, and has been always, in art the only profound realism." This Whitmanesque invocation of Columbus rang with personal significance. After all, Fenollosa himself was half-Spanish by birth, just as Columbus was by choice; also, as he did in his Harvard Class Book, Fenollosa proudly traced his aristocratic origins to the union of a conquistador and an Aztec princess at the time of Cortez.[34] His invocation of Columbus was justified—not because of these romantic claims but because of what he did to expand the cultural horizons of America.

SIX

Hearn

Lafcadio Hearn (1850–1904), the last to join this distinguished company of Yankees, was not even a native of America, though he spent his formative years as a journalist and writer there. (Son of an Anglo-Irish army physician and a Greek woman, he was born in the Ionian islands, raised in Dublin by his great-aunt, and shipped to America in 1869.) When he arrived in Japan in 1890, hoping to write a series of magazine articles on the new civilization in Japan, he was already forty years of age with some literary reputation to his credit. He intended this trans-Pacific journey to be just another expression of his ceaseless wanderlust as a "civilized nomad." But fate apparently decreed otherwise. As he got caught up in a chain of events which included teaching and marriage, one year stretched to fourteen and one book multiplied to a dozen. Even death could not wrest him from Japan. On the contrary, it made him a part of Japan forever.[1] There is something inevitable about this, for of all places it was Japan that had most appealed to his aesthetic sensibility and that had invariably been the destination of his imaginary voyages.

No matter how inevitable, the price was too costly for Hearn to accept without protest. Indeed, he was no lotus-eater. Those fourteen years were in part a life of exile, a life of captivity. To this self-imposed bondage he remained not wholly reconciled to the last.

In his isolation Hearn felt that he was losing his artistic inspiration. Often "in literary despair," he complained of Japan as "a sort of psychological tropic"—a legitimate complaint for the kind of artist he was, an artist highly susceptible to climatic changes.[2] Apart from such a personal factor, there was another, his growing detestation of the New Japan of the 1890s, increasingly arrogant and chauvinistic in its inflated sense of self-confidence—the Japan which sobered Fenollosa during his second sojourn. It was the disillusionment that was bound to come after enthusiasm. This alternation of light and darkness Hearn and his friend B. H. Chamberlain would call "the swing of the pendulum." "Pendulum on the left—," he confided to Chamberlain after having lived nearly four years in Japan: "To make everything that he [the Japanese] adopts small—philosophy, sciences, material, arts, machinery;—everything is modified in many ways, but uniformly diminished for Lilliput. And Lilliput is not

108

tall enough to see far. Cosmic emotions do not come to Lilliputians. Did any Japanese ever feel such an emotion? Will any ever feel one?" "We are *Brobdingnagians!*"[3] Here Hearn was merely voicing what Adams, Lowell, and many other Westerners in Japan had often felt.[4] A little later Hearn wrote to the same friend, this time while visiting Yokohama:

> Another day, and I was in touch with England again. How small suddenly my little Japan became! —how lonesome! What a joy to feel the West! What a great thing is the West! What new appreciations of it are born of isolation! What a horrible place the school!—I was a prisoner released from prison after five years' servitude!
>
> Then I stopped thinking. For I saw my home,—and the lights of its household Gods,—and my boy reaching out his little hands to me,—and all the simple charm and love of old Japan. And the fairy-world seized my soul again, very softly and sweetly,—as a child might catch a butterfly.[5]

Hearn was "a caged cicada," as he characterized his own life in Japan. Consoling him, Chamberlain wrote: "The only thing I don't like is your want of satisfaction with the fame brought by your books. Japan, no doubt, is a small field. Still here you are king; and could any one be more?"[6] He reiterated this point more emphatically in another letter: "You ought, I say, to be the man of all others fitted to form a just opinion,—a final opinion on this land and people. You have been under the spell, and are now disillusioned, and yet not so disillusioned as not to retain much love for that which no longer seems divine. Write another book, and call it "Illusion and Disillusion," and give us *all* Japan,—the lights and the shadows, the native and the bearded foreigners, the dear old Tempo man."[7] Hearn's Japanese books resulted from his renewed response to Chamberlain's challenge.

When, soon after his arrival in Japan, Hearn proceeded to Matsue as an English teacher, he found himself also an interpreter of the West to his Japanese students. By 1896, when he accepted the chair of English literature at Tokyo Imperial University ("Imperial" was added in 1886), Hearn had already played his role of interpreter for several years on more than one level, in more than one place. This time, however, his audience was no longer a local one, but consisted of the cream of a young generation, the intellectual elite groomed to carry forward the destiny of modern Japan. To judge from his students' reaction to his half-forced resignation of 1903, Hearn discharged his professorial duties fully and well, despite his meager academic credentials. They were deeply hurt "to think that even the biggest school of Japan could not afford to keep one Hearn,'' and all agreed that ''there was no greater teacher of literature than Hearn in Japan.''[8] Years later, when selections made from his former students' verbatim notes began to appear, they were greeted with acclaim. John Erskine, who edited the first several volumes of Hearn's university lectures, went so far as to compare them to the best of Coleridge. Norman Foerster, though denying any distinction to Hearn as ''a judge of literature,'' conceded that he must have been ''an illuminating teacher.''[9]

In these lectures Hearn perforce acted as an interpreter of the West as he tried to present English literature as an illustration of Western culture to his Japanese students. Whether in a historical survey of English literature or in a series of special lectures, Hearn approached literature from a global perspective and as the ongoing creative process, for he was convinced that literary studies should be primarily creative in inducing students to produce literature in their own language. Moreover, Hearn defined literature as ''an art of emotional expression,'' and by the term *emotion* he meant something specific, namely, ''organic memory'' or inherited memory, anticipating Jung's concept of the collective unconscious. This emphasis on the universality of emotion as the basis of literature gave his lectures a sense of unity while making him an effective teacher of literature. As Takeshi Saito noted: ''Though he was not an academic scholar or critic, his lectures are said to have had the magic power of transforming the lecture-room into a fairyland where poets and novelists of olden days and new came and went, and each lecture disclosed to students some hidden corners of their hearts. Hearn attracted his pupils with his penetrating insight into others' minds as well as with his unworldly character and love of Japan.''[10]

At the same time he presented the West to his Japanese students, Hearn also interpreted Japan to his readers back at home. For both roles Hearn had long prepared himself—while still in America—as a journalist, writer, and translator. As early as 1883, at the threshold of his literary career, Hearn declared: ''I would give up anything to be a literary Columbus,—to discover a Romantic America in some West Indian or North African or Oriental region,—to describe the life that is only fully treated of in universal geographies or ethnological researches. Won't you sympathize with me?''[11] Certainly, all his American writings were based on his travels, actual and imaginary. There were ''Ozias Midwinter'' letters, ''Floridian Reveries,'' and *Two Years in the French West Indies* (1890), all his firsthand travel accounts; there were also *Stray Leaves from Strange Literature* (1884) and *Some Chinese Ghosts* (1887), both imaginary flights to many a land by way of their colorful myths and legends; and there were *Chita* (1889) and *Youma* (1890), his romances full of local

110

color. All these old and divers interests finally culminated in his Japanese books.

They are no ordinary travelogs. Unlike his university lectures, the Japanese books were rewritten, revised, and polished with care, for they were intended to meet Chamberlain's challenge: "Give us *all* Japan." And they do give us all Japan, and more. They also give us Hearn, all Hearn, for into these dozen volumes he put not only Japan but also himself, as though he had sensed that they would eventually decide whatever claim he might have to literary fame.

Chronicling the fourteen years Hearn lived in Japan as a curious traveler, a foreign teacher, a family man, and a maturing artist, the Japanese books offer anything and everything imaginable about Japan and the Japanese, ranging from the simplest to the most intricate, from the most obvious to the most esoteric. They are, in Chamberlain's words, "perfect mines for the enquirer to dig in." Take, for instance, the Japanese smile, a topic which elicited Adams's remark: "Positively everything in Japan laughs."[12] Since it is one of the most common experiences that mystify Westerners, Adams's reaction was natural enough, no better or no worse than that of many other fellow sojourners. But this same experience made Hearn write "The Japanese Smile," an in-depth study of nearly thirty pages. "A Japanese can smile in the teeth of death, and usually does. But he then smiles for the same reason that he smiles at other times. There is neither defiance nor hypocrisy in the smile; nor is it to be confounded with that smile of sickly resignation which we are apt to associate with weakness of character. It is an elaborate and long-cultivated etiquette. It is also a silent language." This Hearn illustrated with several cases involving Westerners' misunderstanding, often comic and often tragic.[13]

Take another example, nirvana, which Adams found too late for the season, and which Lowell likened to "the idyllic stupefaction of the cow in the stall, or the dog upon the hearth-rug." Having known something about the topic in America, in Japan Hearn determined to come to grips with it once and for all in his more than forty-page-long essay "Nirvana." By exploring this central Buddhist doctrine in terms of relevant scriptural passages and also modern scientific theories, Hearn drove his point home: "Nirvana is no cessation, but an emancipation. It means only the passing of conditioned being into unconditioned being—the fading of all mental and physical phantoms into the light of Formless Omnipotence and Omniscience." Take still another example, Japanese women, about whom Adams found nothing good, much less beautiful: "They are all badly made, awkward in movement, and suggestive of monkeys." This is doubly shocking since the Japanese woman is one thing that rarely disappointed Western travelers in Japan. Hearn had this to say: "It has well been said that the most wonderful aesthetic products of Japan are not its ivories, nor its bronzes, nor its porcelains, nor its swords, nor any of its marvels in metal or lacquer—but its women.''[14]

Hearn's Japanese books are rich in variety, each showing a different combination of four genres: sketch, essay, legend, and prose poem. In terms of the combination of these four genres the Japanese books reveal an interesting pattern. *Glimpses of Unfamiliar Japan* (1894), the first of these, was what Hearn had originally proposed to write. In relating an artist-teacher's initiation into Japan during the period 1890–94, *Glimpses* was meant to be only an introductory book with sketches for the most part and few essays. But with his next book, *Out of the East: Reveries and Studies in New Japan* (1895), more essays began to appear along with sketches. This tendency continued in the two ensuing works, *Kokoro: Hints and Echoes of Japanese Inner Life* (1896) and *Gleanings in Buddha-Fields: Studies of Hand and Soul in the Far East* (1897). Both titles clearly indicated Hearn's attempt to penetrate into the inner life of Japan —far beyond the initial stage of sensations and impressions. His theoretical explorations resulted in *Exotics and Retrospectives* (1898), a series of highly original speculations in poetic prose on the mystery of organic memory in terms of evolutionism and Buddhism.

With the next group of works, *In Ghostly Japan* (1899), *Shadowings* (1900), *A Japanese Miscellany* (1901), and *Kotto* (1902), Hearn passed still another turning point. While pursuing his inner explorations, he was no longer theoretical, but gathered more legends haunted with ghostly shadows and more prose poems laden with personal memories—both from the depths of the psyche, collective and personal. And with the last group of works, *Kwaidan* (1904), *Japan: An Attempt at Interpretation* (1904), and *The Romance of the Milky Way* (1905), Hearn completed the whole cycle. His sense of finality was pervasive: *Kwaidan* was the culmination of his legends; *Japan*, the culmination of his essays; and *The Romance of the Milky Way*, a posthumous collection of legends, memories, letters home, and other pieces.

It was in Japan that Hearn was finally freed from his stylistic obsession, his long-cherished dream of a poetical prose. At last he came to realize that his concept of a literary style was too confining, too narrow to meet his need to register his total response to Japan. Now he was willing to vary his style according to his subject: for sketches and legends he used a pure, simple, colloquial style; for essays a sort of middle style; and for prose poems his old poetical prose. This stylistic freedom insured Hearn's maturation both as an artist and as a man. In a way he matured as he tried to come closer to Japan. By trying to give us all Japan he also gave us all Hearn.

Although he succeeded as well as anyone possibly could in meeting

Chamberlain's challenge, the impression persists that what he gave us is not all Japan but only a part of it. In this even the Japanese are not always the best judges. According to Yoshie Okazaki, for instance, "It was unavoidable that he should have been unable to have a true understanding of Japan and have seen it as a dreamlike world of mystery, in spite of his love for and aspirations with regard to Japan."[15] That is, Hearn, enamored with Old Japan, failed to do justice to New Japan. But such was not the case. As a longtime resident in Japan, first in provincial towns, then in Kobe and Tokyo, Hearn saw as much of New Japan as any foreigner could. He lived through one of the most critical periods of modern Japanese history, the period between the war with China and the war with Russia. In his books he duly registered the pulses and heartbeats of the Japanese ridden with doubts, frustrations, dreams, and aspirations. Sympathetic as he was, Hearn apprehended the course they were single-mindedly pursuing under their historical mandate of modernization and Westernization. That it was a matter of national survival, and that the Japanese had no alternative, Hearn knew full well, yet he could not but voice his misgivings, his personal protest. He feared the tragic consequences sure to follow their wholesale break with tradition. As time went on he became more painfully aware of the shallowness of the young generation fast drifting away from their cultural roots. With this in mind he said in a farewell speech to his Matsue students: "This is an era of great and rapid change; and it is probable that many of you, as you grow up, will not be able to believe everything that your fathers believed before you; though I sincerely trust you will at least continue always to respect the faith, even as you still respect the memory, of your ancestors."[16] This he was saying not merely out of his poetic love for Old Japan. The further he explored Japan the more he became convinced that Japan could and should be understood in terms of its foundations, not its surface. The increasing number of folktales, legends, and myths in his Japanese books does indicate that through them, by retelling them, Hearn hoped to gain access to the psychic structure of Japan, the soul of Japan—in short, Old Japan. Hearn explored Old Japan in order to do full justice to New Japan, as he did in *Japan: An Attempt at Interpretation*.

Japan, originally written for his prospective American lectures, synthesized all his previous attempts, such as "The Genius of Japanese Civilization" and "Some Thoughts on Ancestor-Worship." When the volume appeared shortly after Hearn's death, William E. Griffis hailed it as "the product of long years of thought, of keenest perception, of marvellous comprehension"—"a classic in science, a wonder of interpretation."[17] *Japan*, if anything, should serve as Hearn's final, most balanced opinion about the subject.

Coming directly to the heart of the matter, Hearn declares that "the history of Japan is really the history of her religion." Accepting Spencer's law of religious development he postulates that the cult of ancestor worship is at the root of Japanese culture—its religion, ethics, aesthetics, and all its social institutions. Using Japanese history he illustrates the process in which this ancient cult adopted and absorbed alien beliefs, Chinese and Indian, thereby developing into Shintoism through three stages—family cult, communal cult, and state cult. As he points out, the patriarchal society built on these three levels of ancestor worship turned out to be receptive to Confucianism and Buddhism. Although its original doctrine conflicted with Shinto beliefs, Buddhism could meet the special needs of the Japanese because of its proven adaptability in India, China, and Korea. In Hearn's opinion Buddhism, more than anything else, has humanized and civilized the Japanese without uprooting their indigenous ancestor worship.

This religious conservatism, Hearn continues, accounts for the immense duration of the Japanese imperial dynasty as well as for the relative brevity of its various regencies and shogunates. The Fujiwara rule, for instance, was of comparatively long duration because it represented a religious aristocracy, whereas the Tokugawa, which was noted for its fortified religion of loyalty, collapsed rapidly because of its essentially military foundation. This same conservatism also accounts for the failure of the Jesuit attempt to convert Japan. Because of its monotheistic position, Christianity could not adapt itself to Japanese society, where the religion of filial piety still persisted. In the light of such a historical precedent, Hearn is confident that Japan could and would react similarly to the peril of Western aggression. Even under the pressure of modern Western democracies Japan would sustain itself as long as it relied on "the new national sentiment of trust and duty: the modern sense of patriotism"—"this new religion of loyalty, evolved, through the old, from the ancient religion of the dead."

As a staunch evolutionist Hearn refuses to accept Japan as a unique case, isolated from universal evolution. As Spencer provides him with the necessary theoretical framework, so Fustel de Coulanges supports what Hearn regards as the fundamental parallel between Japanese and Greco-Roman society. Drawing on Coulanges's classic study *La Cité antique*, Hearn looks to the unity of East and West in the history of human evolution. As he emphatically states, Japan managed to maintain its ancient patriarchal social structure whereas Europe lost its own through the industrial revolution. In this sense Japan is "evolutionally young." With this premise Hearn ponders on the present state of Japan and on its future in international competition.

Although the Meiji Restoration freed Japan from the bonds of feudal

114

law and military rule, its social foundations have so far retained their ancient shape largely through the tremendous social pressure on the individual Japanese, Hearn observes. Most typical of this social pressure is official education, which is still conducted upon a traditional plan, after all its modernizations. Hearn cannot but dread the possible consequences of the current educational policy, which has failed to encourage the cultivation of a more ''constructive'' imagination. As a result, home scholarship remains indifferent to the higher emotional and intellectual sides of Western civilization. This indifference, Hearn believes, is a matter of grave concern since Japan must now compete with the West for survival. As Hearn sees it, Japan's dilemma is that, although evolutionally young enough to retain its patriarchal society, it has been compelled to revamp itself in the course of a generation into an industrialized society. Yet the capacity for industrial competition, as Western history testifies, depends on the intelligent freedom of the individual. Recalling Coulanges's thesis that the absence of individual liberty caused the disintegration of Greek society, Hearn concludes that the absence of individual freedom in modern Japan is nothing less than a national danger. ''Only those long accustomed to personal liberty—liberty to think about matters of ethics apart from matters of government—liberty to consider questions of right and wrong, justice and injustice, independently of political authority—are able to face without risk the peril now menacing Japan.'' Therefore, what Japan desperately needs is more personal freedom, ''freedom restrained by wisdom,'' ''freedom to think and act and strive for self as well as for others.''

In 1903, when *Japan* was near completion, Hearn wrote to an old friend in America: ''Lowell's *Soul of the Far East* is the only book of the kind in English; but I have taken a totally different view of the causes and the evolution of things.''[18] Considering his expressed admiration for Lowell's book, Hearn's confidence was unusually high. Indeed, these two books were much alike and yet very different. Although pressing the same evolutionary notion that Japan is young, Lowell and Hearn came up with radically different diagnoses and cures.

As we recall, Lowell warned in the conclusion of *The Soul of the Far East*: ''Unless their newly imported ideas really take root, it is from this whole world that Japanese and Koreans, as well as Chinese, will be inevitably excluded.''[19] This warning was absolutely just in the light of the historical reality that confronted the Far East at the time. But Lowell would not explain how his so-called mysterious mind-seed could be transplanted in the soul made unreceptive by its innate absence of personality; he merely voiced an ultimatum. On the other hand, Hearn's advice was certainly sober, but at least it was positive: he urged more individual freedom for the Japanese, a kind of freedom restrained by wisdom, which alone would ensure their national survival and their cultural integrity. In warning the Japanese about their future without such personal freedom Hearn was certainly prophetic, as recent history has demonstrated.[20]

Again, it was Lowell who declared: "We discover in his [the Far Oriental's] peculiar point of view a new importance,—the possibility of using it stereoptically."[21] In exploring and exploiting this possibility Hearn was not unlike Lowell, in fact, he went further than Lowell. In all his Japanese studies Lowell remained the observer, classifier, analyzer, and synthesizer—in short, a scientist to the last, brilliantly original but without any intimate involvement. This was what Hearn meant by Lowell's "from the top" method and his "scientific mind." Impressed as he was with Lowell's work, Hearn was determined to go his own way, "from the bottom."[22] By living with the Japanese he learned to think and feel as they did. Morse, too, had said a decade earlier: "It is by taking actual lessons in the tea ceremony and in singing that I may learn many things from the Japanese standpoint."[23] This approach which made Morse's *Japan Day by Day* singularly accurate, refreshing, and Japanese, was also Hearn's. Moreover, Hearn possessed another virtue, his "soul sympathy,"[24] which enabled him to identify with his subject—the ultimate secret of the permanence of his Japanese books.

It was not only Japan that Hearn learned to look at from the Japanese point of view; he also learned to look at his own West from the same point of view. A subtle and slow process, it took him more than three years after his arrival in Japan. But when it came it was dramatic, as dramatic as any experience of discovery. In 1893 Hearn wrote to an American friend:

> They send me a paper—the Sunday edition, full of poetry about love, wood-cuts of beautiful fashion; and all sorts of chatter about women and new-styles of undergarments. Today, after three years in the most Eastern East, when I look at that paper, I can hardly believe my eyes. The East has opened my eyes. How affected the whole thing seems! Yet it never seemed so to me before. My students say to me, "Dear Teacher, why are your English novels all filled with nonsense about love and woman?— we do not like such things."[25]

Note the role his teaching also played in this drama. The incident set him thinking about this theme of sexualism from an East-West perspective. In June he confided to Chamberlain: "And here is something else *entre nous*. I am going, in spite of considerable self-distrust, to attempt a

116

philosophical article on L'éternal féminin—in the West, as elucidated by the East. *Ex Oriente Lux*! This idea has encouraged me to the attempt; and I am therefore very careful of the idea,—like one having made a discovery.''[26] Hearn had to overcome many doubts and misgivings as he tried to formulate his central thesis. What resulted was the essay "Of the Eternal Feminine," which appeared in the *Atlantic Monthly* for December.

The essay begins with Hearn's elaboration on the statement: "The East has opened my eyes":

> He who would study impartially the life and thought of the Orient must also study those of the Occident from the Oriental point of view. And the results of such a comparative study he will find to be in no small degree retroactive. According to his character and his faculty of perception, he will be more or less affected by those Oriental influences to which he submits himself. The conditions of Western life will gradually begin to assume for him new, undreamed-of meanings, and to lose not a few of their old familiar aspects. Much that he once deemed right and true he may begin to find abnormal and false. He may begin to doubt whether the moral ideals of the West are really the highest. He may feel more than inclined to dispute the estimate placed by Western custom upon Western civilization. Whether his doubts be final is another matter: they will be at least rational enough and powerful enough to modify permanently some of his prior convictions.[27]

Here Hearn describes in a general way the process of his own transformation. Remarkably enough, he was still capable of such a transformation, though long past the impressionable period of his life. Furthermore, he had to undergo such a process more than once as he tried to come to grips with his own West over those issues which confronted him in his ceaseless explorations of Japan. The first of these issues was sexual idealism in the West, a natural topic for him because he had written about it for many years. With him it had become such an obsession that his one-time friend Dr. George Gould once exclaimed: "*C'est toujours femme!*"[28]

In the essay "Of the Eternal Feminine" Hearn relates the difficulty of making his Japanese students understand love as the dominant force in Western literature. This difficulty, he believes, arises because their culture does not have the kind of sexual idealism—apotheosis of woman—that has characterized the West. Hearn refuses to explain away this Oriental absence of sexual idealism in terms of the alleged low position of woman in Far Eastern society or in terms of Far Eastern religions, since he is familiar with the significant role of the female principle in their tenets and practices. As far as he can determine, this absence of the feminine ideal in Far Eastern art and literature reflects tendencies deeply rooted in racial character, much older than the idea of the family and the oldest religious beliefs and practices.

By contrast, the aesthetic and moral ideal of the Eternal Feminine, Hearn points out, may well be the strongest evidence of the Western genius for apotheosis. This ideal of woman as the unattainable, the incomprehensible, the divine, has permeated every phase of Western civilization, molding its life and character. Many factors, Hearn continues, have contributed to its historical development—the Greek apotheosis of human beauty, the Christian worship of the Mother of God, the exaltations of chivalry, the spirit of the Renaissance, and so on—all of which must have had "their nourishment, if not their birth, in a race feeling ancient as Aryan speech, and as alien to the most eastern East." In this long process the ideal of the Eternal Feminine has turned into an aesthetic abstraction, making even nature feminine. "Thus," Hearn sums up, "out of simple human passion, through influences and transformations innumerable, we have evolved a cosmic emotion, a feminine pantheism."

In this Hearn was not alone. Adams, noting that sex does not exist in Japan, also declared: "Sex begins with the Aryan race."[29] Lowell, too, regretted that woman is not regarded as the source of the Far Eastern imagination, and, resorting to his favorite personality-versus-impersonality theme, he pointed out that the Far Eastern Muse is not woman but nature.[30] Both Lowell and Hearn agreed that to the Far Eastern mind art and nature are inseparable, but they began to diverge the moment Lowell insisted on Western sexual idealism as the norm the Far East should adopt. Hearn posed a series of questions: Is this sexual idealism absolutely necessary to our intellectual health? Is it not possible that because our aesthetic faculties have overdeveloped in one direction, we are left blind to many wonderful aspects of nature? Is ours really the highest possible ideal? Is there not a higher ideal, known perhaps to the Oriental soul?

Coming to his main point, the treatment of nature in art, Hearn asks two specific questions: Are we Western artists capable of perceiving the infinitely varied aspects of nature? Are there not some serious limitations in the Western approach to nature, which is neither masculine nor feminine, but neutral or nameless? Being free of anthropomorphism, Eastern artists can see in nature much that for thousands of years has remained invisible to their Western confreres, Hearn argues. Because of its anthropomorphism and its passional ideal, Western art is rooted in sexual idealism and likely to degenerate into an indifferent realism whenever it takes a realistic approach to nature. Finally, Hearn points to the rocks in his garden, whose value to their owner reflects not the expense of transporting them but their aesthetic suggestiveness. To those who would ask what the Japanese find so beautiful about a common stone, Hearn answers: "Many things; but I will mention only one—irregularity."[31]

While Lowell turned his personality-versus-impersonality theme into a matter of superiority-inferiority, Hearn, starting from his thesis of personification and its absence, came to discover "irregularity," one of the major aesthetic principles of Far Eastern art and culture. Hearn's motive was neither to determine which of these modes is superior or inferior, nor to indulge intellectual speculations for their own sake. As he said, his intent was to explore the contrast between East and West for his own intellectual health by reexamining certain aspects of Western aesthetic thought in the light of Eastern aesthetic thought, so that the former might be readjusted, enlarged, and enriched. From experience he became all the more convinced that this was possible, however slow and often painful the process might be.

The second issue Hearn had to wrestle with, along with that of sexual idealism, was Western individualism. Here, too, Lowell's theory of personality versus impersonality served as his springboard. As early as August 1891 and despite his renewed admiration, Hearn found himself horrified by some of the conclusions set forth in *The Soul of the Far East*. In particular, he thought Lowell's contention that "the degree of the development of individuality in a people necessarily marks its place in the great march of mind" is "not true necessarily." "At least," continued he, "it may be argued about." Frankly, he doubted that the cultivation of individuality is really "a lofty or desirable tendency," for the simple reason that much of so-called personality and individuality is "intensely repellant" and the cause of "the principal misery of Occidental life." To him the term *individuality* connoted aggressive selfishness.[32] Although he subscribed fully to Spencer's view that the highest individuation must coincide with the greatest mutual dependence, and that evolutionary progress tends at once toward the greatest separateness and the greatest union, Hearn wondered whether our Western methods of cultivating individuality are natural and right, and whether we may eventually have to abandon all our present notions about the highest progress and the highest morality. "Personally," Hearn opined, "I think we are dead wrong." The further he pondered over the question the more he wanted to write about "Morbid Individuality," taking issue with Lowell.[33]

After several years in Japan, Hearn came to appreciate this absence of personality which Lowell branded an Oriental phenomenon. His own experience convinced him that what Lowell called impersonality in the Japanese is largely voluntary, a result of their traditional life, which has been "religiously regulated by the spirit of self-suppression for the sake of the family, the community, the nation." As he pointed out, Japanese impersonality reflects an "ancient moral tendency to self-sacrifice for duty's sake," certainly not a lack of personality. Inasmuch as the sacrifice of self for others is the highest possible morality from any religious point of view, Christian or pagan, Hearn observed that the traditional Japanese civilization is morally as far in advance of the Western as it is materially behind it. While conceding that this advance was made at some considerable sacrifice to character and mental evolution, Hearn concluded that "the loss does not signify that the moral policy was wrong."[34]

Like many of his Victorian contemporaries, Hearn was here reexamining one of the burning issues of the day, the moral basis of modern industrial and commercial society. He felt that Christianity offered no solution to the problem, having betrayed its incapacity to tame the all-demanding industrial and commercial materialism in the West. With its spiritual and moral foundation thus weakened, the West would be a mere aggregate of individuals, each striving to expand his own individuality at the expense of everyone else. The future peril of the West would be this unbridled expansion of the individual, Hearn argued.[35] If this moral laxity constitutes the peril from within, there is the other peril the West must face, the peril from without, namely, the industrial competition that is bound to come from the Far East. At issue here is the survival of the West, and surprisingly, it is China rather than Japan that figured in Hearn's panorama of the East-West struggle for survival.

In his article "China and the Western World: a Retrospective and a Prospect" (1896) Hearn speculates on the destiny of China in particular and of humanity in general. Dismissing current views on the causes of the recent Sino-Japanese War as altogether superficial, Hearn states: "The vast tidal wave of Occidental civilization, rolling round the world, had lifted Japan and hurled her against China, with the result that the Chinese Empire is now a hopeless wreck." Yet once industrialized under Western pressure, China would eventually confront the West. The final outcome of the East-West struggle for survival, the struggle between the luxury-loving, pleasure-seeking races and those races struggling for the simple privilege of life, seems obvious. Having fulfilled its historical role on this planet, is the West now doomed to disappear? Does the future belong to the East? The only way out of this crisis of the West, Hearn suggested, would be a sort of internationalization in which East and West could cooperate as partners—"universal brotherhood, without distinctions of country, creed, or blood":

It is neither unscientific nor unreasonable to suppose the world eventually peopled by a race different from any now existing, yet created by the blending of the best types of all races; uniting Western energy with Far-Eastern patience, northern vigor with southern sensibility, the highest ethical feelings developed by all great religions with the largest mental faculties evolved by all civilizations; speaking a single tongue composed from the richest and strongest elements of all preëxisting human speech; and forming a society unimaginably unlike, yet so unimaginably superior to, anything which now is or has ever been.[36]

To those who may wonder about the possibility of such an earthly paradise, Hearn pointed to the ant society as his insect pattern,[37] and to Old Japan as his human pattern. As he wrote in *Japan*, this was the ultimate charm of Old Japan with its ideals: "instinctive unselfishness, a common desire to find the joy of life in making happiness for others, a universal sense of moral beauty." In other words, Old Japan foreshadowed "the possibilities of some higher future, in a world of perfect sympathy."[38] Upholding Old Japan as a symbolic norm, Hearn urged the Japanese to exercise more personal freedom, and at the same time warned his own West against the peril of unbridled individualism.

The third issue Hearn had to deal with was that of science and faith which tore the Victorian world asunder. Like many of his contemporaries, he had lost his faith early in his life, "at the tender age of fifteen," to use his own words,[39] and like them, he had also striven to recover it. In the process he turned to the East and also accepted evolutionism, what he called Spencer's oceanic philosophy. After having lived in Japan for several years, in its Buddhist atmosphere, Hearn came to realize that his whole thinking had changed despite his studies of Spencer. As is evident in his essays "The Stone Buddha," "In Yokohama," "The Idea of Preëxistence," and "Nirvana," Hearn redoubled his efforts to explore some of the central doctrines of Buddhism in terms of evolutionary science. Once again the old pattern of evolutionism and Buddhism asserted itself, with greater clarity and force, converging with his East-West theme.

This dialectical pattern resulted in his chapter "The Higher Buddhism" in *Japan*. Clarifying his position Hearn writes: "I venture to call myself a student of Herbert Spencer; and it was because of my acquaintance with the Synthetic Philosophy that I came to find in Buddhist philosophy a more than romantic interest."[40] As a student of modern philosophy Hearn notes that Buddhism has formulated its basic doctrines through mental process unknown to Western thinking and unaided by any scientific knowledge. After examining Buddhist doctrines of nirvana, self, karma, etc., in terms of Spencer's observations, Hearn points out that Buddhism and evolutionism begin to diverge as regards the ultimate. In admitting their intellectual incapacity for grasping the unknowable reality, Spencer and his fellow evolutionists are agnostic, whereas Buddhism professes to know this. Moreover, evolutionism would "attribute the qualities of the atom merely to a sort of heredity—to the persistency of tendencies developed under chance influences operating throughout an incalculable past," whereas Buddhism "proclaims a purely moral order of the cosmos, and attaches almost infinite consequence to the least of human acts." Despite their common monistic stand, Hearn declares, evolutionism remains amoral, whereas Buddhism postulates a moral universe.

Through his study of evolutionism and Buddhism Hearn came to regard the one as a manifestation of the Western genius and the other as a manifestation of the Eastern genius; he also came to believe their union at once possible and logical, not just because of their complementariness but rather because of their common monistic ground. Although, Hearn noted further, the East has already accepted Western science, the spiritual authorities of the West have for centuries attempted to impede the advance of science and are now alarmed at the possible invasion of Eastern religion. As the most practical solution to this situation Hearn urged the West to respond more positively to the spiritual challenge from the East. "The soft serenity, the passionless tenderness, of these Buddha faces might yet give peace of soul to a West weary of creeds transformed into conventions, eager for the coming of another teacher to proclaim."[41] Hearn wondered if it was absolutely necessary for Christianity to stress its own uniqueness based on its dogmas. As he saw it, Christian dogmas—the hypothesis of special creation, faith in a personal God, belief in the continuation of personality after death—seemed no longer tenable in the light of modern science. Philosophical Buddhism convinced him that faith is still possible without adhering to rigid dogmas, and that faith can embrace science and humanize it with its profound spirituality. When the West ceases to cling to these dogmas, Hearn noted, East and West will be one whole with its universal religion. Insisting on the common ground where all religions converge, Hearn in effect proposed the perennial philosophy, and his call was for a recovery of faith on the divine ground which alone could reconcile religion and science, East and West.

> All of the old barriers set up by dogmatic faith have been broken down. The future is to be a new era of thought, a new era of philosophy. The ultimate questions must, indeed, remain for us as dark as ever—unless we should be able at some enormously remote time to develop new senses. The indications are that in

122

the immediate future Western and Eastern thought will cease to be in opposition, and that a combination is very likely to occur between the fundamental truth of Oriental philosophy and of Occidental science. Should this come about, we might expect the inauguration of what might be called a new universal religion—a religion of humanity, not in the sense of Comte (which was an impossible dream), but in that ethical signification which would represent the unification of all that is best in human knowledge and experience.[42]

Furthermore, Hearn rested this reintegration of East and West on the reintegration of man himself. In his scheme the East, with its emphasis on religious wisdom, represented the feminine, and the West, with its emphasis on scientific knowledge, represented the masculine. As he saw in the symbolic division of East and West both the necessity and the possibility of their union, so did he urge the same completeness and wholeness of man himself. As he wrote in "Suggestion":

A man or a woman is scarcely more than half-a-being,—because in our present imperfect state either sex can be evolved only at the cost of the other. In the mental and the physical composition of every man, there is undeveloped woman; and in the composition of every woman there is undeveloped man. But a being complete would be both perfect man and perfect woman, possessing the highest faculties of both sexes, with the weakness of neither. Some humanity higher than our own,—in other worlds, —might be thus evolved.[43]

That is, every man has East and West, the female and the male within himself. This notion of androgyny here suggests man's dream of wholeness. In connection with those famous fables, Platonic and biblical, it is well to recall the Far Eastern belief that man attains the highest state when *yin* and *yang*, the female and the male principles, are in harmony. Thus Hearn's plea was for healing the awful division characteristic of modern man.

Matthew Josephson once denounced Hearn as "an enemy of the West." According to his charge, Hearn was "a belated romanticist living for his natural emotions, pursuing always, in the face of everything, his scandalous, sensational existence," "a great pattern of flight—toward the blue Gulf, to the tropical islands, ultimately to the Far East." Harry Levin also called him a "deracinated" Bohemian, "a transient contributor to American literature" on "his devious pilgrimage from the Old World toward the Orient.'' ''He never escaped from what he had never found: himself. 'Ironically,' Katherine Anne Porter points out, 'he became the interpreter between two civilizations equally alien to him.' ''[44]

In a way Josephson was right about Hearn's ''great pattern of flight,'' for exoticism was no mere episode of his career; it was his career, his life itself. Levin was also right about Hearn's ''pilgrimage'' from the Old World toward the Orient. And yet their judgments were negative because of their failure to recognize what was behind his ceaseless wanderlust. Hearn explained himself thus: ''the civilized nomad, whose wanderings are not prompted by hope of gain, nor determined by pleasure, but simply compelled by certain necessities of his being,—the man whose inner secret nature is totally at variance with the stable conditions of a society to which he belongs only by accident.''[45] It was this existential drive that turned flight into quest, exile into pilgrimage. And it was in Japan, in the Orient, that Hearn's voyage became a voyage of discovery, a voyage of self-discovery. By fulfilling his old dream of becoming a literary Columbus he extended America's passage to the Orient.

What was the secret of this success? His scientific accuracy and his poetic sensibility make his Japanese books still fresh in spite of the passage of time. He also possessed ''soul sympathy,'' a gift which enabled him to identify with others by thinking and even feeling as they did. In this sense Hearn was a born translator, an artist with the translator's soul. With him, translation was not ''only the first step,'' as he hoped it would be, but also the last, for he remained an interpreter of West to East, East to West. In this dual role he suggested the possibility of restoring the divided world and the divided man to their original wholeness, what he called ''a perfect sphere.''[46] It was this dream of wholeness that haunted him all his life, as his favorite fable of Salmacis and Hermaphroditus indicated.[47]

PART THREE

SEVEN

Babbitt

Naturalism, it has often been pointed out, is the main stream of modern Western thought. Modern American literature is no exception; a history of early twentieth century American literature is a history of naturalism on its triumphant march. While many embraced it ecstatically as their long-awaited liberator, there were some who resisted it valiantly, even though they knew that theirs was a lost cause. Lost cause or not, they felt they had to fight the battle as a matter of honor. These defenders of ideality or the genteel tradition were variously inspired, some intellectually, some sentimentally—but all alike were passionately committed to their lost cause. Most articulate among them was a band of intellectuals called New Humanists, who rallied around Irving Babbitt, Paul Elmer More, and their disciples like T. S. Eliot, Stewart Sherman, and Norman Foerster. These "professors," as they were called, became increasingly aggressive. In 1930, when they came out with *Humanism and America*, a sort of manifesto, their show of force was threatening enough for their foes to counter with *The Critique of Humanism* (1930).[1]

The New Humanism, like any other movement, had its share of defectors and deserters. In spite of More's separate pilgrimage toward Platonism and Christianity, and in spite of Sherman's shift toward a more liberal point of view, the movement survived because of Babbitt. After all, it was his movement, his cause, and his war in that it was conceived, planned, and executed by Babbitt himself. Thus Babbitt and the New Humanism were virtually synonymous in American literary history, though the movement turned out to be part of a larger war involving some European thinkers in their challenge to naturalism.[2] Standing his ground to the last against the onrushing tide of naturalism, Babbitt was a born fighter playing his role to his heart's content.

During his career as a professor of French at Harvard, Irving Babbitt (1865–1933) wrote several volumes of polemics: *Literature and the American College* (1908); *The New Laokoon* (1910); *The Masters of Modern French Criticism* (1912); *Rousseau and Romanticism* (1919); *Democracy and Leadership* (1924); *On Being Creative and Other Essays* (1932); and *Spanish Character and Other Essays* (1940). Taken together, his writings reveal a distinct pattern of thought "widening in concentric circles," to use Louis J. A. Mercier's phrase.[3] Babbitt's steady progress from an observer of American education to a critic of culture reminds us of two of his great Victorian predecessors, Carlyle and Arnold.

The first volume, *Literature and the American College*, contains all of Babbitt's central concerns in embryonic form.[4] Quite contrary to its subtitle, "Essays in Defense of the Humanities," Babbitt launches the offensive against the elective system and the tyranny of philology, which he designates as new evils in American education. With nothing to restrain the all-pervasive democratic spirit, the American college, much to Babbitt's dismay, has turned into "something of everything for everybody." Moreover, literature has turned into a handmaid of science, as is evident in the dry-as-dust philological studies which now control our doctoral programs, causing "a certain incapacity for ideas." Missing from the American college now, Babbitt points out, is the rational study of the classics which should sustain the humane standard.

These alarming symptoms Babbitt traces back to scientific and emotional naturalism which has come to dominate Western thought since the Renaissance. As he explains, modern man, having lost his unique status as the center of the world, found sentimental solace in both the Baconian domination of nature and the Rousseauistic return to nature. As a corrective to the erosion of American education Babbitt proposes humanism. Insisting on the role of discipline in education, and believing in "the perfecting of the individual rather than in schemes for the elevation of mankind as a whole," humanism has nothing to do with humanitarianism. "In short," Babbitt writes, "the most practical way of promoting humanism is to work for a revival of the almost forgotten art of reading. As a general rule, the humane man will be the one who has a memory richly stored with what is best in literature, with the sound sense perfectly expressed that is found only in the masters."

Here Babbitt sounds unmistakably Arnoldian. Worth noting, however, is his emphasis on the value of leisure. By *leisure* Babbitt means nothing like reverie, indolence, or Wordsworth's "wise passiveness," as is apparent in his reference to Aristotle's belief that "the highest good is not the joy in work, but the joy in contemplation"; the term, according to Babbitt, means meditation, an ideal common to East and West, and to their great religions. As he sums up, "What is wanted is neither Oriental quietism, nor again the inhuman strenuousness of a certain type of Occidental; neither pure action nor pure repose, but a blending of the two that will occupy all the space between them,—that activity in repose which has been defined as the humanistic ideal."

The next two volumes, *The New Laokoon* and *The Masters of Modern*

French Criticism, purport to be more scholarly than polemical; yet neither is a conventional academic exercise. Even in the former, where his focus shifts quickly from the neoclassical confusion of the arts to what he calls the Romantic confusion, Babbitt speaks once again as a committed humanist. This posture becomes more pronounced in the latter. While surveying the entire spectrum of modern French criticism from Madame de Staël to Sainte-Beuve, from Chateaubriand to Taine and Renan, Babbitt really concentrates on the nineteenth-century struggle between tradition and naturalism. That is, he presents a French case. His ultimate concern, as he states in the preface, is with the need for a standard in the world of flux and change—the very issue confronting modern critics and philosophers. Once again Babbitt repeats his call for humanism.

Rousseau and Romanticism, his fourth and best-known book, had been anticipated since *Literature and the American College*. After a decade-long search Babbit came at last to face Rousseau, his personal devil, who he believed stands behind all the modern ailments.[5] And Babbitt was ready to slay Rousseau and his multitudinous offspring with his best weapon, his fabulous erudition which supplied illustrations from ancient and modern, from Occidental and Oriental sources.

With a preliminary distinction between the Classic and the Romantic, Babbitt sets out to dissect various Romantic cults—invariably in terms of Rousseau. As this dissection gains its focus, Babbitt begins to prescribe his favorite antidote, a critical humanism. The book opens with the issue of Classicism versus Romanticism, and closes with the issue of naturalism versus humanism—a pattern characteristic of Babbitt.

It should be clear by now that Babbitt really had one central idea, his *idée fixe*, the rest being illustrations for elaboration and refinement. This is no doubt what made More say of Babbitt: "He seems to have sprung up, like Minerva, fully grown and fully armed." As More continued, "There is something almost inhuman in the immobility of his central ideas," "a kind of rotary movement instead of a regular progression."[6] Whether rotary or circular, Babbitt always returned to his version of humanism as he traced the modern ailments to their main source, Rousseau. He did this once and for all in a pair of essays, "What I believe: Rousseau and Religion" and "Humanism: An Essay at Definition," both of which appeared in 1930 and could serve as his final position papers on the New Humanism.

In the first essay Babbitt, as usual, begins by stating: "To debate Rousseau is really to debate the main issues of our contemporary life in literature, politics, education, and, above all, religion."[7] Rousseau's famous vision on the road to Vincennes, a revelation that "man is naturally good and that it is by our institutions alone that men become wicked,'' Babbitt argues, led to his false dualism of man and society. This new myth of man's natural goodness affected the course of the modern world just as Saint Paul's vision on the road to Damascus affected the subsequent course of Christianity. Rousseau's humanitarianism, in time, found its ally in Baconian utilitarianism, and together they undermined not only the religious tradition but also the humanistic tradition inherited from ancient Greece. By insisting on the new social dualism, modern humanitarianism—emotional and scientific—has ignored the older dualism, the true dualism between vital impulse and vital control—the ''civil war in the cave''—which Babbitt regards as the basis of both religion and humanism.

Although Babbitt suggests two alternatives, religion and humanism, as countermeasures, it is obvious that he prefers a positive and a critical humanism, the kind of humanistic movement which should come through education. This slow and long process of education, according to Babbitt, encompasses three stages: the Socratic definition; the coming together of a group of persons on the basis of this definition; and the attempt to make this resultant conviction effective through education. Babbitt attempts to deal with the first stage in the second essay, ''Humanism: An Essay at Definition.''[8]

As Babbitt points out, the term *humanism* has two main meanings—a historical meaning, when it is applied to the Renaissance scholars who turned to the Greeks and Romans for inspiration, and a psychological meaning, when it describes whoever aims at ''proportionateness through a cultivation of the law of measure.'' Babbitt finds this law of measure to be the basis of both Occidental and Oriental humanism. It is what Cicero defines as a ''sense of order and decorum and measure in deeds and words.'' China's independent discovery of the law of measure convinces Babbitt of its universality.[9] And for access to this ''universal norm,'' Babbitt suggests that the humanist turn primarily to tradition or to intuition.

In a war between naturalists and supernaturalists Babbitt would side with the latter. Although humanism can remain effective apart from dogmatic and revealed religion, it does profit from religious insight. And all religious insight, vague as it is, finally centers on the higher will, which Babbitt urges us to ''affirm first of all as a psychological fact, one of the immediate data of consciousness, a perception so primordial that, compared with it, the deterministic denials of man's moral freedom are only a metaphysical dream.'' Such an affirmation on our part, he believes, may enable us to come out of the modernist dilemma and become thoroughly and completely modern.

In traditional Christianity this higher will has been associated with God's will in the form of grace. As Babbitt reasons, ''It is an error to hold

130

that humanism can take the place of religion. Religion indeed may more readily dispense with humanism than humanism with religion." Because of its acceptance of this higher will, on which all religious insight centers, he even suggests that the Catholic and the non-Catholic should be able to cooperate on the humanistic level, and that the great traditional faiths, notably Christianity and Buddhism, may come to agreement on this level.

Furthermore, the kind of positive and critical humanist limned here, Babbitt continues to point out, has a certain tactical superiority over the religious traditionalist in dealing with modern humanitarians. "In the battle of ideas, as in other forms of warfare," says Babbitt, resorting to his favorite military metaphor, "the advantage is on the side of those who take the offensive." "Why not meet them on their ground and having got rid of every ounce of unnecessary metaphysical and theological baggage, oppose to them something that is both immediate and experimental—namely the presence in man of a higher will or power of control?"

In the conclusion Babbitt envisions humanism as perhaps the most positive means of bringing together all sects, all religions, and thereby contributing to the peace of the world. To this end, the humanist must act individually and collectively. Here again Babbitt proposes his three-stage program: right definition, creation of a convention, and education. In his opinion, the last stage should be of paramount interest in America, where economic and other conditions favor the achievement of a truly liberal conception of education—though its current system is controlled by humanitarians upholding the gospel of service. As Babbitt puts it in the last sentence: "One is at all events safe in affirming that the battle that is to determine the fate of American civilization will be fought out first of all in the field of education." By stressing the primary importance of education as the way to implement his humanistic program Babbitt, coming full circle, returns to his point of departure.

In surveying Babbitt's humanism in the making one notices the steady emergence of the Orient, not just as one of the major sources of his illustrations but as one of the cornerstones of his philosophy. Tracing Babbitt's career, Harry Levin once remarked: "One of Babbitt's most farsighted contributions was his insistence that an enlightened world view must come to terms with Asiatic thought," and, regarding his religious view, he added: "Babbitt was keenly interested in Christianity, utterly fascinated by Buddhism, and probably most sympathetic to the secular creed of Confucius."[10]

This should come as no surprise since Babbitt, throughout his career, remained a devoted student of the Orient. He read Sanskrit and Pali with

Professor Sylvain Lévi at the Sorbonne,[11] then with Professor Charles Lanman at Harvard. Even during his last illness Babbitt worked on the *Dhammapada*, a volume on the essence of Buddhist ethics which tradition has attributed to Buddha himself. In a memorial tribute Victor M. Hamm wrote: "If Babbitt had a religion, it was certainly closer to Buddhism."[12] This contention had support from none other than More, whose friendships with Babbitt had been formed in Lanman's graduate seminar. Noting Babbitt's early interest in Buddhism, that is, Hinayana Buddhism, More wrote:

> On the other hand, he was much closer to Buddhism than would appear from his public utterances. I wish not to exaggerate. In private as well in public he refused to be denominated a Buddhist, with perfect sincerity. But in the denial by Buddha (the real Buddha as seen in the authentic texts) of anything corresponding to Grace, in his insistence on the complete moral responsibility of the individual, in the majesty of his dying command, "Work out your own salvation with diligence," Babbitt perceived the quintessential virtue of religion, purged of ephemeral associations, of outworn superstition, of impossible dogma, of obscurantist faith, and based on a positive law which can be verified by experiment, pragmatically, step by step. It was in this way he sought to bring together a positivism in the religious plane with a positivism in what he distinguished as the purely humanistic plane of life and letters.[13]

Under what circumstances Babbitt initially turned to Buddhism, and to the Orient for that matter, we do not know for want of any testimony from him or his friends. As René Wellek suggested, he may have been inspired by the Orientalism of the American Transcendentalists, especially Emerson.[14] What is certain, however, is that Babbitt's interest in Buddhism long preceded his formulation of humanism. William F. Giese, recalling his undergraduate years with Babbitt at Harvard, wrote: "He was already deeply immersed in Buddhism, and its influence in shaping his thought is so plain from the start that other influences (barring Aristotle) need hardly be invoked as enriching tributaries. The ultimate convictions behind his humanism (which seemed then only an emerging aspect of his philosophy) are to be fully understood only in this Oriental light, however Aristotelian his analytic method." Also, Frank Jewett Mather, Jr., who met Babbitt at Williams College when they were first-year instructors, wrote: "As I recall the companionship of that year [1893–94], Irving Babbitt's later watchwords were not then formulated. Rousseau had not yet attained his sinister pre-eminence; Babbitt seldom mentioned him.

The word humanism was rarely on his lips. There were constant reflections of his admiration of the early Buddhist thinking, which he knew at first hand from his study of the original texts; but I doubt if in that year he ever appealed to Confucius or Aristotle. His concern was rather with the problem of education as the major part of the problem of culture."[15]

Whatever the case, his foes recognized this aspect of Babbitt's humanism. C. Hartley Grattan, editor of *The Critique of Humanism*, duly noted: "Dr. Babbitt derives his doctrine that the ethical will takes primacy over the intellect, from Oriental sources." Henry-Russell Hitchcock, Jr., also ridiculed Babbitt's Oriental interest: "In the distance he looks for values and in the near he finds only multiplicity: a defect of eyesight rather than a critical or philosophical principle." Even Henri Massis, a fellow humanist in France, wrote, apparently with More and Babbitt in mind: "Romanticism and Rousseau have become secondary—it is the Buddha that threatens us. The philosophy of the Buddha is creeping over Europe, and undermining our healthy realism, our philosophy of absolute values, our belief in the individual person. We must distrust the 'Hindu Brahman and the Chinese ascetics'—particularly, I might add, since certain American Humanists have been tricked into welcoming these influences."[16] Indeed, if this interest in the Orient set the New Humanism apart from its European counterpart, it also distinguished More and Babbitt from most of their disciples.

In Babbitt's writings, however, the Orient emerged only gradually—India first, China somewhat later, but virtually nothing of Japan at any time.[17] Take, for instance, Babbitt's anonymous review of his friend More's book *A Century of Indian Epigrams* (1898).[18] India, as Babbitt sees it, poses an interesting problem to all thinking men because of its position as a meeting ground of the two extremes of Aryan civilization, namely, English and Hindu, and also because of its slow infiltration into Western thought. If India has a special message to the modern world, it is the insight into what Babbitt calls "this inner sense of the absolute, this constant aspiration toward the central unity of life." By contrasting East and West in terms of repose and activity he points out: "The West tends more and more to pure activity, just as India, when most herself, has tended toward pure repose. Here again the half truth of the East may serve as a corrective to the half truth of the West, and may bring to pass that activity in repose which someone has defined as the classical ideal. We in America, especially, if we are not to spend ourselves in vain surface agitation, might profitably cultivate some feeling for the 'ultimate element of calm.' " The review mentioned neither Bacon nor Rousseau, neither Romanticism nor humanism. Though it anticipated his future direction, Babbitt had not yet found his humanistic vocabulary.

In *Literature and the American College* he begins to see his way more clearly. As he pits humanism against both humanitarianism and naturalism, the Orient emerges, finding its modest but distinct niche. In this first attempt to define humanism Babbitt introduces the concept of measure as the supreme law of life which binds all other laws. He relates measure to Buddha's Middle Way—but not yet to Confucius, as he is to do later. "It was doubtless the perception of this fact that led the most eminent personality of the Far East, Gotama Buddha, to proclaim in the opening sentence of his first sermon that extremes are barbarous. But India as a whole failed to learn the lesson." Greece was in Babbitt's opinion "perhaps the most humane of countries." Greece not only formulated the law of measure but also saw that the avenging Nemesis punished all forms of excess or violation of this law. Babbitt counters Rousseau's doctrine of man's natural goodness, not with the Christian doctrine of original depravity, but with the Buddhist doctrine of original laziness. According to Buddha, he points out, the greatest of all vices is "the lazy yielding to the impulses of temperament," and the greatest virtue "the awakening from the sloth and lethargy of the senses, the consistent exercise of the active will." Then he cites his favorite quotation, Buddha's last command to his disciples: "Work out your own salvation with diligence." Babbitt's increasing emphasis on the value of discipline in his humanistic program clearly derives from what he calls the Buddhist doctrine of original laziness.

As we have already noted, Babbitt's defense of academic leisure resulted from his praise of contemplation, or meditation, which he found common to all religions, Eastern and Western. In *Literature and the American College* he again took up the theme of Eastern repose and Western activity. Going further, he called for their blending, which would "occupy all the space between them,—that activity in repose which has been defined as the humanistic ideal"; earlier he had called this activity in repose "the classical ideal." The difference developed as he tried to formulate his own philosophy during the ten intervening years between his review of *A Century of Indian Epigrams* and his first book.

There was hardly any significant mention of the Orient either in *The New Laokoon* or in *The Masters of Modern French Criticism*. In *Rousseau and Romanticism*, however, the Orient at last asserts its vital role as Babbitt comes to expose the true colors of his personal devil, Rousseau, and thereby stage the full-scale confrontation between humanism and naturalism. By citing at the outset Emerson's "Law for man, and law for thing" passage (which he used as an epigraph for *Literature and the American College*), Babbitt notes his past attempt to establish the distinction between those two laws once and for all, so that we may be com-

---

pletely critical, positive, and modern—in short, truly humanistic. Whoever attempts to oppose "the sinister one-sidedness" of the current naturalism must work out "a truly ecumenical wisdom," and whoever attempts to do this cannot afford to ignore the experience of the Far East which "completes and confirms in a most interesting way that of the Occident." The experience of the Far East, Babbitt believes, may be epitomized in the teachings of two men, Buddha and Confucius.

Following the great teachers of both East and West Babbitt distinguishes three levels of human experience—naturalistic, humanistic, and religious. Much to his delight, Buddhism confirms Christianity, and Confucianism, the teaching of Aristotle, with its Greek emphasis on the law of measure. Thus, the East has in Buddhism a great religious movement and in Confucianism a great humanistic movement. Moreover, the East also has in early Taoism a naturalistic movement which is analogous to the Romantic Movement under discussion. And all great religious and humanistic disciplines, Babbitt further believes, attest to "the element of oneness, the constant element in human experience." Whereas Confucius, with his sense of tradition, is "a moral realist," Buddha is an individualist who urges men to base their belief neither on tradition nor on his authority. Referring to the latter in particular Babbitt declares: "No one has ever made a more serious effort to put religion on a positive and critical basis. It is only proper that I acknowledge my indebtedness to the great Hindu positivist; my treatment of the problem of the One and the Many, for example, is nearer to Buddha than to Plato."

Indeed, the Orient pervades *Rousseau and Romanticism*. While invoking Confucius and Buddha whenever justified, Babbitt also blasts the romantic view of the Orient, especially of India. He dismisses the Schlegels, Schopenhauer, Leconte de Lisle, and Yeats on the grounds that their romantic India has little or nothing to do with India at its best, India at the height of its achievement in the early Buddhist movement. In discussing Buddha's positivism, his psychology of desire, Babbitt introduces his favorite terms: *vital impulse (élan vital)* and *vital control (frein vital)*, the "civil war in the cave," "spiritual vigilence or strenuousness," "inner check," and the like. Turning from the romantic East he also has this to say: "We hear of the fatalistic East, but no doctrine was ever less fatalistic than that of Buddha. No one ever put so squarely upon the individual what the individual is ever seeking to evade—the burden of moral responsibility."

If *Rousseau and Romanticism* marks perhaps the most crucial moment of Babbitt's career, it also reveals the equally crucial role the Orient played as he attempted to rest his kind of humanism on a truly ecumenical wisdom as the key to the survival of human civilization. Not only did he denounce his personal devil, Rousseau; he also accepted Buddha as his personal master. Moreover, with this book Babbitt brought in another master from the Orient, namely, Confucius, whose wisdom rounded out his global scheme of East and West in balance and symmetry.[19]

In this sense Babbitt's fifth book, *Democracy and Leadership*, is a grand synthesis of his two-pronged crusade—his everlasting Nay and his everlasting Yea. The further he pressed his diagnosis of the modern malaise the more resounding his voice of doom became; the more he grew convinced of his humanism as the most effective antidote, the more urgent his voice of hope became. After alternating these two voices, he finally blended them in perfect harmony in *Democracy and Leadership*.

Here, too, Babbitt confronts Rousseau, readily conceding that he raised the right question though he offered the wrong answer. For the moment, however, Babbitt challenges him as "one who is easily first among the theorists of radical democracy," "the most eminent of those who have attacked civilization." As he sees it, Rousseau's theory of man's fall from nature parodied the Christian doctrine of man's fall from God, and this shift of emphasis from God to nature amounted to the shift of moral responsibility from the individual to society. Rejecting the old dualism of good and evil in the heart of the individual—Babbitt's so-called civil war in the cave—Rousseau set up a new dualism of man and society, and this social dualism led in turn to still another dualism, of the natural and artificial. As Babbitt summarizes Rousseau's position, "The only free and legitimate government is that founded upon a true social contract. On this basis, it is possible to combine the advantages of organized government with the liberty, equality, and fraternity that man enjoys, not as the result of moral effort, but as a free gift, in the state of nature. Only, under the social contract, these virtues no longer reside in the individual, but in the general will." Replacing the divine will, which sustained the medieval theocracy, this popular will assumed the form of popular sovereignty.

So arguing, Babbitt inevitably turns to American democracy, in which he finds the most conspicuous signs of "this tendency to put on sympathy a burden that it cannot bear and at the same time to sacrifice a truly human hierarchy and scales of values to the principle of equality." Devoid of a sense of tradition, devoid of a sense of standard, America has no qualitative view of life; in the name of democracy she pursues "standardized mediocrity." As Babbitt puts it, "If democracy means simply the attempt to eliminate the qualitative and selective principle in favor of some general will, based in turn on a theory of natural rights, it may prove to be only a form of the vertigo of the abyss." As far as he can see, "the hope of civilization lies not in the divine average, but in the saving remnant." Only the latter will be able to save America from a danger which combines "the strength of giants with the critical intelligence of children." Certainly not among the saving remnant, America's intellectual and political leaders, from Franklin down to Dewey, have misled America into worshiping service for humanity, not for God. Following a false god, modern man has broken with his tradition and is in danger of losing the truths of the higher will.

At the same time Babbitt defends the veto power—"the most unpopular of all tasks." With this in mind he surveys notable examples of this veto power in history. In the Greco-Roman world the Stoics attempted to formulate "the principle of true spiritual cohesion," and more recently Burke countered Rousseau's idyllic imagination with his moral imagination. But neither the Stoics nor Burke succeeded. Christianity has been more successful, particularly Catholicism, in Babbitt's opinion, despite its dependence on outer authority.

At this point Babbitt reminds us of the Oriental origin of Christianity itself. With Christianity the notion of humility—man's submission to a higher will—came into Europe, for the primacy of will over intellect, Babbitt believes, is eminently Oriental. Yet Christianity represents only part of the total experience of Asia. Insisting on the desirability and also the need of bringing together the two halves of human experience, Babbitt documents the centrality in all religions of a higher will. No exceptions are Buddhism and Christianity, which, while differing in dogmas, resemble each other "when studied experimentally and in their fruits." If the Christian concept of the will is most succinctly summarized in Dante's famous line: "In his will is our peace," Buddhism also finds its unifying principle in will, not intellect. Babbitt calls Buddha "the ultimate Oriental" because Buddha's supreme vision coincides with a supreme act of analysis. This notion of a higher will manifests itself at the humanistic level, too, in the law of measure, on which Confucius and Aristotle agree in spite of all their obvious differences. "It is," says Babbitt, "a part of my own method to put Confucius behind Aristotle and Buddha behind Christ. The best, however, that even these great teachers can do for us is to help us to discover what is already present in ourselves. From this point of view they are well-nigh indispensable."

Babbitt's defense of the veto power eventually turns into a plea for humanism, a new kind of humanism which embraces East and West in its search for a truly ecumenical wisdom, and which is positive enough, critical enough, and experimental enough to enable modern man to regain his proper status in the scheme of things, thereby becoming completely modern. Here at last Babbitt's plea rings with the voice of an everlasting Yea-sayer.

Babbitt, it is clear, defined his humanism in terms of Romanticism and completed it in terms of the Orient. His view of the Orient could best be called humanistic as he attempted to clarify it in another pair of essays: "Romanticism and the Orient" (1931) and "Buddha and the Occident" (1927). In the former piece Babbitt designates the Occidental sense of superiority—racial, scientific, and religious—as the main obstacle to a better understanding between East and West.[20] If this threefold superiority complex occupies one end of the scale, then a variety of romantic Orientalism represents the other end, Babbitt points out. Romantic Orientalism, whether exotic, escapistic, or primitive, misinterprets the Orient, remaining blind to its essence, "the affirmation in the religious form of the truths of the inner life." (Babbitt fears the Orient itself is fast losing this orientation for its survival in the modern world.) By the Orient he means the Asia that mothered all the great religions of the world, whose common emphasis on the higher will alone offers peace. "Though Asia has much to offer the humanist in its Confucian lore, its superlative achievement, I have been trying to make clear, is to have produced a Christ and a Buddha." And according to both, renunciation is the key to peace and brotherhood. This stress on man's inner life, Babbitt believes, is not only religious but also humanistic. "There has been reason in the past, at least, for speaking of the *meditative* East." Babbitt counters this meditative East with the romantic East.

In the same essay, "Romanticism and the Orient," Babbitt called Buddha "the ultimate Oriental"—a phrase he had already used in *Democracy and Leadership*. And Buddha literally marked the culmination of Babbitt's lifelong interest in the Orient, as is borne out by the translation of the *Dhammapada* which he completed shortly before his death. It was the book which Babbitt, in *Rousseau and Romanticism*, called "an anthology of some of the most authentic and authoritative material in early Buddhism." His final tribute to Buddha, the essay "Buddha and the Occident," spelled out his Orientalism once and for all, as the essay "Humanism: An Essay at Definition" did his New Humanism.

"Buddha and the Occident" contained nothing new but simply reaffirmed what Babbitt had been saying for years. With a note of warning about both the Occidental sense of superiority and romantic Orientalism, he comes straight to his point, that the humanism of Confucius and the religion of Buddha, being largely free from dogmas, tend to be positive and experimental in regard to the truths of the inner life. As for Buddha, he may best be described as "a religious empiricist," "a critical and experimental supernaturalist." Neither an emotionalist nor a rationalist, Buddha invariably starts from what Babbitt calls "the immediate data of consciousness." A profound psychologist, Buddha gives the primary place to will. "In its primary emphasis on will," continues Babbitt, "the doctrine of Buddha is not a system in the Occidental sense but a 'path.' " This aspect of Buddhism may seem to be a weakness in the eyes of those who value knowledge for its own sake, but to Babbitt it is precisely what makes Buddhism attractive.

As for Buddha's significance to the Occident, Babbitt reverses the usual question of what we are to think of Buddha and urges us to ask what Buddha would think of us. What characterizes the modern Occident, Babbitt believes, is humanitarianism—both utilitarian and sentimental— which is notorious for its enormous expansiveness. The advocates of this movement "hope to enjoy all the fruits of renunciation, while resolved to renounce nothing," and this tendency has become most manifest in America—"the paradise of the half-educated"—where "substantial material rewards await anyone who can devise some new and painless plan for getting 'in tune with the infinite.' " "America stands for the purely industrial and utilitarian view of life, the cult of power and machinery and material comfort." For this reason Babbitt holds that Buddhism can be most useful as we try to deal with our problems. Being essentially "a psychology of desire," Buddhism begins "at the centre— with the issue of war or peace in the heart of the individual." Here again Babbitt finds the common ground between Buddhism and Christianity in their dualistic acceptance of the higher will, the will to refrain, which comes only through meditation. "Everything will be found to hinge finally on the idea of meditation." Babbitt seriously doubts that religion itself can survive unless we retain "some sense of the wisdom that may, according to Dante, be won by sitting in quiet recollection." As he concludes: "Persons of positive and critical temper who yet perceive the importance of meditation may incline here as elsewhere to put less emphasis on the doctrinal divergence of Christianity and Buddhism than on their psychological agreement."[21] Thus Babbitt gives the ultimate primacy to meditation, convinced that it alone can bring together humanism and religion, Buddhism and Christianity, East and West.

The New Humanism was, by general consensus, a failure, and the reasons cited for this failure were many and varied. Confined more or less to academic and intellectual circles, it failed to recognize those creative endeavors which sustained the modern world with all its ills and enriched modern literature.[22] To contemporary Americans the gospel of the New Humanism sounded altogether negative, even though it was meant to complete, not to deny, the age, as Babbitt stated in his first book.[23]

Whatever happened to the New Humanism, Babbitt has survived both in his writings and in his disciples. The contributors to the memorial volume *Irving Babbitt: Man and Teacher* all agreed on at least one thing, that he was great teacher. (According to More, he was "greater as a teacher than a writer."[24]) No matter how often they disagreed with their teacher in pursuing their separate interests—creative, critical, and academic—they carried on his cause, his spirit of commitment.[25] This aspect of Babbitt's legacy was best stated by T. S. Eliot: "To have been once a pupil of Babbitt's was to remain always in that position, and to be grateful always for (in my case) a very much qualified approval."[26]

As we reexamine his central thesis, humanism versus naturalism from the vantage point of history, we begin to realize that the issue Babbitt raised with such persistence is very much alive today.[27] We cannot afford to ignore his insight into the condition of modern man—spiritual malaise as a result of naturalism—nor can we afford to dismiss his call for "a truly ecumenical wisdom" as the best possible remedy and the basis of his humanism. And what the Asiatic experience represents in his prescribed remedy, we know now. Embracing East and West, this last of our great Puritans, as he often was called, strove to be a complete modern, that is, a humanist, an heir to both traditions.[28]

EIGHT

O'Neill

"One may indeed affirm almost anything of Asia in general compared with the Occident in general. One may even, like Dr. Frederic Ives Carpenter in his recent volume, *Emerson and Asia*, discover an oriental element in the dramas of Eugene O'Neill!" So wrote Babbitt in "Romanticism and the Orient,"[1] in spite of some of O'Neill's works which Carpenter cited in an attempt to place him in the mainstream of American Orientalism since Emerson. Moreover, Babbitt and O'Neill, while pursuing their separate careers, had at least two things in common: their reaction to naturalism and their response to the Orient.

Given his scrupulousness, it is unlikely that Babbitt made the above statement without having read O'Neill. How could he then have missed those Oriental references scattered through O'Neill's plays? In *Beyond the Horizon* Robert Mayo speaks of "the beauty of the far off and unknown, the mystery and spell of the East which lures me in the books I've read"; in *The Great God Brown* Cybel is described as chewing gum "like a sacred cow forgetting time with an eternal end," and Dion Anthony says: "One must do something to pass the time while one is waiting for one's next incarnation"; in *Dynamo* the giant machine with oil switches and their six cupped outstretching arms looks like "queer Hindu idols tortured into scientific supplications"; and, in particular, O'Neill's Chinese play, *Marco Millions*, which had been performed only a couple of years earlier, is a colorful pageant contrasting the material West and the spiritual East. Babbitt's cavalier dismissal was all the more puzzling since O'Neill did seem to exemplify romantic Orientalism, the very thing Babbitt was attacking in that essay.

In spite of Babbitt, the topic of O'Neill's Orientalism has managed to attract some attention over the years.[2] Among the first to take it seriously was Carpenter himself. In the conclusion of *Emerson and Asia* he called O'Neill "most original of all contemporary authors" and "most thoroughly steeped in the tinctures of Hindu literature and thought," and then went on to state: "Perhaps, before the end of the century, a study of 'The Orientalism of Eugene O'Neill' may be undertaken."[3] In 1956 Doris Alexander, in her article "*Lazarus Laughed* and Buddha," found Lazarus a sort of composite hero inspired by Jesus, Dionysus, Zarathustra, and above all Buddha. This she followed up in 1960 with another article, "Eugene O'Neill and *Light on the Path*," tracing O'Neill's Orientalism to a single source—a finding which she reiterated in *The Tempering of Eugene O'Neill* (1962). In 1964 Carpenter himself came out with *Eugene O'Neill*, in which he attempted to interpret the dramatist's three-stage development in terms of Oriental religions. And in 1966, in the essay "Eugene O'Neill, the Orient, and American Transcendentalism," Carpenter again stressed the Oriental pattern in O'Neill's career.

In this essay Carpenter wrote: "O'Neill's Orientalism is—I think—the most important and distinctive aspect of his art, and yet the most difficult to define." And then he quoted O'Neill's own response to his query in this matter. O'Neill replied in 1932:

> As for your question regarding Oriental ideas, I do not think they have influenced my plays at all. Certainly, not consciously. Many years ago I did considerable reading in Oriental philosophy and religion, however, although I never went in for an intensive study of it. I simply did it in order to have some sort of grasp of the subject as part of my philosophical background. The mysticism of Lao-tse and Chuang-Tzu probably interested me more than any other Oriental writing.[4]

As Carpenter pointed out, O'Neill's disclaimer, like his similar disclaimer of the Freudian and Jungian influence, may merely reflect his insistence on his own creative originality, and as such should not be accepted at face value. To write *Marco Millions* alone he must have done extensive background reading in Oriental history, religion, and philosophy. And in 1929 he had also made nineteen pages of summary notes for another Chinese play, this time about Shih Huang Ti, the First Emperor of China, on the theme of his defiance of death and his search for the herb of immortality.[5]

O'Neill's Orientalism finally came under full scrutiny in James A. Robinson's *Eugene O'Neill and Oriental Thought* (1982). Robinson viewed O'Neill's career in terms of the tension between the mystic and tragic, the Eastern and Western sides of his own divided nature. The Eastern side first manifested itself in his early plays, such as *The Fountain* and *Marco Millions*, and then reached a high watermark with his expressionistic, religious plays, notably *Lazarus Laughed*. Following a decade of dormancy, it resurfaced in his last autobiographical plays. O'Neill's ambivalence toward the Orient, Robinson suggested, may help explain his artistic unevenness and his continuing relevance. His "Western" plays, those in the realistic mode, stand among his best, whereas his "Eastern" plays, those on his Oriental intuitions, remain ineffective. As Robinson concluded:

His greatest drama probed the enduring concerns of Western man: the fear of death, the obsession with history, the quest for identity. Though it did so in a form familiar to Western audiences, it simultaneously raised the possibility of Oriental approaches to these problems, while remaining sceptical about Eastern philosophy's ultimate relevance to the Western mind. In this ambivalence, the American playwright represents many modern Europeans and Americans alike—and not just artists. . . . Universal as O'Neill's work may be, it is of course unlikely to bridge the gap between East and West; but his divided vision may further mutual understanding by offering deep and subtle statements of the problem.[6]

Because of this schematic approach Robinson simply by-passed *Mourning Becomes Electra*, O'Neill's most ambitious work; however, his new study established Orientalism as a major aspect of O'Neill's art and thought.

Whenever speaking of the Orient, as in the letter quoted above, O'Neill invariably turned toward China. There is indeed something personal, almost obsessional, about his interest in China. In September 1928, just before sailing for the Far East—"India and way stations on to China"—O'Neill wrote: "I can't tell you how much this trip to the East means to me. It's been the dream of my life to live there for a while and absorb a bit of background. It's going to be infinitely valuable to me in its bearing upon my future work."[7] Although the venture ended in a near nightmare in Shanghai, cutting short what he had intended to be a year-long journey, he became the first major American writer to set foot in the Orient. Despite his harrowing experience O'Neill continued talking about the possibility of another trip, with Somerset Maugham.[8] Still later, in 1937, when O'Neill had his residence built in Danville, California, he named it "Tao House." Even in his last years O'Neill was reportedly haunted with Oriental dreams—"a strange dream laid in China and lasting a thousand years."[9]

As already mentioned, Doris Alexander traced O'Neill's Orientalism, as well as his mysticism, to one specific source, Terry Carlin, and through him to *Light on the Path*, read during the winter of 1915–16, O'Neill's Hell Hole period.[10] According to her, it was largely through this slim collection of Oriental wisdom that he began "his profound readings in Buddhism, Taoism, and Hinduism—in comparative religion, in general— which became his absorbing interest in the next ten years." In addition to this, Robinson pointed out O'Neill's reading of Emerson, Schopenhauer, Nietzsche, Strindberg, and Jung—all known for their interest in the Orient.[11] But we could also suggest that Kipling and Conrad, among

143

O'Neill's favorite writers during boyhood, may have kindled his romantic interest in the Orient, or even that his Irish heritage, the well-known love of the romantic and the mysterious, may have driven this disillusioned Catholic toward the Orient, whose philosophy and religion tend to merge in mysticism.

Whatever the case, the first significant reference to the Orient appears in *Beyond the Horizon* (1920), O'Neill's first full-length play that assured his career as a playwright. In the opening scene Robert Mayo speaks to his prosaic-minded brother, Andrew: "Supposing I was to tell you that it's just Beauty that's calling me, the beauty of the far off and unknown, the mystery and spell of the East which lures me in the books I've read, the need of the freedom of great wide spaces, the joy of wandering on and on—in quest of the secret which is hidden over there, beyond the horizon? Suppose I told you that was the one and only reason for my going?"[12] And when Andrew calls him "nutty," Robert protests: "Don't, Andy. I'm serious." Ironically, it is Andrew who sails in his brother's place. Upon his return three years later, Andrew makes the point of reminding Robert: "And as for the East you used to rave about—well, you ought to see it, and *smell* it! One walk down one of their filthy narrow streets with the tropic sun beating on it would sicken you for life with the 'wonder and mystery' you used to dream of." With Robert responding in aversion: "So all you found in the East was a stench?" Andrew continues driving his point home: "*A Stench!* Ten thousand of them!" Apart from the irreconcilable difference between the Andrews and the Roberts, the prosaic and the poetic, the materialistic and the idealistic, one thing is certain: despite his sympathetic identification with Robert, O'Neill was already exhibiting a greater awareness than his hero, regarding the East with both sides, beauty and stench—a pattern peculiar to O'Neill, who continued to be drawn toward China in spite of his experience in Shanghai. His Orientalism is made of stuff tougher than Robert's, is tougher than it appears.

This image of the East, with both its beauty and its stench, was realistic enough, in keeping with the overall tone of *Beyond the Horizon*. In *The Fountain* (written in 1921–22, produced in 1925), however, the East assumed an exalted status, at once mythical and mystical—no doubt because the mythical Fountain of Youth transforms itself into a mystical vision, a passionate reaffirmation of beauty, love, life, and eternity as the protagonist, Juan Ponce de León, progresses from youth through middle age to death. As O'Neill himself pointed out, the play sought to "express the urging spirit" of that great period of discovery.[13] And he dramatized this urging spirit in the figure of Juan Ponce de León against the background of Columbus's quest for a passage to the East.

Although a failure as a drama, *The Fountain* was the kind of work O'Neill had to write at this stage of his career. While identifying the source of O'Neill's mysticism and Orientalism, Alexander observed that "no other single play would reflect the 'light' from *Light on the Path* as strongly as this one," and to prove her point she cited some interesting parallels between the slim collection of Oriental wisdom and *The Fountain*, especially Juan's vision of the fountain.[14] In order to fight off the figure of death, the dying Juan invokes Beatriz, daughter of his old love, and as she sings, the fountain itself, in the flooding mystical light, turns into "a gigantic fountain, whose waters, arched with rainbows, seem to join earth and sky, forming a shimmering veil, which hides the background of forest." In the ensuing phantom show the rapt Juan finds Beatriz rising from the spring itself. As she vanishes, various other forms appear—a Chinese poet, a Moorish minstrel, his Indian guide Nano, and his old friend Luis. While Beatriz's voice is singing the fountain song, the Chinese poet holds the Indian by one hand and the Moor by the other, and these latter in turn stretch out their hands, completing the circle. Soon these four forms disappear, but when they reappear as if responding to the puzzled Juan, the Chinese poet is robed as a Buddhist priest, the Moorish minstrel as a priest of Islam, Nano as a Medicine Man, and Luis as a Dominican priest. At this point Juan exclaims: "All faiths—they vanish—are one and equal—within—What are you, Fountain? That from which all life springs and to which it must return—God! Are all dreams of you but the one dream? I do not know. Come back, Youth. Tell me this secret!"

The scene embodies O'Neill's conviction that all religions are "the most illuminating 'case histories' of the inner life of man."[15] The fountain, the source of this inner life of man, represents "the impelling, inscrutable forces behind life,"[16] or "the Force behind—Fate, God, our biological past creating our present, whatever one calls it—Mystery certainly," that which O'Neill said he attempted to recapture in his plays.[17] Juan had learned of the fountain long before while he was dreaming of Spain's wealth, fame, and glory. As Juan and his fellow nobles were chatting about Columbus's attempt to find the Western passage to the Orient, his friend Luis interpreted a Moorish minstrel's song of "treasure in the East":

> He sang of treasure—but strange to your longing. There is in some far country of the East—Cathay, Cipango, who knows—a spot that Nature has set apart from men and blessed with peace. It is a sacred grove where all things live in the old harmony they knew before man came. Beauty resides there and is articulate.

Each sound is music, and every sight a vision. The trees bear golden fruit. And in the center of the grove, there is a fountain—beautiful beyond human dreams, in whose rainbows all of life is mirrored. In that fountain's waters, young maidens play and sing and tend it everlastingly for very joy in being one with it. This is the Fountain of Youth, he said. The wise men of that far-off land have known it many ages. They make it their last pilgrimage when sick with years and weary of their lives. Here they drink, and the years drop from them like a worn-out robe. Body and mind know youth again, and these young men, who had been old, leap up and join the handmaids' dance. Then they go back to life, but with hearts purified, and the old discords trouble them no more, but they are holy and the folk revere them. (*With a sigh*) That's his tale, my friends—but he added it is hard to find that fountain. Only to the chosen does it reveal itself.

The whole play revolves around this fabled fountain in the sacred grove. As Luis pointed out, the fable originally came from some wandering poet from Cathay. Did O'Neill perhaps have in mind Tao Yuan-ming's celebrated description of the Peach Blossom Fountain?[18] Whatever his source, the passage here suggests something unmistakably Taoistic in its emphasis on the prelapsarian harmony and the curative, regenerative, and miraculous power of water as the source of life. What is really significant is O'Neill's poetic vision, which transforms Juan's and Columbus's quest into a mystical affirmation of life itself.

With the Orient emerging as a symbol of life, it was natural that O'Neill wrote *Marco Millions*, immediately following *The Fountain*. As we know, the idea of this Chinese pageant had been on his mind for some time. After all, Marco Polo was the one who had originated the myth of the fabulous Orient, thereby inspiring Columbus to seek his Western passage. Then came Otto Kahn's suggestion that O'Neill write a play in praise of American big business and the American businessman,[19] and he complied with this suggestion by whitewashing "the good soul of that maligned Venetian"—as he said in his foreword to the play—by "render[ing] poetic justice to one long famous as a traveler, unjustly world-renowned as a liar, but sadly recognized by posterity in his true eminence as a man and a citizen." The result was his Chinese play, *Marco Millions* (written in 1923–25, first produced in 1927), a merciless satire of Polo's illustrious career.

When the young Polo arrives in China his self-confidence impresses the Great Kaan so much that he keeps Polo in his service, hoping to observe his unique soul. In the next fifteen years Polo amasses his desired millions. By now thoroughly disgusted with what he calls Polo's spiritual hump, the Kaan concludes: "He has not even a mortal soul, he has only an acquisitive instinct. We have given him every opportunity to learn. He has memorized everything and learned nothing. He has looked at everything and seen nothing. He has lusted for everything and loved nothing. He is only a shrewd and crafty greed. I shall send him home to his native wallow." In short, Polo has won the world but lost his soul.

On his passage home Polo delivers Princess Kukachin to the King of Persia. During the voyage he duly performs his daily task of gazing into her eyes—completely unaware of her passionate love, not to mention her beauty. While she dies of despair, Polo arrives home and marries his obese Donata in pomp. Observing this triumphant end of Polo's progress through a crystal ball, the Kaan exclaims: "The Word became their flesh, they say. Now all is flesh! And can their flesh become the Word again?"

In this play, too, O'Neill's characters are molded to serve his particular purposes. He magnifies only certain aspects of his characters—Polo's love of statistics and Kublai's sense of humanity—and thereby contrasts the material West and the spiritual East.[20] As Kublai embodies the spiritual wisdom of the East—Taoistic, Buddhistic, and Confucian—so does Kukachin personify youth, love, and poetry—all symbolic of an affirmation of life.

Relating the episode of Otto Kahn's suggestion, George Jean Nathan remarked that O'Neill's answer was "to write *Marco Millions*, the sourest and most magnificent poke in the jaw that American big business and the American business man have ever got." In the epilogue O'Neill sees that the audience makes no mistake about his satirical target. With the play over, a bored man dressed as a Venetian merchant of the later thirteenth century rises from the first row; he is none other than Marco Polo, which means that Marco Polo is still much alive among us. Yet he is no American monopoly, nor a Western monopoly. He stands as a universal symbol of crass materialism which pollutes poetry, beauty, love, wisdom, and life itself. This is what the prologue suggests. At a sacred tree in Persia near the Indian border three medieval merchants, Christian, Magian, and Buddhist, chance to meet together. As they fight over the religious significance of the tree, a group of soldiers bearing the dead Kukachin in a coffin arrives. Much to their fascination, "her calm expression seems to glow with the intense peace of a life beyond death." Suddenly a voice comes from the coffin. It is Kukachin's—"more musical than a human voice": "Say this, I loved and died. Now I am love, and live. And living, have forgotten, and loving, can forgive." As O'Neill carefully notes: "A sound of tender laughter, of an intoxicating, supernatural gaiety, comes from her lips and is taken up in chorus in the branches of the tree as if every harp-leaf were laughing in music with her. The laughter recedes heavenward and dies as the halo of light about her face fades and noonday rushes back in a blaze of baking plain." *Marco Millions* is a satire and at the same time transcends satire by reaffirming life whose meaning has been all but lost to modern man in his blind pursuit of gold. All this O'Neill articulates through the Orient in his colorful pageant.

The year 1925 was perhaps the most fertile of O'Neill's golden decade. That year *The Great God Brown* was written, *Marco Millions* completed at last, and *Lazarus Laughed* begun. These three plays, conceived and composed almost simultaneously, attest to O'Neill's creative drive. Experimental in form and content, they echo one another. For instance, the dying Brown exclaims: "It's an age of miracles. The streets are full of Lazaruses"; and 'Blessed are they that weep, for they shall laugh!' Only he that has wept can laugh! The laughter of Heaven sows earth with a rain of tears, and out of Earth's transfigured birth-pain the laughter of Man returns to bless and play again in innumerable dancing gales of flame upon the knees of God!'' Even the dead Princess Kukachin, as has been noted above, laughs "a sound of tender laughter, of an intoxicating, supernatural gaiety" which eventually rises heavenward. Through laughter both plays sustain the miracle of life, and this mystical affirmation of life, which appeared first in *The Fountain*, finally culminates in *Lazarus Laughed*.

The play follows the career of Lazarus, who was raised from the dead by Jesus. To the crowd demanding to know what is beyond, Lazarus responds: "There is only life! I heard the heart of Jesus laughing in my heart; 'There is Eternal Life in No,' it said, 'and there is the same Eternal Life in Yes! Death is the fear between!' And my heart reborn to love of life cried 'Yes!' and I laughed in the laughter of God." As he begins to preach this new gospel of life, his home at Bethany becomes known as the House of Laughter. Soon after the crucifixion of Jesus, however, Lazarus and his followers suffer persecution at the hands of the orthodox. With his wife, Miriam, Lazarus proceeds from Judea to Athens, where he is hailed as a reincarnation of the God Dionysus. Whereas Miriam gets older, he grows younger—with the countenance of "the positive masculine Dionysus, closest to the soil of the Grecian Gods, a Son of Man, born of a mortal." When he carries his gospel on to Rome, Lazarus grows even younger, his face "exalted and calm and beautiful" and his eyes shining with "an unearthly glory." Once in Rome, he goes through a series of ordeals: Pompeia has Miriam killed, Tiberius orders him burned at a stake, and Caligula, stabbing Tiberius, now has Lazarus killed. To this terror-stricken Caligula the dying Lazarus declares: "Fear not, Caligula! There is no death." As O'Neill notes: "His voice is heard in a gentle, expiring sigh of compassion, followed by a faint dying note of laughter that rises and is lost in the sky like the flight of his soul back into the womb of Infinity.''

In theme and form *Lazarus Laughed* is perhaps the most imaginative of all O'Neill plays, whether or not, as he himself believed, it was his most successful work to date. The entire play, or rather the entire pageant, revolves around its protagonist, Lazarus, who has seen what is beyond. To create such a mystical hero with his gospel of laughter, with his death-defying and life-giving laughter, must have posed an enormous challenge to O'Neill.

Lazarus is a Christian. As he journeys westward, however, he assumes new aspects. Critics have noted his resemblance to savior figures such as the Nietzschean superman, which suggests that Lazarus is a composite of various saviors. While agreeing to this, Doris Alexander nonetheless pointed out that in Rome, during the last phase of his career, Lazarus exhibits certain familiar traits of Buddha—a halo, contemplative and calm abstraction, and compassion embracing even animals.[21]

Ringing throughout the play is Lazarus's laughter, a mystical affirmation of life which O'Neill has come to find common to all religions. With Lazarus's divine laughter, the play comes close to articulating what O'Neill called the Force—''the one eternal tragedy of Man in his glorious, self-destructive struggle to make the Force express him instead of being, as an animal is, an infinitesimal incident in its expression.''[22] The third act opens at Tiberius's villa-palace at Capri, which has a triumphal arch over the marble terrace. O'Neill notes that ''in the exact center of the arch a cross is set up on which a full grown male lion has been crucified''; the cross bears the inscription: ''From the East, land of false gods and superstitions, this lion was brought to Rome to amuse Caesar.'' Touching on this note, Carpenter wrote: ''When the dying lion licks Lazarus's hand, the double identity of the laughter of Lazarus with the religious mysticism of the East and with the tragic religion of Christ crucified is realized in the single, unforgettable image.''[23] In pointing to O'Neill's intention Carpenter was probably right. Going even further, however, one could suggest that *Lazarus Laughed* was conceived in the spirit of *Ex oriente lux*. As Irving Babbitt observed, Christianity, in its original form, represents the Asiatic experience of the human race.[24] The Romans not only killed Lazarus but turned his joyous gospel into something less positive. Interesting in this regard is the time of day O'Neill has Lazarus burned at the stake—''just before dawn,'' the time of the day's first light—a favorite motif, one he had already used for the ending of *Beyond the Horizon* and would use again in *A Moon for the Misbegotten*.

Mourning Becomes Electra (written in 1929–31, produced in 1931) was, by general consensus, the most ambitious of O'Neill's plays in that by orchestrating all of his major concerns at the zenith of his career he dared to challenge the ancient masters of dramatic literature. Here, as in *Lazarus Laughed*, O'Neill exploited the tension between life and death; here, as in *Strange Interlude* (1928), he probed into the borderland between the conscious and the subconscious; here, as in *Desire Under the Elms* (1924), he employed what Eliot called a mythical method; and here he finally confronted what he had pursued in these and other works: "the Force behind—Fate, God, our biological past creating our present." In so doing he worked out the problem he had raised in a note of 1926: "Modern psychological drama using one of the old legend plots of Greek tragedy for its basic theme—the Electra story?—the Medea? Is it possible to get modern psychological approximation of the Greek sense of fate into such a play, which an intelligent audience of today, possessed of no belief in gods or supernatural retribution, could accept and be moved by?"[25]

For this purpose O'Neill returned to Aeschylus's *Oresteia*, the only extant Greed trilogy, or rather to its source, the myth of the House of Atreus. And yet *Mourning Becomes Electra* and *The Oresteia* differ far more than they resemble each other.[26] O'Neill's trilogy, unlike his ancient model, is often internalized in Freudian and Jungian terms—in keeping with his attempt at "modern psychological approximation of the Greek sense of fate." Aeschylus's solution, namely, Orestes' acquittal in the court of Athens, whatever its appeal to his Greek audience, is definitely a letdown and altogether unconvincing to the modern audience. O'Neill's trilogy is female-centered in the way Aeschylus's is male-centered. In his characterization of Lavinia he is in fact Sophoclean and Euripidean. Unlike Aeschylus's Electra, whose significance diminishes toward the end of *The Oresteia*, Lavinia comes to dominate *Mourning Becomes Electra*. While Orin is driven to self-destruction, Lavinia sustains herself to the last, willing to choose her own way—a rare moment in modern drama suggesting the possibility of a tragedy and a tragic character in the naturalistic age.

The tragedy of the Mannons is clearly suggested in the mansion itself. Set off by its surrounding green, it is a sort of prison, a sort of tomb, thus standing for Puritan negation, a negation of life. Yet the Mannons, through their family business, have the sea as their route of escape. It is Brant, a sea captain, who sets the keynote when he speaks of the natives in the South Seas: "And they live in as near the Garden of Paradise before sin was discovered as you'll find on this earth! Unless you've seen it, you can't picture the green beauty of their land set in the blue of the sea! The clouds like down on the mountain tops, the sun drowsing in your blood, and always the surf on the barrier reef singing a croon in your ears like a lullaby! The Blessed Isles, I'd call them! You can forget there all men's dirty dreams of greed and power!'' Antithetical to the prisonlike, tomb-like House, the South Seas with their blessed isles beckon to every Mannon. Even Ezra, "sick of death," dreams of getting away to some island with Christine. Orin, too, longs for the South Sea Islands, which he read about in Melville's *Typee* and which he came to identify with his mother. Christine is no exception. Learning Brant's intention of giving up the sea, she declares: "Don't talk like that! You have me, Adam! You have me! And we will be happy—once we're safe on your Blessed Islands!'' Indeed, this countermotif of the Blessed Islands recurs over a dozen times throughout the trilogy. Remembering what he wrote in his work diary for March 1930, O'Neill exploits the dramatic contrast between the Mannon House and the Blessed Islands: "Develop South Sea Island motive—its appeal for them all (in various aspects)—release, peace, security, beauty, freedom of conscience, sinlessness, etc.—longing for the primitive—and mother symbol—yearning for prenatal non-competitive freedom from fear—make this Island theme recurrent motive.''[27] Clearly reminiscent of that dream of old harmony which haunted Paddy in *The Hairy Ape* and Juan in *The Fountain*, the Blessed Islands symbolize innocence and free-dom in contrast to sin and imprisonment, which the Mannon House re-presents. If the one negates life, the other affirms it.

All the while longing for the Blessed Islands, they die one after another —Ezra is poisoned, Brant gets shot, and Christine kills herself. Only Orin and Lavinia reach their Blessed Islands on their way back from the East, a voyage which hardens Orin into another Mannon but frees Lavinia. As she relates: "I loved those islands. They finished setting me free. There was something there mysterious and beautiful—a good spirit—of love—coming out of the land and sea. It made me forget death. There was no hereafter. There was only this world—the warm earth in the moonlight—the trade wind in the coco palms—the surf on the reef—the fires at night and the drum throbbing in my heart—the natives dancing naked and innocent—without knowledge of sin." Admitting that he is "too much of a Mannon, after all, to turn into a pagan," Orin chooses death by declar-ing: "Darkness without a star to guide us!" Lavinia's taste of innocence, love, beauty, peace, and freedom does not last either, for she is another Mannon, even if "only half." With this knowledge of life and death she is willing to live out the tragic history of the Mannons.

In *Mourning Becomes Electra*, especially its contrast of the Mannon House and the Blessed Islands, O'Neill brought together two recurring themes in American literature: the accursed Houses of Poe, Hawthorne, and Faulkner, on the one hand, and the South Sea Paradise of Melville and Adams, on the other. Their tragic division O'Neill sought to resolve with his mystical transcendence, which he had embodied in that "sacred grove" with its fabled fountain, "where all things live in the old harmony they knew before man came," "in some far country of the East." In this trilogy, too, the East looms over the horizon, remote and yet distinct. Christine appeals to Brant: "Can't we go on another ship—as passengers —to the East—we could be married out there." In reply Brant mentions the *Atlantis*, bound for China. Orin and Lavinia, it may be recalled, originally sail for the East—the voyage which Orin points out has brought about a miraculous change in his sister. What matters here is their instinct which turns to the East. Whether O'Neill was aware or not, the South Seas constitute the age-old passage to Asia, their mother continent.[28] There was Henry Adams's persistent dream of journeying to China while relishing the idyllic paradise of the South Seas; there was Fenollosa's Pacific School of Art linking Asia and Oceania; and there was O'Neill's own recurring dream of China. All these may suggest the irrepressible urge deep down in the American psyche, an urge to complete Columbus's unfinished passage to the Orient by way of the prehistoric route across the Pacific.

After *Mourning Becomes Electra* the Orient seems to disappear altogether from O'Neill's writings;[29] his later plays are either historical or autobiographical, quite different from his earlier ones, which center on philosophical and religious themes. But what became of his interest in the Taoist mysticism of Laotzu and Chuangtzu? What are we to make of his Tao House, where he wrote most of his last plays? And what are we to make of those Chinese dreams which continued haunting him toward the end of his life? The first scholar to take O'Neill's Orientalism seriously, Carpenter suggested in his study *Eugene O'Neill* the familiar Hindu triune pattern of Shiva, Brahma, and Vishnu to describe the three different aspects of O'Neill's character and also the three succeeding stages of his career. Although this suggested pattern is general enough to fit any number of other cases, what he said of O'Neill's last plays is worth quoting:

> The "transcendental" tragedy of the later O'Neill achieves a goal much like that of the Oriental religion and philosophy which "lured" O'Neill throughout his life, and which found final expression in "Tao House." In the final tragedies, the veil of Maya seems to be torn aside and all the illusions of human life laid bare. Romantic dreams are exposed as the delusions they are. And yet, unlike O'Neill's earlier dramas and unlike all the romantic literature of the modern Occident, these dreams are no longer seen as beautiful, nor are they seen as evil. Rather, they are recognized as the very substance of human life.[30]

From 1934 to 1943 O'Neill worked on his ever-expanding cycle, *A Tale of Possessors Self-Dispossessed*, only to abandon the whole project. Obsessed as he was with this "story of America," a failure of the American Dream, he interrupted it in order to write two autobiographical plays, *The Iceman Cometh* (1939) and *A Long Day's Journey Into Night* (1940–41). This return to his roots inevitably led him to his own self, as he once quoted from *Thus Spake Zarathustra*: "In the end one experienceth nothing but one's self."[31]

Common to both groups of plays, historical and autobiographical, was O'Neill's readiness to strip away any veil, any illusion. If in the former he attempted to strip the American Dream of its glamor and show it as it is, the dream of material things, in the latter he was determined to confront his own past, his own youth in its stark nakedness. In both he was bent on unmasking, an ironic contrast to his earlier practice of masking characters for his kind of drama. As he said in "Memoranda on Masks" (1932): "For what, at bottom, is the new psychological insight into human cause and effect but a study in masks, an exercise in unmasking?"[32] In these last plays O'Neill strove to achieve the same, but without the aid of masks or any other devices. Bare-handed, as it were, he undertook the most difficult task—unmasking himself. The moment O'Neill the man and O'Neill the artist at last came face to face, he returned to the roots of his own being, significantly, in conventional, realistic settings.

The Iceman Cometh is the play O'Neill had wanted to write ever since the 1920s about his old haunt, the Hell Hole.[33] It had taken him a quarter of a century to get ready to confront the nightmare of his youth. O'Neill needed aesthetic distance, as he said in an interview: "I don't think you can write anything of value or understanding about the present. You can only write about if it is far enough in the past. The present is too mixed with superficial values; you don't know which thing is important and which is not. The past which I have chosen is one I knew."[34]

The Iceman Cometh is a drama of revelation—to use O'Neill's own words, "an exercise in unmasking." By unmasking all the characters separately and together, the play moves inexorably toward its climactic revelation that Hicky killed his wife out of hatred for her infinite trust. Following this, other revelations come. Even Harry's sentimental love for his dead wife turns out to be something else as he now calls her "that nagging bitch" or "that nagging old hag." Parritt, out of hatred, also betrayed his mother and their anarchist cause, a revelation which drives him to self-destruction. The underlying philosophy, as O'Neill himself pointed out in the same interview, is that "there is always one dream left, one final dream, no matter how low you have fallen, down there at the bottom of the bottle I know, because I saw it."[35] Life is such stuff made of "pipe dreams," illusions and delusions, and Death alone unmasks its last dream, its last illusion. In the omnipresence of Death, the ultimate unmasker, the play unfolds a vision of life as it is—a living hell. The whole process of this unmasking, which is the play's action, can best be called Oriental, more specifically Buddhistic, for more than any other Oriental religion, Buddhism insists on its doctrine of maya, viewing life primarily as a living hell—where man clings to his illusions and delusions to the last, even when death comes—unless he attains his nirvana. From this Buddhist point of view, there is nothing especially pessimistic about *The Iceman Cometh*. To recognize life as it is means a first step toward enlightenment or release.

Larry Slade is believed to have been modeled on Terry Carlin, a Nietzschean anarchist, who introduced the young O'Neill not only to *Light on the Path* but also to the Provincetown group, thus playing a decisive role in his career. Slade sustains the burden of the play's meaning.[36] A sort of *raisonneur* of the play, he often speaks for O'Neill. The only one to challenge the newly converted Hickey, Slade destroys his illusions and exposes his true nature. If anyone in the play is relatively free of illusions, it is this one-time syndicalist-anarchist who remains almost pitiless, as when he does nothing to prevent Parritt's suicide. He is "done with judging," he says. As O'Neill takes pains to point out: "He is the only occupant of the room who is not asleep. He stares in front of him, an expression of tired tolerance giving his face the quality of a pitying but weary old priest's." Slade is indeed unique in the play. At the beginning of the play, when asked why he abandoned his anarchist cause after thirty years' dedication, he lists three reasons among others: himself, his comrades, and men in general. Admitting that he was "never made for it," he says: "I was born condemned to be one of those who has to see all sides of a question. When you're damned like that, the questions multiply for you until in the end it's all question and no answer." And then at the end of the play, when learning of Parritt's suicide, Slade says in a whisper of horrified pity: "Life is too much for me! I'll be a weak fool looking with pity at the two sides of everything till I die! May that day come soon!"[37] Born "to see all sides of a question" or look at "the two sides of everything," he comes close to embodying Emerson's bipolar vision, and singularly resembles Whitman's all seeing figure in the poem "I Sit and Look Out." There is something Oriental about Slade's vision, and yet it had long ago been anticipated by O'Neill himself, in *Beyond the Horizon*, when he saw both beauty and stench in the Orient. It was this double vision that enabled O'Neill to look steadily at what he went through at the Hell Hole and dramatize what it meant, for the first time in his life.

There is something amiss in *The Iceman Cometh*, however. There is no

O'Neill, there is no single character who represents the young O'Neill who stood on the brink of self-destruction at the time. Even more curious is *A Long Day's Journey Into Night*, a sort of sequel to *The Iceman Cometh*. In this play, which is more autobiographical than its predecessor, O'Neill, while having Edmund portray him, gives his name, Eugene, to a long-dead brother who was called Edmund. This curious name-switching seems to have something to do with the darkest moment of the young O'Neill's life out of which he was to be born again—the moment O'Neill regarded as the beginning of his career as a playwright. In short, the agony of rebirth. After all, the name Eugene means "well-born," a fact O'Neill doubtless had in mind when he wrote the play, the hardest and most painful task he had ever tackled in his life as a man and as a writer.

A Long Day's Journey Into Night is another exercise in unmasking. If this relentless unmasking were all there is to it, however, the play would be simply unbearable. Yet it is profoundly moving, as T. S. Eliot, among others, has testified.[38] This is because of its countermotif, another kind of unmasking that comes only in flashes, later in the play. But when it comes it brings the much-needed relief to the terribly depressing Tyrone household. These moments of relief are rare but powerful enough, intense enough, to offset their sense of hopelessness. They are epiphanies in that they suggest the promise of these tortured characters and what they might have become.[39] Even Mary momentarily relives her youthful dreams of becoming a nun or a concert pianist; Tyrone, dropping his habitual self-defense, does what he has never done—confesses that, spoiled by his initial success, he prostituted his talent for money. With this candid confession Tyrone wins Edmund's sympathy, putting an end to their day-long quarrel.

This countermotif of unmasking comes to its climax when Edmund, touched by his father's confession, responds ecstatically:

> You've just told me some high spots in your memories. Want to hear mine? They're all connected with the sea. Here's one. When I was on the Squarehead square rigger, bound for Buenos Aires. Full moon in the Trades. The old hooker driving fourteen knots. I lay on the bowsprit, facing astern, with the water foaming into spume under me, the masts with every sail white in the moonlight, towering high above me. I became drunk with the beauty and singing rhythm of it, and for a moment I lost myself—actually lost my life. I was set free! I dissolved in the sea, became white sails and flying spray, became beauty and rhythm, became moonlight and the ship and the high-dim-starred sky! I belonged without past or future, within peace and unity and a

wild joy, within something greater than my own life, or the life of Man, to Life itself! To God, if you want to put it that way. Then another time, on the American line, when I was lookout on the crow's nest in the dawn watch. A calm sea, that time. Only a lazy ground swell and a slow drowsy roll of the ship. The passengers asleep and none of the crew in sight. No sound of man. Black smoke pouring from the funnels behind and beneath me. Dreaming, not keeping lookout, feeling alone, and above, and apart, watching the dawn creep like a painted dream over the sky and sea which slept together. Then the moment of ecstatic freedom came. The peace, the end of the quest, the last harbor, the joy of belonging to a fulfillment beyond men's lousy, pitiful, greedy fears and hopes and dreams! And several other times in my life, when I was swimming far out, or lying alone on the beach, I have had the same experience. Became the sun, the hot sand, green seaweed anchored to a rock, swaying in the tide. Like a saint's vision of beatitude. Like the veil of things as they seem drawn back by an unseen hand. For a second you see—and seeing the secret, are the secret. For a second there is meaning! Then the hand lets the veil fall and you are alone, lost in the fog again, and you stumble on toward nowhere, for no good reason! It was a great mistake, my being born a man. I would have been much more successful as a seagull or a fish. As it is, I will always be a stranger who never feels at home, who does not really want and is not really wanted, who can never belong, who must always be a little in love with death!

Unlike the memories of the other characters, which are nothing but memories of the past, Edmund's, all connected with the sea, encompass entry, liberation, merging, and belonging, distinct stages of mystical experience.[40] While unmistakably pantheistic, his memories transcend time and space, aspiring, in Edmund's own words, toward "a saint's vision of beatitude." A Zen anthology singled out this particular passage as "one of the most sensitive and recent expressions of No-Knowledge in the Occidental literature."[41]

The source of Edmund's vision here is the source of O'Neill's drama. It is this vision that Paddy longed for in *The Hairy Ape*; it is this vision that Juan pursued in *The Fountain*; it is this vision that Lazarus reaffirmed with his gospel of eternal life; and it is this vision that Orin and Lavinia groped for vainly in *Mourning Becomes Electra*. Without this vision Marco Polo ended with nothing but his nickname Marco Millions; without this vision Nina in *Strange Interlude* declared: "Our lives are merely strange interludes in the electrical dispay of God the Father"; without this vision

Reuben in *Dynamo* also exclaimed: "There is no God. No god but Electricity"; and without this vision all those characters in *The Iceman Cometh* were lost souls. As Edmund said, it is this vision that insured his sense of belonging—"within peace and unity and a wild joy, within something greater than my own life, or the life of Man, to Life itself! To God, if you want to put it that way." This is what O'Neill himself, as early as 1919, meant by "my feeling for the impelling, inscrutable forces behind life" which it is "my ambition to at least faintly shadow at their work in my plays"; this is also what O'Neill meant by "the Force behind —Fate, God, our biological past creating our present, whatever one calls it—Mystery certainly—and of the one eternal tragedy of Man in his glorious, self-destructive struggle to make the Force express him instead of being, as an animal is, an infinitesimal incident in its expression." Being acutely conscious of this Force, O'Neill called himself "a most confirmed mystic."[42]

His art, then, was created out of his ceaseless attempt to translate such an experience, such a vision, into his chosen medium. To confirm its authenticity O'Neill studied the history of all religions "with immense interest as being—for me, at least—the most illuminating 'case histories' of the inner life of man."[43] If, as he also said, Taoist mysticism interested him more than any other Oriental religion, it was undoubtedly because of its special emphasis on primal harmony, what he called "the old harmony they knew before man came." In this sense the Orient did not vanish with *Mourning Becomes Electra* but rather turned inward, nurturing his mystical vision itself.

A Long Day's Journey Into Night was written at Tao House, as O'Neill recorded in a dedicatory note. Referring to "this play of old sorrow, written in tears and blood," he said: "I mean it as a tribute to your love and tenderness which gave me the faith in love that enabled me to face my dead at last and write this play—write it with deep pity and understanding and forgiveness for all the four haunted Tyrones." Because of this rare sense of reconciliation which he achieved at the virtual end of his writing career, the play takes a special place in the O'Neill canon. In particular the phrase "this play of old sorrow, written in tears and blood" echoes the opening passage of *Light on the Path*: "Before the eyes can see they must be incapable of tears. Before the ear can hear it must have lost its sensitiveness. Before the voice can speak in the presence of the Masters it must have lost the power to wound. Before the soul can stand in the presence of the Masters its feet must be washed in the blood of the heart."[44] It may be recalled that one of the first things O'Neill decided to do when he went to Provincetown with Terry Carlin in 1916 was to paint these lines onto the rafters of his apartment.[45] If such was the promise he had made to himself at the threshold of his career, he kept it well. That is why he could say ''this play of old sorrow, written in tears and blood'' without sounding hollow.

NINE

Eliot

Eliot's quarrel with his old teacher Babbitt was, after all, a family quarrel in that they knew they shared common ground. This relationship Eliot himself described thus: "Having myself begun as a disciple of Mr. Babbitt, and feeling, as I do, that I have rejected nothing that seems to me positive in his teaching, I was hardly qualified to 'attack' humanism."[1] Although their relationship needs to be examined afresh, it can be said that Eliot inherited Babbitt's legacy in at least two areas: his outlook on the modern world and his interest in the Orient.

While at Harvard, the young Eliot came under Babbitt's influence. He already knew *Literature and the American College* when, as a Master's candidate in English, he took Babbitt's course in French literary criticism, the subject of his third book, *The Masters of Modern French Criticism*.[2] As we recall, in the former volume Babbitt, deploring the decline of the humanities in American higher education, insisted on tradition and discipline as a way of combating the modern malaise—namely, naturalism—which he believed had over the centuries been eroding the foundations of Western civilization; in the latter volume he illustrated his thesis specifically in terms of nineteenth century French literary criticism. Such was the intellectual background from which Eliot emerged with his essay of 1919, "Tradition and the Individual Talent," which advocated the primacy of tradition over originality. Calling it "the germinal essay of Eliot's whole thought, especially of his literary thought," Austin Warren remarked that it could "best be understood as an artist's version of *Rousseau and Romanticism*," the best known of Babbitt's books, which appeared in the same year.[3] As late as 1928, when he discussed religion in relation to humanism, Eliot still referred to Babbitt, in this instance to his fifth book, *Democracy and Leadership*. "I believe," concluded Eliot, "that it is better to recognize the weaknesses of humanism at once, and allow for them, so that the structure may not crash beneath an excessive weight; and so that we may arrive at an enduring recognition of its value for us, and of our obligation to its author."[4] And in the same year Eliot decided to write his own prescription: "classicist in literature, royalist in politics, and anglo-catholic in religion." While accepting Babbitt's as an

159

accurate diagnosis of the condition of modern man, Eliot went beyond his teacher's humanism, charting his own path.

Another legacy of Babbitt's was his interest in Indian philosophy and religion. In 1911, when he returned to Harvard from Paris, Eliot took up his two-year study of Sanskrit and Pali with Professor Charles Lanman, as Babbitt had done seventeen years earlier. During the second year Eliot read Indian philosophy with Professor James Woods, who was then working on his *Yoga System of Patanjali*. Thus Eliot became the first American, indeed, the first Western poet of major stature, to devote his formative years to an academic study of Indian philosophy and religion.

All this is by now a matter of common knowledge. Eliot himself spoke of his experience on several occasions in connection with modern Orientalism. For instance, touching on the current populariy of Confucius in *After Strange Gods* (1934), he wondered how anyone could understand him without "some knowledge of Chinese and a long frequentation of the best Chinese society." "Confucius," continued Eliot, "has become the philosopher of the rebellious Protestant. And I cannot but feel that in some respects Irving Babbitt, with the noblest intentions, has merely made matters worse instead of better." Driving his point home, Eliot then related his own experience:

> Two years spent in the study of Sanskrit under Charles Lanman, and a year in the mazes of Patanjali's metaphysics under the guidance of James Woods, left me in a state of enlightened mystification. A good half of the effort of understanding what the Indian philosphers were after—and their subtleties make most of the great European philosophers look like schoolboys—lay in trying to erase from my mind all the categories and kinds of distinction common to European philosophy from the time of the Greeks. My previous and concomitant study of European philosophy was hardly better than an obstacle. And I came to the conclusion—seeing also that the "influence" of Brahmin and Buddhist thought upon Europe, as in Schopenhauer, Hartmann, and Deussen, had largely been through romantic misunderstanding—that my only hope of really penetrating to the heart of that mystery would lie in forgetting how to think and feel as an American or a European: which, for practical as well as sentimental reasons, I did not wish to do.

The passage is noteworthy for various reasons. First, in dismissing Schopenhauer, for instance, as a case of romantic misunderstanding Eliot echoes Babbitt.[5] Second, his phrase "a state of enlightened mystification," though highly quotable, seems deliberately ambiguous; what is certain is his tone—modest, almost self-deprecatory, and ironic. And third, his fear of losing his sense of identity as an American or a European stands in sharp contrast to his friend Pound's devotion to Confucius. Whether or not this fear was typical of Eliot, in his intellectual endeavors he was serious enough and advanced enough to feel the danger.[6] Years later, in *Notes towards the Definition of Culture* (1949), Eliot no doubt had this experience in mind when he generalized: "What we ordinarily mean by understanding of another people, of course, is an approximation towards understanding which stops short at the point at which the student would begin to lose some essential of his own culture. The man who, in order to understand the inner world of a cannibal tribe, has partaken of the practice of cannibalism, has probably gone too far: he can never quite be one of his own folk again."[7] And in his address "The Unity of European Culture" (1946) Eliot summed up his case once and for all: "Long ago I studied the ancient Indian languages, and while I was deeply interested at that time in Philosophy, I read a little poetry too; and I know that my own poetry shows the influences of Indian thought and sensibility."[8]

It is clear from these personal testimonies that the Orient, in Eliot's case, was exclusively Indian. Even so, it was not immediately visible in his early poems, say, in "The Love Song of J. Alfred Prufrock." With *The Waste Land*, however, India finally and fully surfaced from the depths of the poet's psyche, long after he had abandoned his academic study of Indian religion and philosophy.

The Waste Land has too often been read as the poem of the lost generation, that disillusioned generation of World War I, in spite of Eliot's repeated denial of the poem's alleged intention. As he said simply in an interview: "One wants to get something off one's chest."[9] That is, *The Waste Land* is a personal poem in that it began as a personal rather than as a cultural document. From those scattered, often buried, biographical passages throughout the poem one can sense that Eliot was going through a personal crisis—so serious that he considered becoming a Buddhist. The crisis came in the form of a twofold impasse: his domestic hell with the mentally unstable Vivienne and his despair over his own artistic sterility.[10] Eliot managed to find his way out of this impasse as he came to view his personal crisis in a larger perspective, by identifying his sense of impotence both with the chaotic ruins of postwar Europe and with the mythic wasteland of the Fisher King involving the mystery of the Holy Grail. By relating this medieval Christian myth to its origin in nature myth, Eliot completed what he called a mythical method. In a review of Joyce's *Ulysses*, which appeared in 1922, the same year as his own poem, he pointed out that this use of myth, this manipulation of "a continuous

161

parallel between contemporaneity and antiquity," signified "simply a way of controlling, of ordering, of giving a shape and a significance to the immense panorama of futility and anarchy which is contemporary history." With this method Eliot was able to transform those scattered and seemingly unrelated fragments into a unified whole. Viewing a personal situation from a universal frame of reference was more than a method; it was also a vision, as Elizabeth Drew pointed out.[11] Read from this perspective, *The Waste Land* should easily dispel its alleged pessimism and defeatism, for this mythical method or vision does transcend that sort of sentimentalism.

The Oriental references in *The Waste Land* have received much critical attention, because of their conspicuousness and because of the poet's accompanying notes. To Raymond Tschumi, for instance, "more than a disguise of Eliot's convictions as a Christian the allusions to Indian rituals are the whole foundation of the poem." Reporting Eliot's confession that at the time of its composition he was seriously considering becoming a Buddhist, Stephen Spender also observed that "a Buddhist is as immanent as a Christian." G. Nageswara Rao suggested that these Indian references, neither out of place nor unexpected, constitute part of the poem's structural design, which is basically Upanishadic.[12]

The first major Oriental reference appears in the third section, "The Fire Sermon." Thanks to Eliot's notes on Buddha's famous sermon and on Eastern and Western asceticism, we have little difficulty in grasping the overall theme of lust. The section comes to focus on the love scene between a typist and a clerk against the background of the polluted river and city, symbolic of the modern world as a wasteland. Through the all-seeing Tiresias we quickly perceive the sterile nature of their relationship and of countless other affairs, no matter how romantic and glamorous. Common to them all is lust, "a cauldron of unholy loves," to use Saint Augustine's metaphor. Here lust burns as the ultimate symbol of the world. As Buddha himself declares in his sermon, all things human are burning with the fire of passions—"with the fire of hatred, with the fire of infatuation; with birth, old age, death, sorrow, lamentation, misery, grief, and despair."[13] This symbol of all-consuming fire brings Buddha and Saint Augustine together in the final lines of the section:

> To Carthage then I came
>
> Burning burning burning burning
> O Lord Thou pluckest me out
> O Lord Thou pluckest
>
> burning

162

To recognize life as a burning hell is the first step toward the total cure, the precondition of salvation or release which represents the aim of asceticism, Buddhist and Christian, Eastern and Western. Insisting on an aversion for all human passions, Buddha concludes his sermon: "And in conceiving this aversion, he becomes divested of passion, and by the absence of passion he becomes free, and when he is free he becomes aware that he is free; and he knows that rebirth is exhausted, that he has lived the holy life, that he has done what it behooved him to do, and that he is no more for this world." And those thousand priests, while listening, are said to have become "free from attachment and delivered from the depravities." What is suggested here is that fire destroys as well as purifies, and this twofold symbolism of fire is reinforced by water, the central symbol of the ensuing section, "Death by Water," while anticipating the last section, "What the Thunder Said."

The last section, according to Eliot, is "not only the best part, but the only part that justifies the whole, at all."[14] Yet over this section critics are sharply divided, for it finally determines the meaning of *The Waste Land*. At the climax of this last section, indeed, of the entire poem, the second major Oriental reference appears, this time to a Upanishadic fable. The fable relates how gods, men, and demons, having lived as students of sacred knowledge, each understood their father Prajapati's monosyllabic *Da*. To the gods it meant *damyata*, "be self-controlled"; to the men *datta*, "be charitable"; and to the demons *davyadhavam*, "be compassionate." The fable ends: "The storm cloud thunders: 'Da! Da! Da!'— 'Be self-controlled! Be charitable! Be compassionate!' "[15] Hence the section title, "What the Thunder Said."

F. O. Matthiessen, who sees no need to read Buddha and Saint Augustine in order to understand *The Waste Land*, says about this particular passage: "I have not yet read the Upanishad from which Eliot borrowed the onomatopoeic representation of 'what the thunder said'; but it is perfectly clear from his own lines what an excellent 'objective correlative' he found in that legend."[16] Nor does Cleanth Brooks bother to consult the Upanishadic source, though he says of *datta, davydhavam, damyata*: "words which will seem to many apparently meaningless babble, but which contain the oldest and most permanent truth of the race." Yet for the Hieronymo line he returns to its source, Kyd's *Spanish Tragedy*.[17] Elizabeth Drew even fails to mention the fable, though she discusses Buddha's sermon in connection with the third section and also notes that Eliot's mind absorbed "the whole literary and cultural tradition of Europe, as well as a great deal of Asiatic religion and philosophy." And yet she rests her case on this unexamined Indian reference: "But it is impossible to feel peace in the concluding passage. It is a *formal* ending only.

. . . But they are in foreign tongues, not translated into his own inner experience and so become a part of himself. *Give, Sympathize, Control, Peace*, remain abstract ideas; none of them has been transfigured into a redeeming symbol. The surrender has been made, but it still seems a surrender to death, and the possibility of rebirth is still without substance or outline.''[18]

More helpful in this regard is what Indian critics have to say about the passage in question. Duly noting Eliot's knowledge of Indian religion and philosophy, C. D. Narasimhaiah points to the waste land which appears in the *Veda*—eagerly awaiting rain, which the gods bestow in response to a mendicant sage's prayer. Within this overall framework Narasimhaiah examines the third section and then proceeds to the last section. As for Eliot's change of the order in which the three Sanskrit words appear in the original—namely, from *damyata, datta, davyadhavam* to *datta, davyadhavam, damyata*, Narasimhaiah, while granting the change is justified by the requirements of the poem, nonetheless takes a hint from the *Upanishad* itself—that whereas the gods and devils keep their mottoes, only men forget. "And finally," he concludes, "the benediction of Shantih, Shantih, Shantih is itself the rain to the Waste Land." G. Nageswara Rao, likewise examining many parallels between *The Waste Land* and the *Upanishads*, comes to reject both F. R. Leavis's view that the poem shows no progress, and I. A. Richards's that the poem presents the disillusionment of a generation. According to Rao, even Tiresias has his Upanishadic counterpart. "Tiresias," says Rao, "is like the *Drasta* (Seer) in the Upanishads. As in Prajapati both the sexes meet in him and Eliot says what Tiresias *sees*, in fact, is the substance of the poem. What Prajapati saw and expounded is the Upanishads." As, continues Rao, the seemingly chaotic *Upanishads* owe their unity to the seer-narrator, whose free and varying discourses always aim at bringing home the complex nature of the absolute, so *The Waste Land*, like the *Upanishads*, is "a secret message delivered to the people in the Waste Land to liberate themselves." The progression of *The Waste Land* as a poem of quest is cyclic. "It is not surprising then, that the poem appears to end where it began, though the cycle is complete and the protagonist is not the same person he was at the beginning of the poem." At the end of his quest there is the promise of rain.[19]

Whether or not Narasimhaiah and Rao are carried away by their natural enthusiasm, they are certainly not guilty of negligence or ignorance, as many Western critics are. Be that as it may, it is significant that the Oriental references, when read properly, do reinforce Eliot's mythical method and lead us far beyond the pessimism of the lost generation.

If *The Waste Land* represents what we may call Eliot's Indian period, *Four Quartets* (1936–43) belongs to his Christian period, the period of his career which commenced with his declaring himself an Anglo-Catholic in religion. *Four Quartets*, by critical consensus, is a religious poem, a Christian poem at that. While not denying this, Indian critics still find in them much that is Indian. Narasimhaiah does admit the possibility of reading the poem in terms of Heraclitus or the Christian tradition, but at the same time he relates its central theme of time and action directly to the *Gita*.[20] Kamal Wood is more emphatic. "Eliot's own devotion to the person of Jesus runs like an undertone through the *Quartets*." With this opening statement, however, she attempts to read it as a poem of search and arrival, the pattern characteristic of the *Upanishads*, the *Gita*, and other Indian works.[21] In this Indian critics are not alone. Some Western critics are in fact more positive. Harold E. McCarthy, for one, regards *Four Quartets* as Eliot's crowning achievement, which "brings together in a concentrated form a lifetime of thought, reflection, feeling, hope, and despair," and then observes: "Of all Eliot's works, taken separately, it is the *Four Quartets* which is closest to the spirit of Buddhism." Russell T. Fowler, on the other hand, singles out the *Gita*: "Its influence, however, has a central importance, both structurally and thematically, to the last of the four and to the *Quartets* as a whole."[22]

Four Quartets is also a personal poem. A poetic expression of Eliot's mature middle age, it is candid, intimate, confessional, and yet subtle. Here too, the Orient appears, though not as conspicuously as in *The Waste Land*. At the outset of "Burnt Norton" we note the lotus rising quietly in the rose garden, and further on, the stillness of a Chinese jar. Nothing is obtrusive as memories culminate in meditations over time and eternity. Forever torn between these two, man must reconcile their conflicting claims in terms of action. In all humility the poet says in "East Coker": "For us, there is only the trying. The rest is not our business." This inevitably leads to the *Gita* passage in "The Dry Salvages."

In this passage, which begins "I sometimes wonder if that is what Krishna meant— / Among other things—or one way of putting the same thing," Eliot interweaves the voyage imagery and Krishna's admonitions to Arjuna the warrior, who in confusion refuses to act:

> "Fare forward, you who think that you are voyaging;
> You are not those who saw the harbour
> Receding, or those who will disembark.
> Here between the hither and the farther shore
> While time is withdrawn, consider the future

And the past with an equal mind.
At the moment which is not of action or inaction
You can receive this: 'on whatever sphere of being
The mind of a man may be intent
At the time of death'—that is the one action
(And the time of death is every moment)
Which shall fructify in the lives of others:
And do not think of the fruit of action.
Fare forward.

     O voyagers, O seamen,
You who come to port, and you whose bodies
Will suffer the trial and judgement of the sea,
Or whatever event, this is your real destination.''
So Krishna, as when he admonished Arjuna
On the field of battle.
     Not fare well,
But fare forward, voyagers.

In the eighth chapter of the *Bhagavad-Gita*, referred to here, Arjuna asks his charioteer, Krishna, one of the reincarnations of Vishnu the Preserver, about the nature of the self and action, among other things. In reply Krishna explains Brahman the Absolute and Atman the Self, and also karma, the creative force which brings beings into existence. Then he comes to the nature of action in this relative world.

> Therefore you must remember me at all times, and do your duty. If your mind and heart are set upon me constantly, you will come to me. Never doubt this.
> Make a habit of practising meditation, and do not let your mind be distracted. In this way you will come finally to the Lord, who is the light-giver, the highest of the high.[23]

Krishna urges Arjuna to act, that is, in this instance, to fight, the only proper thing he can do as a member of the warrior caste. There is no other way. When he acts, however, he must do so with no thoughts of the fruit of action—the sort of selfless act which alone brings him freedom.[24] Through this right action Arjuna then can reconcile the conflicting claims of the relative and the absolute, of time and eternity. Toward the end of ''The Dry Salvages'' Eliot once again writes, with a sense of humility:

    And right action is freedom
From past and future also.
For most of us, this is the aim

166

Never here to be realised;
Who are only undefeated
Because we have gone on trying;
We, content at the last
If our temporal reversions nourish
(Not too far from the yew-tree)
The life of significant soil.

While admitting that the *Gita* passage fits perfectly the poem's theme of
annunciation, Helen Gardner nevertheless believes that "to introduce
Krishna at this point is an error and destroys the imaginative harmony of
the poem, since it is precisely in their view of history and the time process
that Christianity and Hinduism are most opposed." "I imagine," she
continues, "that the reason for the introduction of the *Gita* here is that the
poem contains so much of Mr Eliot's past that inevitably his explorations
of Hindu metaphysics find a place in it. He has owned that two years'
study of Sanskrit and 'a year in the mazes of Patanjali's metaphysics' left
him 'in the state of enlightened mystification,' and I must own that is the
feeling the passage leaves me with. It is introduced rather tentatively, as a
piece of speculation."[25] It seems a bit naive of her to take Eliot's statement at face value and further to lump Patanjali and the *Gita* together. We
may as well recall what Eliot said about the *Gita*—in his experience the
greatest philosophical poem after the *Divine Comedy*[26]—and also what he
said about Arjuna—"That balance of mind which a few highly-civilized
individuals such as Arjuna, the hero of the *Bhavagad Gita*, can maintain
in action, is difficult for most of us even as observers."[27] Indeed, no other
work could justify Eliot's meditation on time and eternity better than the
Gita, because of its central message: selfless action as a way of reconciling the relative and the absolute in terms of mysticism, yogic discipline
which helps man transcend time and place.

According to Fowler, Krishna and Arjuna do not really disappear even
after this passage, for the themes thus introduced become the main
concerns of the rest of "The Dry Salvages" and of "Little Gidding."
"Krishna, like Christ, moves below the surface of 'Little Gidding,' exerting an influence through his words and the nature of his own existence,"
Fowler concludes.[28] This amounts to saying that *Four Quartets* is as
much Hindu as it is Christian. Undoubtedly this aspect of *Four Quartets*
made one reviewer comment that the poem, though superior to *Murder in
the Cathedral*, shows "less Christianity," and go on to ask if it is "possible that the level reached . . . is beyond Christianity?"[29] There is no
real contradiction here, however. What these observations suggest is that
Four Quartets is ultimately a mystical poem. To such a label Eliot himself

would have objected, but we may recall what he said about Pascal: "Pascal was not a mystic, and his works are not to be classified amongst mystical writings; but what can be called mystical experience happens to many men who do not become mystics."[30] And we may also recall what he meant by "the kind of unexplainable experience which many of us have had, once or twice in our lives, and have been unable to put into words."[31] Helen Gardner, in her conclusion, calls Eliot "a poet of vision," to be in the company with his master Dante. Robert Sencourt, who personally knew Eliot's religious quest, is more positive and specific: "In a unique personal way, they [*Four Quartets*] express his ardours for mystical experience and for the expression of mysticism. They reveal also the fidelity with which he still turned from the Anglican liturgy to the *Divina Comedia* and the *Bhagavad Gita*, classics which were now even more familiar companions than they had been twenty years earlier."[32]

At the heart of Eliot's poetry is this mystical experience or vision, a moment of ecstasy and illumination, a point of silence and stillness. And it often takes garden and light imagery. In *The Waste Land* there is this passage: "—Yet when we came back, late, from the hyacinth garden, / Your arms full, and your hair wet, I could not / Speak, and my eyes failed, I was neither / Living nor dead, and I knew nothing, / Looking into the heart of light, the silence." In *The Family Reunion* there is the rose garden with associations of innocent love. Agatha relates such a remembered moment: "I only looked through the little door / When the sun was shining on the rose garden." And in *Four Quartets* the rose garden appears again: "And the pool was filled with water out of sunlight, / And the lotos rose, quietly, quietly, / The surface glittered out of heart of light." As a matter of fact, it is in *Four Quartets* that these recurring symbols culminate:

> At the still point of the turning world. Neither flesh nor flesh-
> less;
> Neither from nor towards; at the still point, there the dance is,
> But neither arrest nor movement. And do not call it fixity,
> Where past and future are gathered. Neither movement from nor
> towards,
> Neither ascent nor decline. Except for the point, the still point,
> There would be no dance, and there is only the dance.
> I can only say, *there* we have been: but I cannot say where.
> And I cannot say, how long, for that is to place it in time.

Eliot's still point here resembles Dante's point of light at the end of the *Paradiso*, just as his "turning world" suggests the familiar Buddhist image of the world of time. Together they symbolize man's paradoxical condition, the paradox of living in history and out of history, in the intersection of time and eternity. As W. T. Stace points out, a mystical vision which embraces such a paradox of action and inaction, while directly apprehended by acknowledged mystics, also appears in poetry. With specific reference to Eliot's metaphor, "the still point of the turning world," he then says: "There is no specific reference to any regular or mystical conception here. But the inner meaning of the metaphor of the motionless axis of the spinning planet is plain. It is that the world of sense—to use Plato's phrase—is a perpetual flux, yet at the heart of things there is stillness and silence."[33] Coming from a deeper source than Eliot's personal consciousness, this mystical vision makes *Four Quartets* what it is—the greatest achievement of his career as a man and as a poet. Indeed, he said of *Four Quartets*: "I stand or fall on them."[34]

As we know, Eliot's interest in poetic drama continued to increase throughout his career. After *Four Quartets*, poetic drama became his central literary concern. While justifying the legitimacy of this interest and articulating his thoughts on the subject, Eliot tried his hand at writing verse drama. After his early attempts, he finally wrote *Murder in the Cathedral* (1935), which established him as a playwright of no mean order. In the ensuing years he wrote four more verse plays: *The Family Reunion* (1939), *The Cocktail Party* (1949), *The Confidential Clerk* (1953), and *The Elder Statesman* (1958). In theory and practice alike, he played a significant role in the modern revival of poetic drama.

Poetic drama is a severely limited form, especially Eliot's kind of poetic drama which deliberately turned away from the Elizabethan, Shakespearean tradition in favor of the older, medieval and classical, while extending the range of the English comedy of manners. From this we may conclude that the Orient would be out of place in his dramatic writings. At first glance such seems to be the case. A closer examination, however, reveals quite otherwise. This is true even of *Murder in the Cathedral*, a Christian play about the martyrdom of Thomas à Becket, Archbishop of Canterbury, at the hands of his former friend King Henry II.

Well aware of the difficulty of treating the theme of religious martyrdom, Eliot has four tempters approach Becket as he prepares himself for the final confrontation, and following his murder, four knights come forward with their various justifications. Whereas the four tempters, representing his youthful pleasures, his political power, his new alliance with the feudal barons, and above all his desire for martyrdom, each help bare Becket's deepening inner conflict, the four knights each plead their case by appealing to the British sense of fair play, insisting on their complete

169

disinterestedness, pointing out Becket's desire to put the church above the state, and declaring "a verdict of Suicide while of Unsound Mind."

More than anything else, the fourth tempter and the fourth knight together point to the nature of Eliot's difficulty. In order to present properly a case of religious martyrdom he must exonerate Becket from a twofold charge: he must appear to a post-Freudian audience to be free of a martyr complex, and to a traditional Christian audience not to be courting martyrdom out of the sin of pride. In short, Eliot's task is to make Becket convincing as a genuine martyr. Judging from the play's popularity which reached far beyond the immediate Christian audience, Eliot succeeded.

Being familiar with what they come to offer, Becket can easily dismiss the first three tempters. But the unexpected fourth is something else. In his urging: "Seek the way of martyrdom, make yourself the lowest / On earth, to be high in heaven," Becket recognizes his own inmost desire. Once past this friendly tempter, he sees his way, declaring:

> The last temptation is the greatest treason:
> To do the right deed for the wrong reason
>
> .   .   .   .   .
>
> I shall no longer act or suffer, to the sword's end.
> Now my good Angel, whom God appoints
> To be my guardian, hover over the swords' points.

In his Christmas sermon Becket reiterates this point: "A Christian martyrdom is never an accident, for Saints are not made by accident. Still less is a Christian martyrdom the effect of a man's will to become a Saint, as a man by willing and contriving may become a ruler of men. A martyrdom is always the design of God." Neither courting nor avoiding, he now accepts his own martyrdom as part of God's design.

Only by doing the right deed for the right reason does Becket become a genuine martyr. The whole concept here anticipates Eliot's words in "The Dry Salvages" (1941): "And right action is freedom / From past and future also," which in turn hark back to Krishna's in the *Gita*: "Action rightly renounced brings freedom; / Action rightly performed brings freedom: / Both are better / Than mere shunning of action."[35] As David E. Jones observed,[36] Becket follows Krishna's advice—in Eliot's words: "And do not think of the fruit of action. / Fare forward." In order to make a Christian martyrdom convincing dramatically and psychologically Eliot turns to the *Gita*. That is, the Christian martyr Thomas à Becket, in this play, has his model in the Hindu warrior-hero Arjuna, whose rare mental balance in action Eliot noted with admiration.

With his second play, *The Family Reunion*, Eliot turned to the contemporary world, while using Greek drama as his point of departure—a practice he was to continue in all his later plays. As the play progresses what may be called a hierarchical pattern of psychological, moral, and spiritual insight begins to emerge. While most of the characters remain in the dark about what really happens, Mary and Agatha become more aware of the situation, and Harry gains insight into the roots of his identity. Especially interesting in this connection is Harry's servant-chauffeur, Downing, who seems to see all and understand all. Not only is he the first one to see the Furies as Mary and Agatha do, but he also calls Harry "psychic." He even foretells what the future has in store for his master:

> But with people like him, there's something inside them
> That accounts for what happens to them. You get a feeling of it.
> So I seem to know beforehand, when something's going to
>   happen,
> And it seems quite natural, being his Lordship.
> And that's why I say now, I have a feeling
> That he won't want me long, and he won't want anybody.

A most unusual servant-chauffer he is! Downing may remind us of Tiresias, who observes all in *The Waste Land*, or Krishna, who serves as Arjuna's charioteer.[37] And since the play as a whole anticipates *The Cocktail Party*, he points to Dr. Reilly.

Consistent with its upper-middle-class setting, Eliot's third play opens with one cocktail party and closes with another. Also consistent with its witty and gossipy comedy-of-manners style, it centers around love affairs: Edward Chamberlayne in love with Celia Coplestone; his wife, Lavinia, in love with Peter Quilpe; and Peter in love with Celia. Out of this entanglement they each find their way. Edward and Lavinia realize that they have something in common—being unloving and unlovable—and agree to "make the best of a bad job." Peter leaves London for his new career as a scriptwriter in Hollywood. And Celia joins a religious order as a nurse and goes off to the tropics where she is martyred—a fitting end for one who has suffered from her sense of solitude and her sense of sin. Thus one becomes a saint, one an artist, and the others continue their marriage with a little more awareness. They each attain their proper status according to their inborn inclination and capacity. With this theme of search for identity and vocation defining itself, the play reveals its rich implications: no ordinary cocktail party but, finally, a sort of libation.

They cannot initiate this search by themselves, however; they must be led by another group of characters: Julia Schuttlethwaite, Alexander Mac-Cologie Gibbs, and Sir Henry Harcourt-Reilly. As characters they differ

171

from one another: Julia is garrulous, meddlesome, often silly; Alex, somehow acquainted with everyone everywhere and capable of creating something out of very little; and Sir Henry, mysterious, humorous, and ready with his more than professional wisdom. Because of their experience and insight they are able to help each of the four characters with his or her separate search. This second group of characters, called "guardians" because of their conspicuous role in the play, have baffled critics. For their wisdom, wordly and otherwise, they have been compared to the guardians in Plato's *Republic* or to the "clerisy"—the "charismatic" personalities referred to in Eliot's own essay *The Idea of a Christian Society*.[38] By the same token, they may be compared to Krishna or more familiar Hindu gurus who guide students in spiritual matters.

Alex, for instance, claims to have learned his culinary art in the East. "Ah, but that's my special gift— / Concocting a toothsome meal out of nothing. / Any scraps you have will do. I learned that in the East." He is forever in touch with the East, and one gets the impression that, settled in the East, he occasionally visits London. He brings the news of Celia's martyrdom. More intriguing is Sir Henry, a psychiatrist, who diagnoses his patients' cases and prescribes cures for their particular ailments. Sending them off, he repeats his benediction: "Go in peace. And work out your salvation with diligence." "Work out your salvation with diligence," we remember, was Buddha's deathbed advice to his disciples. Apparently, Sir Henry is intended to be more than a psychiatrist. He has been likened not just to Buddha but also to God, to the Devil, and to an Anglican priest. Noting all this, Philip R. Headings observes: "Reilly is an enlightened mid-twentieth-century psychiatrist who recognizes the parallel insights of Eastern mysticism, Christian mysticism, and Jungian psychology and uses them as he is able in his efforts to help his patients."[39]

Celia, an example of this search for identity and vocation, represents the highest spiritual status man is capable of. Being not of her kind, the Chamberlaynes must be content with learning to "make the best of a bad job." Peter Quilpe is more fortunate. Learning of Celia's death, he blurts out that he understands nothing, and Sir Henry points out: "You understand your *métier*, Mr. Quilpe— / Which is the most that any of us can ask for." The search for identity and the search for vocation at this point tend to merge into each other. Everyone is born with a particular destiny to fulfill, a particular calling to perform.

The Chamberlaynes take a mediocre place in this spiritual hierarchy. Mediocre as they are, their occasional insight saves them from being hopeless. In a moment of rare candor Edward shows his share of insight:

The self that can say "I want this—or want that"—
The self that wills—he is a feeble creature;
He has to come to terms in the end
With the obstinate, the tougher self; who does not speak,
Who never talks, who cannot argue;
And who in some men may be the *guardian*—
but in men like me, the dull, the implacable,
The indomitable spirit of mediocrity.
The willing self can contrive the disaster
Of this unwilling partnership—but can only flourish
In submission to the ruler of the stronger partner.

The notion of man as a sort of partnership of two selves—the social and the solitary, the willing and the unwilling, the illusory and the authentic—echoes those similar notions voiced by Emerson, Thoreau, and Whitman. Once again we may recall the Upanishadic parable of two birds, the one eating and the other observing on the same tree, or better still of the *Gita*, which dramatizes the way Arjuna, the relative self, finally submits to Krishna, the Absolute.[40]

Eliot's next play, *The Confidential Clerk*, is Wildean in its familiar situation of lost children, searching parents, and mistaken identity. (This is no surprise since Eliot used for a springboard Euripides's *Ion*, the play which inaugurated the long tradition of European comedy.) Sir Claude and Lady Elizabeth Mulhammer each believe that Colby Simkins, a replacement for the retiring confidential clerk Eggerson, is their child born out of wedlock. As it turns out, however, Sir Claude's child never saw the light; Lady Elizabeth's is Barnabas Kaghan, fiancé of her husband's acknowledged illegitimate daughter, Lucasta; as for Colby, he is the son of Mrs. Guzzard, Sir Claude's widowed sister. With these complications resolved, all ends well.

The play ends happily in yet another and more serious sense. Upon discovering that his father was a musician, Colby decides to pursue his long-cherished dream. As he declares to Sir Claude:

I want to be an organist.
It doesn't matter about success—
I aimed too high—beyond my capacity.
I thought I didn't want to be an organist
When I found I had no chance of getting to the top—
That is, to become the organist of a cathedral.
But my father was an unsuccessful organist.

By discovering his true identity, Colby also discovers his true vocation.

With one stroke he succeeds in realizing his twofold search for identity and vocation. Having groped through the dark, he has finally found his "secret garden." As Lucasta points out, he can now retire to this secret garden, apart from the rest of the world. "He doesn't need anyone. He's fascinating, / But he's undependable. He has his own world." At the critical moment of his life Colby does indeed prove his tougher self by refusing Sir Claude's business offer. Aware of his own heritage, he chooses to be a musician, even a second-rate musician, rather than a successful businessman, thus avoiding the error of Sir Claude, who, realizing the impossibility of his becoming a first-rate potter, decided to become a successful financier. Here Colby follows Krishna's advice: "It is better to do your own duty, however imperfectly, than to assume the duties of another person, however successfully. Prefer to die doing your own duty: the duty of another will bring you into great spiritual danger."[41]

This mention of the *Gita* is no mere coincidence; the play rings with echoes of the *Gita*. Lady Elizabeth's interest in mysticism is more comprehensible and Eggerson's role is less puzzling once he is understood as a Krishna figure.[42] Throughout the play Eggerson plays a role rather out of the ordinary for a confidential clerk. He helps untangle all the characters' complicated relationships; moreover, he shows the way for Colby. Eggerson gets him a church organist's position in his own parish and invites him to live with his family until he is settled. In taking Colby under his wing, Eggerson assumes the role of guide, guardian, and father. All this he does with a peculiar sense of premonition. As he says to Colby: "I don't see your spending a lifetime as an organist. / I think you'll come to find you've another vocation." In this role Eggerson clearly succeeds Downing of *The Famly Reunion* and Sir Henry of *The Cocktail Party*. They are all versions of Krishna.

The Elder Statesman, Eliot's fifth and last play, dispenses altogether with the comic paraphernalia characteristic of its immediate predecessor. Like its model, *Oedipus at Colonus*, the play sustains an austere simplicity, befitting the protagonist who has outlived his political career and is now facing death. In the midst of seeming serenity Lord Claverton becomes uneasy as his ghosts begin to close in on him in the persons of Frederico Gomez, his Oxford classmate, and Mrs. Cargill, the old musical comedy star he had deserted. Referring to their dark secret—their car had once run over an old man on the road, though he was already dead—Gomez calls him a failure, the worst kind of failure, because all his life he has kept on "pretending to himself / That he's a success." Mrs. Cargill, in turn, tells him what a friend of hers once said about him: "He'd give you the slip: he's not to be trusted. / That man is hollow." By admitting his old mistakes to his daughter, Monica, Lord Claverton for the first time experiences a sense of freedom. He even begins to learn again; from Monica and her fiancé he learns the meaning of love, and from his defiant son, Michael, he learns the meaning of being himself. By accepting himself for what he is, by accepting his children for what they are, he finally finds peace. As he declares at the end: "I've been freed from the self that pretends to be someone; / And in becoming no one, I begin to live. / It is worth while dying, to find out what life is."

In other words, Lord Claverton comes to terms with his tougher self. Early in the play he confides to Monica his dissatisfaction with himself:

> What is this self inside us, this silent observer,
> Severe and speechless critic, who can terrorize us
> And urge us on to futile activity,
> And in the end, judge us still more severely
> For the errors into which his own reproaches drove us?

As if to avoid this real self, he had adopted his wife's name when they married. Similarly, Fred Culverwell, a convicted forger, became Frederico Gomez, the señor from San Marco; and Maisie Montjoy became the wealthy widow Mrs. Cargill. In a way *The Elder Statesman* is a comedy of masking and unmasking. Eliot transforms this worn-out comic device into a subtle vehicle for his perennial theme of search for identity, search for self-knowledge. At the end of his life Lord Claverton admits his old mistakes and begins to learn again, thereby showing his children not only how to avoid his kinds of mistake but also how to heed their own tougher selves. In this role he himself seems to become a Krishna figure, having no need for another Downing, another Sir Henry, or another Eggerson.

A series of programmatic writings Eliot published throughout his career attests to a certain consistency in his expanding view of society and culture. In the first essay, "Tradition and the Individual Talent" (1919), Eliot posed as a literary critic declaring his allegiance to the tradition which seemed to his contemporaries all but bankrupt; in *After Strange Gods* (1934), venturing beyond his literary concerns, he defined tradition as "a way of feeling and acting which characterizes a group throughout generations"; in *The Idea of a Christian Society* (1940) he proposed the community of Christians as the core of a Christian society; and finally in *Notes towards the Definition of Culture* (1949) he presented his notion of a class-oriented society. As his view of society and culture broadened and deepened, moved by an increasing sense of urgency, it steadily assumed a utopian outlook, and because of his sense of roots, it remained the kind of utopian vision that is available only to a traditionalist.

Critics have traced Eliot's view of society and culture to three major traditions: American (Adams, Babbitt); English (Burke, Coleridge, Arnold); and French (Maurras, Maritain). But it would seem equally possible to trace it further back to both Hindu and medieval traditions represented by the *Bhagavad-Gita* and the *Divine Comedy*.[43]

Eliot's devotion to Dante as his major source of inspiration is well known. To Eliot, Dante is not only the most European of all poets but, indeed, *the* poet. He freely acknowledged Dante as "the most persistent and deepest influence" on his poetry. His interest in Indian religion and philosophy, especially the *Gita*, as its central document, is borne out in his poetry and drama. As Philip R. Headings said: "No serious student of Eliot's poetry can afford to ignore his early and continued interest in the *Bhagavad-Gita*. No work is more relevant except Dante's *Divine Comedy*.[44] Yet this juxtaposition of both classics is Eliot's own. In his seminal essay on Dante (1929) he called the *Gita* "the next greatest philosophical poem to the *Divine Comedy* within my experience." Both the *Gita* and the *Comedy*, Eliot pointed out, stand as more than testaments of personal philosophy and find their ultimate authority in the religious tradition each represents. Eliot is not alone in stressing what is common to both, many commentators having noted the compatibility of the *Gita* with Christian philosophy.[45]

The *Gita* appears in the *Mahabharata*, at the most decisive moment of the war of dynastic succession. For the benefit of the confused Arjuna his charioteer, Krishna develops his discourse on both the absolute and the relative level, thereby urging him to go forward and perform his soldierly duty, but with no thoughts of the fruit of action. Only through such renunciation can man become one with Brahman while still in this world and satisfy his binary nature, divine and human. As Krishna continues to explain, these two doctrines of duty and renunciation derive from the caste system; and in this divinely ordained hierarchy of functional groups, heredity (doctrine of the *gunas*) and training (doctrine of *karma*) are responsible for his station in life generally and his vocation particularly. By remaining faithful to his own nature and at the same time taking an active part in society man can attain his salvation while on earth. As "an attempt to regulate society with a view to actual differences and ideal unity"—in S. Radhakrishnan's phrase—such a noncompetitive, nonacquisitive social organization is undoubtedly a utopian vision.[46] What is peculiar to this vision is that it is at once natural and organic, finally grounded in worship. Only such a total way of life as the *Gita* envisions could have created a religious culture of remarkable durability.

If this metaphysical principle of hierarchy underlies the *Gita*'s utopian vision, it also operates in the *Comedy*, encompassing the entire range of spirituality, from damnation to beatitude, of which man is capable. In particular, the *Paradiso*, stressing its heavenly hierarchy of nine angelic orders with their spheres, is meant to serve as an ideal kingdom established in the light of divine justice.[47] In envisioning an ideal social, cultural scheme, one that would insure stages of spiritual transformation, Dante is utopian, as utopian as the author of the *Gita*.

Like all other utopian schemes, those of the *Gita* and the *Comedy* seek to harmonize the individual and society. In heeding individual differences they are realistic, and in relating these individual differences to an ideal unity they are also idealistic. One obvious advantage of such a utopia as the *Gita* and the *Comedy* propose is that, being grounded in worship, it can best satisfy man's innermost hunger, his persistent questions: to what purpose was he born? And what is his end?—in short, man's search for identity and vocation, the theme to which Eliot returns in his poetry and drama time and time again.

In his prose tracts Eliot often refers to Hindu India. In fact, Indian culture is the only non-Western, non-Christian culture to which he pays any degree of sustained attention, and which he chooses to discuss with a measure of familiarity. He repeatedly invokes the Hindu caste system whenever he attempts to delineate his Christian society and its expanded version of a class-oriented society. In *After Strange Gods* Eliot takes pains to separate caste from class by stating that a caste system, based on original distinctions of race, as in India, differs from a system of social classes, which presupposes homogeneity of race and fundamental equality. Again in *The Idea of a Christian Society* he separates his "Community of Christians" from Coleridge's "clerisy," which he fears tends to become a Brahmanic caste. And in *Notes towards the Definition of Culture* he distinguishes a caste from a class system by pointing out that in the former the dominant class tends to consider itself a superior race. Eliot speaks of "ossification into a caste, as in India, of what may have been originally only a hierarchy of functions"—a tendency which, along with cultural specialization, threatens contemporary society with radical disintegration. These and other similar references indicate Eliot's awareness of the alleged historical origins and the generally accepted significance of the caste system in India;[48] they also indicate his sensitivity to the difference between his proposed class system and the caste system, which seems delicate enough to require his elaboration. It is more than probable that in proposing his kind of society Eliot has the Indian caste system in mind for comparison; it is also appropriate that he refers to Hindu India, or Indian culture based on Hinduism, because it is perhaps the most conspicuous example of a religious culture now extant.

As a traditionalist Eliot is convinced that the kind of religious wisdom both the *Gita* and the *Comedy* represent can best help us incorporate the past into the present and guide the present through the uncertain future. This sense of tradition sets him apart from many utopian visionaries and also from contemporary economic, political, and social reformers. If his position seems not radical enough from the one point of view and too reactionary from the other, it is because he is at heart a traditionalist pursuing the *via media*, which is eminently the way of wisdom, traditional religious wisdom, Eastern and Western.[49] Like both visionaries and reformers, Eliot takes no comfort in modern democracy, which he believes has proven itself inadequate as a philosophy of life. Unlike them, however, Eliot ascribes this failure of democracy to yield a positive culture to its lack of genuine religious foundations. As he sees it, only a philosophy —or rather a religion, with its coherent system of values—can give meaning to life, provide the basis for a culture, and shield the mass of humanity from boredom and despair. What he calls for is not a religious revival, which seems to him superficial, but a recovery of faith in its deepest sense, the mode of faith which, as a total way of life, could sustain the structure of modern civilization and revitalize it with a sense of direction.

Eliot's view of culture is organicistic in that he regards culture as "something that must grow," not something we can set about to create or improve. All we can do is to help a contemporary culture grow from the old roots which extend beyond history, reaching down toward the world of nature.[50] This we can do by willing those means or conditions which are favorable to culture: a graded society, cultural regionalism, and orthodoxy with a variety of cults and devotions. What is significant is Eliot's organicistic insistence on unity and diversity, which together form the operating mode of nature, and whose "tension" or "friction" may serve as a principal safeguard for the creative preservation of society and culture as a whole. As for his much-criticized "graded society" as one of the three means to a better culture, it simply reflects both his acceptance of the mystery of inequality and his recognition of actual differences as the basis of unity. By this class system he means a society with a hierarchy of functions, a society in which all positions, high and low, are "occupied by those who are best fitted to exercise the functions of the positions." Out of his concern with the whole, Eliot refuses to exaggerate the importance of one particular organ of society. While realistic enough to recognize natural aristocracy, he does not defend aristocracy as such. As he puts it, his is "a plea on behalf of a form of society in which an aristocracy should have a peculiar and essential function, as peculiar and essential as the function of any other part of society." "In such a society as I envisage," Eliot sums up, "each individual would inherit greater or less responsibility towards the commonwealth, according to the position in society which he inherited—each class would have somewhat different responsibilities. A democracy in which everybody has an equal responsibility in everything would be oppressive for the conscientious and licentious for the rest.'' In such a hereditary society the family could once again play its original role as the primary vehicle for the transmission of culture.[51] Only when each individual performs his proper function as a part of his family, group, class, community, and region can we say that the whole population participates in the creative continuity of culture at all levels. Only in such a society is the rectification of injustice possible and meaningful, Eliot concludes.

What Eliot proposes here comes close to the utopian vision which sustains both the *Bhagavad-Gita* and the *Divine Comedy*. As the culmination of his long quest, this view of society and culture integrates his sense of nature and tradition. And in reaffirming man's original relation to his society, culture, world, and universe it accords with the insight and wisdom of sages, saints, and mystics the world over. Like all other utopian proposals since Plato's *Republic*, Eliot's is vulnerable. But we can neither doubt the integrity of his intentions nor afford to dismiss his proposal, because the kind of society based on justice, on the balance of unity and variety, which makes it possible for the individual to fulfill his destiny according to his potential capacities and thereby to partake of the healthy growth of the total organism, in no way conflicts with the professed ideal of democracy. In this regard Eliot poses a serious challenge to democracy. The issues he raises are the kind which democracy must deal with in one way or another if it is to survive.[52]

What finally emerges from his prose tracts is Eliot, a man of commitment. He attempts to reconcile man with his cosmos and turn his tragic alienation into full participation. All his writing, prose as well as poetry, are impregnated with this sense of urgency. In response to this call of urgency Eliot matured from a poet to a moralist, determined to view personal and contemporary situations *sub specie aeternitatis*. And in this maturation he owed a great deal to India. By discovering India he discovered his own self, his own world—thus bringing East and West together to enrich ''the life of significant soil,'' as he said in *Four Quartets*.

TEN

Pound

Although Eliot and Pound have often been paired together in our literary history, they were in many ways different, often antipodal, as in their reponses to the Orient. In 1933, while relating his experience in "the mazes of Patanjali's metaphysics," Eliot singled out his friend as Babbitt's peer in cosmopolitanism and questioned their wisdom of making Confucius "a mainstay."[1] In 1962 Pound himself put their divergence in a historical perspective: "There's the whole problem of the relation of Chistianity to Confucianism, and there's the whole problem of the different brands of Christianity. There is the struggle for orthodoxy—Eliot for the Church, me gunning round for particular theologians. In one sense Eliot's curiosity would appear to have been focused on a smaller number of problems. Even that is too much to say. The actual outlook of the experimental generation was all a question of the private ethos."[2]

It was in this generation's search for the private ethos that Eliot and Pound turned to the East, one to India and the other to China. We have already seen how characteristically Eliot resisted its spell lest he should lose his sense of identity. But there was no such resistance or restraint as far as Pound was concerned. Ever since his declaration of 1914—"It is possible that this century may find a new Greece in China"[3]—he had devoted his time, energy, and talent to turning this possibility into a reality. In his all-out devotion to China, especially to Confucius, Pound resembled the *philosophes* of the Enlightenment, which was his intellectual cradle.

As Noel Stock said, Pound may have owed his initial interest in China to his parents,[4] but his serious encounter first began with Japan, in 1910 or thereabouts, some years before his discovery of Fenollosa—that is, at the time he was furiously working out his own poetics.[5] "In a Station of the Metro," one of his poetic attempts during the period, is revealing in this connection.

According to Pound's own account in the essay "Vorticism" (1914),[6] his momentary emotional experience at a metro station resulted, first, in a color equation. Following this first equation for the emotion came a thirty-line poem, six months later a poem half that length, and a year later its final form—a two-line poem: "The apparition of these faces in the crowd;

/ Petals on a wet, black bough.'' Pound owed this success, by his own admission, to Japanese haiku poetry. ''The Japanese have the sense of exploration,'' he wrote. ''They have understood the beauty of this sort of knowing. A Chinaman said long ago that if a man can't say what he has to say in twelve lines he had better keep quiet. The Japanese have evolved the still shorter form of the haiku.''

In the same essay Pound also revealed what was close to his heart at the moment: his Vorticism. ''Every concept, every emotion, presents itself to the vivid consciousness in some primary form. It belongs to the art of this form.'' With this reminder, Pound went on: ''My experience in Paris should have gone into paint. If instead of colour I had perceived sound or planes in relation, I should have expressed it in music or in sculpture. Colour was, in that instance, the 'primary pigment'; I mean that it was the first adequate equation that came into consciousness. The vorticist uses the 'primary pigment.' Vorticism is art before it has spread itself into flacidity, into elaboration and secondary applications.'' For further clarification Pound turned to poetry, his own medium. ''All poetic language is the language of exploration. Since the beginning of bad writing, writers have used images *as ornaments*. The point of Imagisme is that it does not use images *as ornaments*. The image is itself the speech. The image is the word beyond formulated language.''

In other words, Vorticism resulted as Pound continued to explore his Imagism in search of an adequate aesthetics capable of embracing all art forms. As far as poetry was concerned, Imagism still served as the base of Vorticism. What is important here is that at this point Pound referred to the Japanese, along with the Chinese. Obviously, the Orient played a decisive role in this developing process from Imagism to Vorticism. The Orient came to Pound at the most opportune time in the form of the Fenollosa manuscripts. As he said in retrospect: ''Fenollosa's work was given me in manuscript when I was ready for it. It saved me a great deal of time.''[7]

This historic transmission of the Fenollosa manuscripts has been told many times with a slight variation each time. Most recently, Hugh Kenner suggested that Mrs. Mary Fenollosa initiated the whole matter after reading Pound's metro poem and others in the April 1913 issue of *Poetry*.[8] In any case, ''all old Fenollosa's treasures in mss.''—to use Pound's own words—were already in his possession by December 1913. During the next couple of years he immersed himself in the manuscripts.[9] As Pound himself admitted later, it was a ''windfall,''[10] perhaps the greatest breakthrough in his long career, producing *Cathay* (1915), *Certain Noble Plays of Japan* (1916), and ''The Chinese Written Character as a Medium for Poetry'' (1919).

Pound created—or rather re-created—those fourteen poems in the original *Cathay* from the notes—glosses, paraphrases, and comments—which Fenollosa kept while reading Chinese poetry with Professor Kainan Mori through an interpreter during his second Japanese sojourn. Even though Fenollosa enlisted the help of perhaps the best available Japanese authority at the time, the fact remains that he was twice or thrice removed from the original not only because of his ignorance of Japanese and Chinese but also because of the peculiar Japanese tradition of Chinese studies. These factors were responsible for those by now well-documented blunders Pound made in *Cathay*. Considering the enormous odds against which he labored, his was a rare poetic feat.

If his sense of discovery launched him into what seemed an impossible task, it was his experience and conviction as a translator that helped him pull off this poetic feat. An old hand in this time-honored art of translation, Pound entertained his own theory. According to him, there are three kinds of poetry: melopoeia, phanopoeia, and logopoeia. Whereas the first kind defies translation, the second can be rendered "almost, or wholly, intact," and even the third—"the dance of the intellect"—can be paraphrased. He believed that Chinese poets, especially Li Po (Rihaku) and Wang Wei (Omakitsu), attained the known maximum of phanopoeia, owing perhaps to the nature of their ideographic language.[11] With Fenollosa's notes at his disposal, Pound must have felt that he could not possibly ruin the original. Furthermore, he was convinced that the poet, no mere linguist, should translate poetry.

Much has been written about *Cathay* since its publication. In recent years Achilles Fang and Wai-lim Yip have examined Pound's translations in the light of their Chinese originals, and Hugh Kenner has done the same in the light of the Fenollosa manuscripts. They have all helped clear up the confusion over Pound's errors: some were traceable to Pound's ignorance, misreading, or misunderstanding, and some to Fenollosa's, even though he had the best available assistance at his disposal. More often than not, however, Pound's errors seemed deliberate, as Kenner pointed out.[12] Take, for instance, "Separation on the River Kiang," one of Li Po's quatrains:

> Ko-jin goes west from Ko-kaku-ro,
> The smoke-flowers are blurred over the river.
> His lone sail blots the far sky.
> And now I see only the river,
> > The long Kiang, reaching heaven.

In the light of Fenollosa's notes on the poem we can see what Pound did with his material.[13] From the second line of the original he omitted two specifics: the month of March, and Yo-shu (Yangchou in Chinese), the traveler's destination. In the third line he changed "the blue sky" to "the far sky." And he broke the last line in two—no doubt for the sake of putting emphasis on the river. With such omissions, changes, and additions Pound apparently sought to focus on the emotional poignancy of separation, a recurrent theme of Chinese poetry.

Pound has been criticized not for these liberties he took as poet but for the blunders he made as translator. First, he left "Ko-jin" untranslated, as if it were a personal name, despite Fenollosa's correct "an old acquaintance." Second, the oft-ridiculed "goes west" resulted as Pound followed Fenollosa's ambiguous paraphrase "starting further west" rather than his gloss "west leave." That is, the first was plainly deliberate and the second was perhaps unavoidable. (Or was this also deliberate?) More intriguing is "The long Kiang," which is another name for the Yangtze River. To be consistent with his use of "Ko-jin" and "Ko-kaku-ro," Pound could have used the Japanese "Cho-ko" rather than the Chinese "Kiang," though both forms appeared in the original notes. It is possible that his choice of "Kiang" was also deliberate, as deliberate as his choice of "Ko-kaku-ro" over the customary "Yellow Crane Pavilion." Here he may have hoped to approximate what he believed to be the melopoeic aspect of the original quatrain. These blunders, whether deliberate or not, remain blunders only when we approach the poem as a *translation*. When we read it as a *poem*, however, they cease to be blunders. (Whether he leaves the west or goes west would make no difference to most readers. Or they might prefer the latter for its rich connotations.) In Pound's hands, linguistic errors often turned into poetic assets.

Of these translations in *Cathay* Pound himself said: "They are, I should say, closer than the *Rubaiyat*, but then the ideographs leave one wholly free as to phrase."[14] Close and yet free—with this paradoxical statement he accurately summed up his situation. His ignorance of Chinese kept him close to the original, but at the same time the ideographs left him free. This happened no doubt because he depended on Fenollosa's particular method. And this peculiar combination of factors and circumstances made him "the inventor of Chinese poetry for our time," to use Eliot's phrase.[15] With those fourteen Chinese poems in *Cathay* Pound set the pattern for subsequent translators to follow, as John Gould Fletcher said: "This form—ignoring the 'rhymes' and the 'tones' of the Chinese originals—directly follows the Chinese construction of the phrase and is therefore the most nearly correct vehicle for translating Chinese poetry we have." The impact of *Cathay* extended far beyond this, affecting the course of modern English poetry itself. According to Kenner, *Cathay* also maximized three criteria at once: "the *vers-libre* principle, that the single line is the unit of composition; the Imagist principle, that a poem may build its effects out of things it sets before the mind's eye by naming them; and the lyrical principle, that words or names, being ordered in time, are bound together and recalled into each other's presence by recurrent sound."[16] Whatever its historical significance, *Cathay* meant something very personal to Pound himself. As Eliot pointed out, "Good translation like this is not merely translation, for the translator is giving the original through himself, and finding himself through the original." In this sense *Cathay* marked —to use Eliot's words once again—"a necessary stage in the progress towards the *Cantos*, which are wholly himself."[17]

Pound probably started to work on the Noh plays as soon as he got the Fenollosa manuscripts. By the end of January 1914 he already had two plays ready for magazine publication.[18] His project progessed rapidly enough, and in 1916 he came out with *Certain Noble Plays of Japan* (*Noh, or Accomplishment* in the American edition), a collection of over a dozen plays with an introduction and appendices. In a note Pound gave credit to Fenollosa for the book's vision and plan. "In the prose," he wrote, "I have had the part of literary executor; in the plays my work has been that of translator who has found all the heavy work done for him and who has had but the pleasure of arranging beauty into the words." Although Pound sounded breezy, it was "an impossible task," as Earl Miner observed,[19] since he simply did not possess the necessary theoretical and practical knowledge of the subject; nor were Fenollosa's manuscripts in ideal condition. Moreover, contemporary Noh scholarship itself, especially in the West, left much to be desired.

Take, for instance, *Awoi No Uye*, an example of what is commonly called a "wig-play," which features a woman as the principal character. This drama of female jealousy is based on one of the episodes in *The Tale of Genji*. Princess Rokujo, hopelessly in love with Prince Genji, becomes jealous of whoever enjoys his favors. Indeed, her jealousy is such that it assumes the form of a living phantom, striking down her rivals. Not only did it strike Yugao dead but it is ready to strike Princess Awoi, wife of Prince Genji. Some time ago, at the festival, an incident occurred involving both ladies. Eager for a full view of the handsome prince in the procession, they rushed their carriages, blocking each other's way. In the ensuing scuffle Awoi's carriage made it to the front place, leaving Rokujo's with broken wheels. Soon after, Princess Awoi fell ill, and at this point the play begins.[20]

Apparently Fenollosa was confused about the whole situation; so was Pound. Confused as he was, Pound did not fail to recognize the beauty of certain passages. "Several passages," said he, referring to *Awoi No Uye*

184

and another play, "which are, however, quite lucid in themselves, seem to me as beautiful as anything I have found in Fenollosa's Japanese notes and these passages must be my justification." Pound may have had in mind the words spoken by Princess Rokujo's phantom: "It may be, it may be, I come from the gate of hell in three coaches. I am sorry for Yugawo and the carriage with broken wheels. And the world is ploughed with sorrow as a field is furrowed with oxen. Man's life is a wheel on the axle, there is no turn whereby to escape. His hold is light as dew on the Basho leaf. It seems that the last spring's blossoms are only a dream in the mind. And we fools take it all, take it all as a matter of course. Oh, I am grown envious from sorrow. I come to seek consolation." What Pound did not recognize was the allusion to the coaches in the famous Buddhist parable of life as a Burning House. Had he known the underlying Buddhist sentiment, Pound could have intensified the symbolic link of Rokujo's obsession with the carriage and the Buddhist Wheel of life, thereby turning the passage into one imagistic whole. Not knowing this, he rendered this potentially poetic material in prose. Arthur Waley, in his *Nō Plays of Japan*, wrote: "The versions of E. P. seem to have been fragmentary and inaccurate; but wherever Mr. Pound had adequate material to work upon he has used it admirably." [21] The fact is that Pound too often missed his opportunity because of his inadequate material. As Eliot said: "The work is not so solid, so firm. *Cathay* will, I believe, rank with the 'Seafarer' in the future among Mr Pound's original work; the Noh will rank among his translations." [22]

Yet, to Pound, *Certain Noble Plays of Japan* was not a waste of time. As these Noh plays convinced Yeats of the possibility of creating a form of poetic drama, even "a certain possibility of the Irish dramatic movement," [23] so did they reassure Pound of the essential validity of his shaping poetics. To his own credit, Pound perceived not only the emotional unity of Noh drama but especially its unity of image. "At least," he said, "the better plays are all built into the intensification of a single Image: the red maple leaves and the snow flurry in Nishikigi, the pines in Takasago, the blue-grey waves and wave pattern in Suma Genji, the mantle of feathers in the play of that name, Hagoromo." And as he added in a footnote: "This intensification of the Image, this manner of construction, is very interesting to me personally, as an Imagiste, for we Imagistes knew nothing of these plays when we set out in our manner. These plays are also an answer to a question that has several times been put to me: 'Could one do a long Imagiste poem, or even a long poem in vers libre?' " In other words, Noh drama reinforced the theoretical basis of his Imagism; furthermore, it suggested the possibility of a long poem in free verse, say, the *Cantos*, which he had launched two years before. Contrary to Eliot's verdict, one could say that *Certain Noble Plays of Japan*, like *Cathay*, served as a necessary step in Pound's poetic career.[24]

The essay "The Chinese Written Character" was apparently the first Fenollosa manuscript Pound had ready for publication yet the last one he managed to place, and then only after great difficulty. The experience was all the more frustrating because he was dead sure of its significance. In June 1915 he had already referred to Fenollosa's "most enlightening essay on the written character (a whole basis of aesthetic, in reality)."[25] In 1917 he was no more hopeful about its publication: "It is one of the most important essays of our time. But they will probably reject it on the ground of its being exotic. Fenollosa saw and anticipated a good deal of what has happened in art (painting and poetry) during the last ten years, and his essay is basic for all aesthetics, but I doubt if that will cut much ice."[26] Pound's misgivings were well founded. Since its publication in 1919 Fenollosa's little essay has remained a piece of exotica to the students of aesthetics and a piece of anachronism to professional Sinologues. Yet to the last Pound remained convinced of its significance, and it was this little essay, of all Fenollosa manuscripts, that continued to exert an enduring influence on Pound's creative career.

In the essay Fenollosa, we may recall, began by basing his philosophy of language on its original source, nature.[27] As syntax reflects the process, so does metaphor represent a vital part of language, "the very substance of poetry," because metaphor keeps language close to the "concreteness of natural process." In Fenollosa's opinion this makes the poet "the only one for whom the accumulated treasures of the race-words are real and active." Since Fenollosa attempted to locate the source of poetic language in the creative process of nature itself, he saw no familiar schism between poetry and science. Poetry may disagree with logic, but not with science, which also aims at describing nature's process. At this point Fenollosa referred to the Chinese language as the most eloquent illustration of what he was driving at—an ideal poetic language. Its ideogrammic origin, he argued, is the ultimate reason that Chinese has kept close to nature, thus remaining concrete, strong, and alive, while developing "a second work of metaphor" capable of expressing the unseen, such as lofty thoughts, spiritual suggestions, and obscure relations. The advantage of this kind of language when compared with phonetic languages, should be obvious. As he concluded: "Such a pictorial method, whether the Chinese exemplified it or not, would be the ideal language of the world." By way of Chinese Fenollosa pointed to the possibility of a new poetic language.

In a prefatory note of 1918 Pound said of Fenollosa: "His mind was constantly filled with parallels and comparison between Eastern and

186

Western art. To him the exotic was always a means of fructification. He looked to an American renaissance.'' The vitality of his outlook, Pound added, was borne out in the latest movement in art. Revealing in this regard were Pound's notes scattered over the essay. Consider Fenollosa's passage on metaphor: ''Poetry only does consciously what the primitive race did unconsciously. The chief work of literary men in dealing with language, and of poets especially, lies in feeling back along the ancient lines of advance.'' For the first statement Pound quickly provided a note referring to his own article ''Vorticism'' in the *Fortnightly Review* for September 1914, and again to the same piece included in his memoir of Gaudier-Brzeska (1916). For the second statement he offered the following: ''The poet, in dealing with his own time, must also see to it that language does not petrify on his hands. He must prepare for new advances along the lines of true metaphor, that is interpretative metaphor, or image, as diametrically opposed to untrue, or ornamental, metaphor.'' It was in this same article on Vorticism that Pound defined all poetic language as the language of exploration and declared that Imagism does not use images as ornaments. With this concept of image Pound could not but be enthusiastic about what Fenollosa had to say about the ideographic nature of the Chinese language.

Pound duly carried this enthusiasm into *ABC of Reading* (1934), announcing that the proper method of studying poetry is the method of contemporary biology. Fenollosa had been the first to suggest this possibility, he asserted with specific reference to the essay ''The Chinese Written Character.'' According to Pound, Fenollosa got to the root of the matter, to the root of the difference between what is valid in Chinese thinking and what is invalid or misleading in much of European thinking. Contrasting the medieval method of abstraction with the method of modern science, Pound, in the manner of Fenollosa, pointed out that the latter method agrees with the method of poetry and also with the way the Chinese go about it in their ideography, or abbreviated picture writing. Recalling Gaudier-Brzeska's ability to read some Chinese writing without any special study, Pound illustrated how three characters, 人 (man), 木 (tree), and 日 (sun), came to form a new character 東 , namely, ''sun tangled in the tree's branches, as at sunrise, meaning now the East.'' Although Fenollosa tried to tell how and why a language written in this way had to stay poetic, he died before proclaiming his method as a method. ''This,'' Pound concluded, ''is nevertheless the RIGHT WAY to study poetry, or literature, or painting.'' Pound took it upon himself to proclaim it in a typically Poundian way: ''THE IDEOGRAMMIC METHOD OR THE METHOD OF SCIENCE.'' And this was what he found in Fenollosa's essay—at the culminating point of his long search for an adequate poetics.

187

In a letter of June 1915 Pound, reporting his difficulty in getting the Fenollosa essay printed, copied two Chinese characters as "merely an exquisite example of the way the Chinese mind works." In another letter, of January 1917 he confided: "China is fundamental, Japan is not. Japan is a special interest, like Provence, or 12–13th Century Italy (apart from Dante). . . . But China is solid. One can't go back of the 'Exile's Letter,' or the 'Song of the Bowmen,' or the 'North Gate.' " At the same time he was drawn toward Confucius and thinking of doing an essay on him[28]—an interesting contrast to Fenollosa's rejection of Confucianism. From ideograms to the Chinese mind to Confucius, Pound's interest rapidly gravitated toward its center.

Once having found the center of his gravitation in Confucius, Pound held to it for the rest of his career. With the passage of time this interest, becoming only deeper and wider, produced a series of Confucian translations: "Ta Hio" (1928); "Digest of the Analects" (1937); *The Unwobbling Pivot & The Great Digest* (1947); *The Analects* (1951); and *The Confucian Odes* (1954). For this task Pound turned constantly to the well-known Chinese-English dictionaries by Morrison and Matthews, on the one hand, and to the translations by Pauthier, Legge, and Karlgren, on the other. In spite of his respect for Pauthier and Legge (he called the former "a magnificent scholar" and the latter's work "a *monument*"),[29] Pound differed from them freely and stood by his ideogrammic method, which set him apart from them and made him unique among the translators of Confucius.[30]

The *Ta Hsieh*, which Pound translated under the title *The Great Digest* ("Ta Hio" was an excerpt made from Pauthier's French version), was originally a chapter of the *Li Chi* (*Book of Rites*), a collection of treatises written by the Confucianists in the third and second centuries B.C., and later, during the Sung dynasty, designated by the Neo-Confucianists to be one of the Four Books. In a prefatory note to the *Great Digest* Pound said that throughout Chinese history the tranquillity of the empire had invariably depended on whether the rulers understood the principles defined therein. In a preliminary section on terminology he ideogrammically redefined the several radicals and characters which recur throughout the text, and proceeded to the opening passage:

> The great learning [adult study, grinding the corn in the heads'
> mortar to fit it for use] takes root in identifying the way wherein
> the intelligence increases through the process of looking straight
> into one's heart and acting on the results; it is rooted in watching
> with affection the way people grow; it is rooted in coming to rest,
> being at ease in perfect equity.

Know the point of rest and then have an orderly mode of procedure; having this orderly procedure one can 'grasp the azure,' that is, take hold of a clear concept; holding a clear concept one can be at peace [internally], being thus calm one can keep one's head in moments of danger; he who can keep his head in the presence of a tiger is qualified to come to his deed in due hour.

Things have roots and branches; affairs have scopes and beginnings. To know what precedes and what follows, is nearly as good as having a head and feet.

The men of old wanting to clarify and diffuse throughout the empire that light which comes from looking straight into the heart and then acting, first set up good government in their own states; wanting good government in their states, they first established order in their own families; wanting order in the home, they first disciplined themselves; desiring self-discipline, they rectified their own hearts; and wanting to rectify their hearts, they sought precise verbal definitions of their inarticulate thoughts [the tones given off by the heart]; wishing to attain precise verbal definitions, they set to extend their knowledge to the utmost. This completion of knowledge is rooted in sorting things into organic categories.

When things had been classified in organic categories, knowledge moved toward fulfillment; given the extreme knowable points, the inarticulate thoughts were defined with precision [The sun's lance coming to rest on the precise spot verbally]. Having attained this precise verbal definition [*aliter*, this sincerity], they then stabilized their hearts, they disciplined themselves; having attained self-discipline, they set their own homes, they brought good government to their own states; and when their states were well governed, the empire was brought into equilibrium.

From the Emperor, Son of Heaven, down to the common man, singly and all together, this self-discipline is the root.

If the root be in confusion, nothing will be well governed. The solid cannot be swept away as trivial, nor can trash be established as solid. It just doesn't happen.

"Take not cliff for morass and treacherous bramble."

In this celebrated passage (all the brackets are Pound's) Confucius sets forth his central principle and further proposes the eight-step process to realize it: the investigation of things (Pound's "sorting things into organic categories"); the completion of knowledge; the sincerity of thoughts (the rectification of the heart); the cultivation of the person (Pound's "self-discipline"); the regulation of the family; the government of the state; and the tranquillity of the empire. This sense of order in a concentric pattern

189

which derives from the classical notion of the microcosm-macrocosm, no doubt, has made the *Ta Hsieh* a favorite of the Chinese. Sun Yat-sen used this book to illustrate "the sort of ancient political philosophy that must be guarded as 'a national treasure,' the like of which no foreign nation possessed."[31] Fung Yu-lan, from a perspective of world politics and world peace, observed: "It is unnecessary that one should be head of a state or of some world organization, before one can do something to bring good order to the state and peace to the world. One should merely do one's best to do good for the state as a member of the state, and do good for the world as a member of the world. One is then doing one's full share of bringing good order to the state and peace to the world. By thus sincerely trying to do one's best, one is resting in the highest good." The real significance of the book, Fung added, lies in its systematic thinking.[32] But Pauthier merely called these opening paragraphs "instances of the sorites, or abridged syllogism"—to which Legge retorted: "But they belong to *rhetoric*, and not to *logic*." Furthermore, unable to see any relevancy of the concept to the ordinary man, Legge concluded that the student of it should be a sovereign.[33]

Unlike Pauthier and Legge, Pound was convinced from the start of the significance of the *Ta Hsieh*. It was this book that he said he believed in in response to Eliot's query: What does Mr. Pound believe? It was also this book that he said he translated so that those who read only English could learn where to start thinking.[34] In his essay "Immediate Need of Confucius" (1937) Pound declared: "But the whole of Western idealism is a jungle. Christian theology is a jungle. To think through it, to reduce it to some semblance of order, there is no better axe than the *Ta Hio*"—more specifically, the first chapter, "which you may treat as a *mantram*, or as a *mantram* reinforced, a *mantram* elaborated so that the meditation may gradually be concentrated into contemplation." In *Guide to Kulchur* (1938) he returned to the *Ta Hsieh*: "The Confucian Great Learning, the examination of motivation, is an examination with clear purpose." Then he added: "It is a root, the centre of steadily out-circling causations from immediate order to a whole series of harmonies and good conducts."[35]

The *Chung Yung*, or Pound's *Unwobbling Pivot*, was also one of the chapters in the *Li Chi*. Presumably composed by Tzu-ssu, the grandson of Confucius, the work has been revered since Sung times as one of the Four Books. As Chu Hsi stated in his preface: "At its start the book speaks of the one principle, it then spreads into a discussion of things in general, and concludes by uniting all this in the one principle. Spread it out and its arrows reach to the six ends of the universe, zenith and nadir; fold it again and it withdraws to serve you in secret as faithful minister. Its savour is inexhaustible. It is, all of it, solid wisdom." That is, with the aid of this

190

one fundamental principle man can achieve perfection—harmony with heaven and earth. To Legge, the *Chung Yung* was less than satisfactory. Although sensing something intuitional, mystical, and mysterious about it, he nonetheless concluded: "He [the author] has eminently contributed to nourish the pride of his countrymen. He has exalted their sages above all that is called God or is worshipped, and taught the masses of the people that with them they have need of nothing from without. In the meantime it is antagonistic to Christianity. By-and-by, when Christianity has prevailed in China, men will refer to it as a striking proof how their wisdom knew neither God nor themselves."[36] Nowhere did Legge so glaringly betray his Christian bias which rendered him blind to the central doctrine of the book.

Without such a bias Pound responded to the *Chung Yung* more properly. As is apparent in his note, he was enthusiastic about the all-embracing Confucian philosophy, which he divided into three parts: the axis, the process, and sincerity—in other words, metaphysics, politics, and ethics. Here, as elsewhere, he proceeded ideogrammically. One of the key passages on "sincerity" he translated thus: "Sincerity, this precision of terms is heaven's process. What comes from the process [is] human ethics. The sincere man finds the axis without forcing himself to do so. He arrives at it without thinking and goes along naturally in the midst of the process [Ts'ung yung chung tao], he is a wise man. He who is sincere seizes goodness, gripping it firmly from all sides" (the second brackets are Pound's). Perhaps the most sublime passage of the entire book he translated thus: "He who possesses this sincerity does not lull himself to somnolence perfecting himself with egocentric aim, but he has a further efficiency in perfecting something outside himself. Fulfilling himself he attains full manhood, perfecting things outside himself he attains knowledge. The inborn nature begets this activity naturally, this looking straight into oneself and thence acting. These two activities constitute the process which unites outer and inner, object and subject, and thence constitute a harmony with the seasons of earth and heaven."

According to Fung, the *Chung Yung*, together with "Appendices" in the *I Ching* or *Book of Changes*, represented the last phase in the metaphysical development of ancient Confucianism, namely, Neo-Confucianism, which absorbed Taoism and Buddhism.[37] Here, as in the *Great Digest*, Pound defined the term *Tao* as the process, based on his ideogrammic reading: "The process. Footprints and the foot carrying the head; the head conducting the feet, an orderly movement under lead of the intelligence." The opening passage became in his translation: "What heaven has disposed and sealed is called the inborn nature. The realization of this nature is called the process. The clarification of this process [the understanding or making intelligible of this process] is called education'' (the brackets are Pound's). This Taoistic strain became even more pronounced in the last chapter; such passages as ''Hence the highest grade of this clarifying activity has no limit, it neither stops nor stays'' and ''Being thus in its nature; unseen it causes harmony; unmoving it transforms; unmoved it perfects'' sound unmistakably Taoistic in thought, echoing the *Tao Te Ching*.

In *Guide to Kulchur* Pound declared: ''Rightly or wrongly we feel that Confucius offers a way of life, an Anschauung or disposition toward nature and man and a system for dealing with both.''[38] One can see why Pound was so much drawn to the *Ta Hsieh* and *Chung Yung*, with their sense of cosmic order and harmony. Within this general framework, however, he invariably focused on the key term *sincerity*. In the *Great Digest* he defined the character 誠 as '' 'Sincerity.' The precise definition of the word, pictorially the sun's lance coming to rest on the precise spot verbally. The right-hand half of this compound means: to perfect, bring to focus.'' In the *Unwobbling Pivot* he made the following translation: ''He who does not attain to this [perfect harmony with heaven and earth] can at least cultivate the good shoots within him, and in cultivating them arrive at precision in his own terminology, that is, at sincerity, at clear definitions. The sincerity will begin to take form; being formed it will manifest; manifest, it will start to illuminate, illuminating to function, functioning to effect changes. Only the most absolute sincerity under heaven can effect any change [in things, in conditions]'' (the second brackets are Pound's). This last sentence Pound quoted, saying: ''Twenty-four centuries ago Tsze Sze needed to continue his comment with a profession of faith, stating what the Confucian idea *would* effect; looking back over the milllennial history of China there is need neither of adjectives nor of comment.'' Then he added: ''And for that reason I end my translation at this point, temporarily at least.''

In time Pound resumed his self-appointed task and brought out two more volumes: *The Analects* and *The Confucian Odes*. The *Analects*, the first of the Four Books, consists chiefly of the sayings of Confucius which were compiled by his disciples and even by theirs, long after his death. In Legge's words, it is the ''digested conversations'' of Confucius, his disciples, and others, as the Chinese title *Lun Yu* suggests. Pound pointed out that despite its lack of ''coherence or orderly sequence,'' this collection of oddments has been revered as *the* Book, just as Confucius has been as *the* Teacher.

As he further pointed out, the study of Confucian philosophy is far more profitable than that of Greek philosophy because ''no time is wasted in idle discussion of errors.'' The *Analects* offers ''a set of measures whereby, at the end of a day, to learn whether the day has been worth living.'' While some translators thought of everything—except what the original author was driving at—Pound was determined to give "the flavour of laconism and the sense of the live man speaking.''

Obsessed as ever with definitions of words and terms, Pound warned in a note to the *Analects*: "It is an error to seek aphorisms and bright saying in sentences that should be considered rather as definitions of words, and a number of them should be taken rather as lexicography, as examples of how Kung had used a given expression in defining a man or a condition.'' Pound was right since language was one of Confucius's central concerns, as Fung observed.[39] More than once Confucius returned to this rectification of names as the first step toward good government. When once asked about government, he replied: "Prince to be prince; minister, minister; father, father; son, son.'' When these names fail to correspond to their actualities, confusion is bound to result in society generally and government particularly. Pound completely agreed with Confucius about the primacy of this correspondence between name and actuality, as is evinced in his repeated reference to the notion in the *Cantos*. The original passage is worth quoting in its entirety:

1. Tzu-lu said: The Lord of Wei is waiting for you to form a government, what are you going to do first?
2. He said: Settle the names (determine a precise terminology).
3. Tzu-lu said: How's this, you're divagating, why fix'em?
4. He said: You bumpkin! Sprout! When a proper man don't know a thing, he shows some reserve.
5. If words (terminology) are not (is not) precise, they cannot be followed out, or completed in action according to specifications.
6. When the services (actions) are not brought to true focus, the ceremonies and music will not prosper; where rites and music do not flourish punishments will be misapplied, not make bullseye, and the people won't know how to move hand or foot (what to lay hand on, or stand on).
7. Therefore the proper man must have terms that can be spoken, and when uttered be carried into effect; the proper man's words must cohere to things, correspond to them (exactly) and no more fuss about it.

Compared with his earlier version in the "Digest" (1937), this one is less conventional, that is, freer and more Poundian, because of his ideogrammic method.

It was inevitable that Pound's study of Confucius conclude with his translation of the *Shi Ching*. Although one of the Five Classics, this ancient anthology of 305 poems has attained scriptural importance in the Confucian canon. The Four Books do indeed make innumerable references to the *Shi Ching* as the ultimate authority, and in the *Analects* Confucius prizes it more than anything else, summing up its central message: "The anthology of 300 poems can be gathered into the one sentence: Have no twisty thoughts." The later Confucians have always approached it with reverence, whether their reading be literal, allegorical, or symbolic.

Whether Pound initially knew that the "Song of the Bowmen of Shu," the first poem in his *Cathay*, really came from the *Shi Ching* is not certain. By 1934, however, he must have discovered its existence. Preferring Père Lacharme's eighteenth-century Latin version to Legge's, which he called "an infamy," Pound exclaimed: "Dust on my head, that I trod the earth 50 years and have not read them in the original. But no reason for leaving others unwarned." In 1937 he complained that "translations of the *Odes* are so bare one thinks the translator must have missed something and very annoying not to be able to see *what*."[40] As he learned to read Chinese characters he was now able to see *what*. And in 1954 he finally brought out his version, *The Classic Anthology Defined by Confucius*.

If in the previous Confucian translations he had acted as a translator-interpreter, in this one Pound played his full role as a translator-interpreter-poet. With this in mind, no doubt, Kenner suggested that Pound's *Anthology* is not the *Shi Ching* Chinese readers know—because it is first of all a book of poems in English.[41] Even here Pound was an Imagist, rejecting abstraction. To achieve this imagistic concreteness Pound, needless to say, had his ideogrammic method at his disposal. Consider Poem #274, one of the Odes of the Temple and Altar:

Great	hand	King	Wu
vied	not,	made	heat.
He	drew	not as	sun
rest	from	work	done
Shang	Ti	(over	sky)
king'd	our	Ch'eng and	K'ang;
bound	all	four	coigns;
hacked	clear	their	light.
Gong,	drum,	sound	out,
stone,	flute,	clear in	tone
ring	in	strong	grain;
bring	here	hard	ears.

194

Work,	true,	shall	pay.
As we've	drunk	we are	full,
Luck	ev-er	is and	shall
Come	with	new	grain.

At first glance this seems to have come right out of the Fenollosa manuscripts, one of those glosses which had accompanied the original Chinese and out of which Pound had created *Cathay* forty years earlier. But his procedure here is thoroughly deliberate, which is obvious because it remains the only example in the entire anthology. No longer ignorantly groping in the dark, Pound was now able to handle Chinese characters and read them ideogrammically. While he expanded the original fourteen lines into sixteen, he regulated each line with four stresses, in keeping with the original phonic form, four characters in each line. Stark and dignified in predominantly monosyllabic words of Old English origin, it could be intoned (all the songs in the anthology were supposedly sung)—a sheer *tour de force*.

Equally interesting is Poem #167, one of the Elegantiae, or Smaller Odes, whose opening stanza reads:

> Pick a fern, pick a fern, ferns are high,
> "Home," I'll say: home, the year's gone by,
> No house, no roof, these huns on the hoof.
> Work, work, work, that's how it runs,
> We are here because of these huns.

A sort of ballad sung by soldiers weary of the borderguard and longing for home, Pound translated this poem for *Cathay* under the title "Song of the Bowmen of Shu." Not knowing how to handle Chinese characters, he had to rely entirely on Fenollosa's notes for the following version:

> Here we are, picking the first fern-shoots
> And saying: When shall we get back to our country?
> Here we are because we have the Ken-nin for our foemen,
> We have no comfort because of these Mongols.

Whereas Kenner considered the later version "a much more convincing soldier's song," L. S. Dembo could see no qualitative change. Conceding that the new version caught the rhythm of a marching song, he nonetheless pointed out: "It is still too contrived to be really effective; one is not convinced that he is listening to a soldier."[42] Whichever our preference, it is well to note what separates the one from the other. The earlier version

195

is prosaic, for all that Pound could do with Fenollosa's notes was more or less to paraphrase. The later version, on the other hand, departs from the original as often as it follows it, for Pound knew what he was doing. More mature in age and knowledge, he could now command a greater sense of perspective, a Chinese perspective. The contrivance Dembo detected in the later version may have resulted from this new perspective Pound had at last come to command after years of absorption in the Confucian classics.

Having completed the *Confucian Odes*, Pound saw to it that three Chinese characters, 思無邪 (ssu wu hsieh), appeared on its last page. He did not have to invent his epigraph. These were the very words with which Confucius, in the *Analects*, summed up the spirit of the *Odes*, signifying "Have no twisty thoughts." As Dembo observed, in this categorical imperative lies the first and last principle of the Confucian view of life.[43] "For me," said Confucius, "there is one thing that flows through, holds things together, germinates." In fact, it runs through all the Confucian classics. In the *Great Digest* and *Unwobbling Pivot* it appears as "sincerity," which alone makes man a partner with heaven and earth. Akin to Tao, which Pound consistently translated as "the process" rather than "the way," it is the source of creativity from which our poetic and our moral imagination derives. This is what Confucius must have meant, and also what Pound must have understood.[44]

As a translator of the Confucian classics Pound stands in the long tradition of Chu Hsi (1130–1200). Like his predecessors, Pauthier in French and Legge in English, Pound was indebted to this founder of Neo-Confucianism. It was Chu Hsi, also known as Chutzu, who grouped together the *Lun Yu, Mengtzu, Chung Yung,* and *Ta Hseih* as the Four Books, with his commentaries. And after the Yuan Dynasty had made these books the main text in the state examinations and his commentaries their official interpretations, his school remained the most influential single system of philosophy in China—until the introduction of Western philosophy.[45] In a way, Pound approached Confucius through Chu Hsi. He saw Confucius with the eye of orthodox China, or rather in terms of Chinese civilization, for Neo-Confucianism, more than a new brand of Confucianism, synthesized three major Chinese traditions: Confucianism, Taoism, and Buddhism. Earlier, Emerson had been reintroduced to China through Legge; Thoreau, through Pauthier; and now Pound went beyond Pauthier and Legge because he knew Chu Hsi. But because of his ideogrammic method he went beyond Chu Hsi, reading Confucius and the mind of China at first hand—in the Chinese language itself.

In 1936, when he finally managed to publish Fenollosa's essay on the Chinese written character in book form, Pound did not forget to mention the "infamy" of the modern monetary system which was not only starving out the masses but also strangulating intellectual life. The following year, when he brought out his "Digest of the Analects," he returned to the same point: "Rapacity is the main force in our time in the occident. In measure as a book contains wisdom it is nearly impossible to force any printer to issue it. My usual publishers refused the *Ta Hio*. What hope have I with a translation of the whole Analects?" And in 1938, in *Guide to Kulchur*, he also declared: "Take the whole ambience of the Analects (of Kung fu Tseu), you have the main character filled with a sense of responsibility. He and his interlocutors live in a responsible world, they think for the whole social order. You may, by contrast, contend that Christian thought has never offered a balanced system."[46]

Armed with such a conviction Pound persisted in his study of Confucius. At the end of the *Great Digest* he duly underlined the recurring message: "A state does not profit by profits. Honesty is the treasure of states." At the end of the *Unwobbling Pivot* he underscored the passage: "Only the most absolute sincerity under heaven can effect any change [in things, in conditions]" (the brackets are Pound's). Throughout the *Analects* he saw Confucius as the one who exemplified these ideas. And finally in the *Odes* he envisioned the kind of culture which would complete man's civilizing process. That is, in the Confucian classics Pound found a utopian vision, a vision of the ideal government, the ideal social order, and the ideal world, capable of realizing man's oldest dream, his partnership with heaven and earth—much as Eliot found his in both the *Comedy* and the *Gita*. Undoubtedly, it is this utopian vision that helped sustain Pound through those years of discontent and search, nurturing his views of history, economics, and culture as he continued to weave them all into his life work, the *Cantos*.

Throughout his long career Pound had many obsessions, and the greatest of them was his *Cantos*. Some critics have hailed it as one of the major poetic achievements of this century, whereas others have felt that, no matter how colossal in scope and magnificent in intention, the *Cantos* has no unifying center and remains a series of fragments.[47] Pound himself, the old Pound at least, seemed to think of it as a failure. In 1962, while pointing out the difficulty of writing a paradiso in this age of ours, he admitted that he was more or less "stuck," and again in 1968 he went even further to declare: "It's a botch."[48]

Whatever ultimate judgment time may pass, it is well to remember the initial intention Pound spelled out in "Three Cantos" (1917), his initial concept of "a rag-bag" ("the modern world / Needs such a rag-bag to stuff all its thought in"). It is this concept of "rag-bag" that underlay the

Homeric and Dantean structure of the *Cantos* throughout its vicissitudes. With this in mind, Eliot wrote in 1918: "In appearance, it is a rag-bag of Mr. Pound's reading in various languages. . . . And yet the thing has, after one has read it once or twice, a positive coherence; it is an objective and reticent autobiography."[49] What Eliot here said of Pound's early cantos holds true for the entire work, for the hero who finally emerges from the *Cantos* is Ezra Pound himself, and his life journey or his intellectual odyssey unifies those divers elements and strands which appear and reappear throughout. As a poetic autobiography the *Cantos* resembles Whitman's *Leaves of Grass*—a resemblance which is more than coincidental inasmuch as Pound felt that Whitman was to America what Dante was to Italy, and that it was his birthright to synthesize both.[50] Starting from America, Pound attempted to log his encounter with history as it happened. Like Whitman, Pound attempted to complete Columbus's unfinished passage to the Orient.

If the polyglot is one salient characteristic of modern literature, the *Cantos* certainly qualifies as perhaps the most conspicuous case. Throughout the *Cantos* all sorts of European languages appear, ancient and modern, in quotations and otherwise, as we might expect from this one-time student of comparative literature steeped in several literary traditions. There are also other forms, such as hieroglyphics, which are as visual as those pictorial designs scattered over the *Cantos*. And finally there are Chinese characters or ideograms, which reflect Pound's interest in Confucius and Chinese civilization. Even more than Eliot's *Waste Land*, the *Cantos* represents a global perspective embracing East and West.

As for the Chinese characters in the *Cantos*, together they indicate Pound's progressive involvement with the Orient. Despite our initial impression that these four-hundred-odd characters are scattered all over, they do not appear until the end of Canto 51.[51] Thus, in Canto 13, the Confucian Canto, all the Chinese proper names, including that of Confucius, follow the French system of pronunciation since at that stage Pound relied heavily on Pauthier's translation. Then, in Canto 49, the "Seven Lakes" Canto, the legendary Emperor Shun's quatrain, beginning with "Kei Men Ran Kei," appears in Japanese transliteration, just as Pound had used Rihaku in Japanese form for Li Po. In his later cantos Pound on occasion merely transliterates Chinese, not bothering with ideograms, which suggests that by then he knew Chinese characters well enough to use Chinese-English dictionaries. Otherwise, the Chinese characters are concentrated in *Cantos* 52–71 (1940), the *Pisan Cantos* 74–84 (1948), the *Rock-Drill* 85–95 (1955), the *Thrones* 96–109 (1959), and *Drafts and Fragments* 110–17 (1969).

Except for dynastic and personal names, all the Chinese characters represent certain key concepts, some of them appearing more than once for repeated emphasis. The first Chinese characters to appear in the *Cantos* are 正名 (chêng⁴ ming²), meaning rectification of language—a concept which Confucius in the *Analects* expounded as the first step toward good government.[52] The term appears first in Canto 51, and then four more times, thrice in the History Cantos and once in the *Thrones*. The term appears for the second time in Canto 60 with reference to Kang Hi, or Kang Hsi, second emperor of the Manchu dynasty, whose virtues as a ruler placed him in the tradition of Sage Emperors Yao, Shun, and Yü. The compilation of the *Kang Hsi Dictionary* was foremost among his contributions.

> He ordered 'em to prepare a total anatomy, et
> qu'ils veillèrent à la pureté du langage
> et qu'on n'employât que des termes propres
> (namely CH'ing ming)
> 正名

With this abrupt shift to French Pound must have wished to remind us of the French Academy's similar project. The same term appears for the fourth time in Canto 68, this time in connection with John Adams, second president of the United States, a Poundian hero whose political vision perhaps came closest to the Confucian ideal of good government in American history.

> to show U.S. the importance of an early attention to language
> for ascertaining the language.
> 正名 Ching
> Ming

One of the most repeated key terms is *chung*[1]—for the first time in Canto 70, where John Adams declares:

> Americans more rapidly disposed to corruption in elections
> than I thought in '74
> fraudulent use of words monarchy and republic
> I am for balance 中

For the third time it appears in Canto 77:

> le beau monde gouverne
> if not toujours at any rate it is a level of
> some sort whereto things tend to return

Chung 中
in the middle
whether upright or horizontal

And for the fourth time, in Canto 84, once again in connection with John Adams and his descendants:

John Adams, the Brothers Adam
there is our norm of spirit
our 中 chung[1]
whereto we may pay our
homage

The term *chung* means "middle," "center," "mean," or "axis." It is the central concept of the *Chung Yung*. As Pound explains in the *Unwobbling Pivot, chung*, like *yung*, represents "most definitely a process in motion, an axis round which something turns." There is no question that he exploits what seems to be most obviously ideogrammic.

In a letter of 1939 Pound explained the presence of foreign words in his work in progress: "I believe that when finished, *all* foreign words in the Cantos, Gk., etc., will be underlinings, not necessary to the sense, in one way. I mean a complete sense will exist without them; it will be there in the American text, but the Greek, ideograms, etc., will indicate a *duration* from whence or since when. If you can find any *briefer* means of getting this repeat or resonance, tell papa, and I will try to employ it."[53] All the same, these foreign words are indispensable, as Pound himself quickly qualified. Without these underlinings there would be no *Cantos*, for its vitality derives from the various traditions these underlinings represent. In indicating a sense of duration no other language could surpass Chinese, which is at once ancient and still alive in its ideograms. As Kenner pointed out, Pound had no intention of standardizing those spellings and pronunciations of Chinese, at times even retaining Japanese and French forms. Their variance was meant to indicate not only the stages of his journey to Cathay but also the strange, roundabout way in which tradition had been transmitted to the modern American poet that is Ezra Pound.[54]

China makes its full-scale appearance in Canto 13, generally known as the Confucian Canto. "Kung wallked / by the dynastic temple / and into the cedar grove, / and then out by the lower river, / And with him . . ." The canto begins in a direct and yet leisurely manner—quite a relief after a character sketch of the American businessman Baldy Bacon in the preceding canto. Emerging from a tapestry of a dozen or so familiar

200

quotations and anecdotes is Confucius, a teacher of insight and discern-
ment, a humanist of order and moderation, an individual of character and
integrity—a human being profoundly alive with his sense of moral and
aesthetic values.

Pound is rather free with quotations, making whatever adaptations fit
his particular purposes. In the first quotation, for example, a loose paraphrase of the *Analects*, XI, 25, Confucius asks four disciples what each
would propose to do once in office. One disciple says he would "put the
defenses in order"; another says he would put his province "in better
order"; the third says he would serve in a small mountain temple; the
fourth, however, puts his lute aside and says: "The old swimming hole, /
And the boys flopping off the planks, / Or sitting in the underbrush
playing mandolins." There are several omissions from the original, the
most interesting being Confucius's comments: "They have all answered
correctly, / That is to say, each in his nature"—quite emphatic in comparison with the original, which says simply: "Each one expressed his
preference, that's all." Noteworthy here is Pound's attempt to reinforce
what he believes typical of Confucius while eliminating anything contrary
and irrelevant—an attempt to portray the humanist, the type more Confucian than Confucius himself.

Following Canto 45, the incantatory canto on usury, "sin against nature," comes another relief, with Canto 49, the "Seven Lakes" Canto,
which begins:

> For the seven lakes, and by no man these verses:
> Rain; empty river; a voyage,
> Fire from frozen cloud, heavy rain in the twilight
> Under the cabin roof was one lantern.
> The reeds are heavy; bent;
> And the bamboos speak as if weeping.

A familiar Chinese landscape painting. This initial impression grows
stronger as the canto unfolds its second verse on an autumn moon, its third
on the sunset, its fourth on snow and wild geese, and so on—all set in the
Seven Lakes region of China. Then, with the fifth verse, a tone of disso-
nance creeps in: "State by creating riches shd. thereby get into debt? /
This is infamy; this is Geryon." But it quickly gives way to the legendary
sage Emperor Shun's song in praise of the diurnal arrival of the resplen-
dent dawn, and further to another song sung by contented peasants under
the reign of his predecessor, Emperor Yao: "Sun up; work / sundown; to
rest / dig well and drink of the water / dig field; eat of the grain / Imperial
power is? and to us what is it?" Stressing the overall mood of serenity, the

canto now moves toward its climax: "The fourth; the dimension of stillness. / And the power over wild beasts." Recreating natural tranquillity,
Canto 49 marks a rare moment in the entire work. According to Kenner, it
resulted from Pound's attempt to translate a Chinese picture book. Designating these scenes as paradigms of natural tranquillity, Kenner also calls
the canto "the still point at the heart of the work."[55] What Canto 49
recaptures is authentic China, with her familiar scenes, motifs, themes,
and moods; timeless China, which has transcended history.

It is the ceaseless struggle between these two Chinas which dramatizes
the Chinese History Cantos (52–61), a sweeping view of those numerous
dynasties over five millennia, with occasional glances at Korea and Japan.
There is nothing novel about this view of Chinese civilization in terms of
the creative contention between the Confucian and the Taoist, the humanistic and the naturalistic tradition. Although Kenner suggested that later in
his career Pound was Taoist "in his deepest impulses," in these cantos he
translated their struggle into one of light versus darkness, good versus
evil, order versus chaos. Pound owed this Confucian bias to both Chu Hsi
and his own intellectual background, the eighteenth-century Enlightenment. As Kenner pointed out, "China, the Enlightenment, the *Cantos*: it
was like the conjunction of three planets."[56]

Pound made no distinction between mystical-philosophical and magical
Taoism. While the one has been largely responsible for China's artistic
achievements, the other has allied itself with alchemy and hygiene, and
with their common search for the elixir of life.[57] By concentrating on this
aspect of popular Taoism Pound transformed Taoism itself into the arch-
rival of Confucianism as the latter attempted to bring light, order, justice,
and peace into the empire. Throughout the Chinese History Cantos Pound
took every opportunity to downgrade the Taoist, whichever form he might
take—Lao Tse, Taotse, or Taozer—often in the company of court eu-
nuchs and Buddhist *hochangs*, or monks. In Canto 56, for instance,
Pound condensed the swift succession of dynasties:

> Hochang, eunuchs, taoists and ballets
> night-clubs, gimcracks, debauchery
>> Down, down! Han is down
>> Sung is down
> Hochang, eunuchs, and taozers
> empresses' relatives, came then a founder
> saying nothing superfluous
> cleared out the taozers and grafters, gave grain
>> opened the mountains
> Came taozers, hochang and debauchery

202

The Enlightenment was confident and optimistic about history's march toward Reason. Likewise, Pound believed in Confucius as a solution to history. No mere summary of Chinese history, these cantos move toward their dramatic climax with the reign of Yong Tching, fifth emperor of the Ch'ing Dynasty. Canto 61 begins:

> Yong Tching
> his fourth son, to honour his forebears
> and spirits of fields
> of earth
> heaven
> utility public
> sought good of the people, active, absolute, loved
> No death sentence save a man were thrice tried

During his reign Christian missionary activities in China were firmly controlled; "No new temples for any hochang, taoists or similars" were allowed. When this exemplary ruler molded in the Confucian tradition died in 1835 at the age of fifty-eight, after his reign of thirteen years, he declared with a profound sense of humility: "A man's happiness depends on himself, / not on his Emperor."

Time and again Pound defined an epic as "a poem including history." And history without monetary intelligence was "mere twaddle," as he wrote to Eliot.[58] The *Cantos* is, in a way, an epic including economic history. Whenever there is a historical reference it is reinforced with economic data. Earl Davis argued that economics is Pound's "ultimate theme."[59] Whether or not we agree with Davis, it is no exaggeration that Pound conceived of evil primarily in terms of economics, and Hell in terms of economic evils.

Early in his career Pound imbibed the English engineer-economist Major Clifford Hugh Douglas's Social Credit as a possible cure of the economic ills long accumulated through the practice of usury. Pound believed that history points to the perennial conflict between the forces of special privilege and the rest of society. Usury is merely another name for the practices of social privilege, the practices of profiting by manipulation of values or the means of production. According to him, it is usury that causes depression, the general decline of national vitality, and international conflicts which result in destructive wars. For these reasons he respected those political leaders who attempted to create a political economy which would prevent the usurious aristocracy from controlling society. In the *Cantos* he memorialized their historical precedents or models:

Mussolini in modern Italy; Jefferson, Adams, Jackson, Van Buren, and Lincoln in America; Pietro Leopoldo and Ferdinando in Tuscany; the Medici and Malatesta in Italy; and Confucius and his followers in China.[60]

To Pound, Confucius and his followers in China particularly exemplified notions of economic management, political tolerance, and social guidance in the interest of the whole society. Pound tried to illustrate this ideal of social utopia in the Chinese History Cantos, as Davis pointed out.[61] In stressing Confucius's moral philosophy, however, Pound did not overlook his other side, the Confucius who suggested in the *Analects*, XIII, 9 that people be first enriched and then educated. Confucius's vision, combining morality and economy, continued to inspire his followers over the centuries, while sustaining the whole structure of Chinese society and civilization in the face of its ever-present danger of corruption and chaos. In this sense Pound's utopian vision was unmistakably Confucian; he returned to Emperor Yong Tching long after the Chinese Cantos—this time in the *Thrones*, Canto 99:

> Sage men have plans
> simplicity a thousand generations, no man can change.
> The Sage Emperor's heart is our heart,
> His government is our government
> $\qquad$ yao^2 high, hsiao^3 dawn
> The Venerated Emperor
> $\qquad$ watched things grow with affection,

Coming after massive clusters of historical details and economic data, a passage such as this brings a sense of relief, even a flash of illumination.

Long ago Pound said that the image is "an intellectual and emotional complex in an instant of time" responsible for "that sense of sudden liberation; that sense of freedom from time limits and space limits; that sense of sudden growth, which we experience in the presence of the greatest works of art." He also described the vortex as "a radiant node or luster," "from which, and through which, ideas are constantly rushing." Each of those "magic" moments which from time to time illuminate the *Cantos* corresponds to what Pound called "an era of brilliance" in human history when "the vortices of power and the vortices of culture coincide."[62]

"Ideogram is essential to the exposition of certain kinds of thought," Pound wrote in 1940. "Greek philosophy was mostly a mere splitting, an impoverishment of understanding, though it ultimately led to development of particular sciences. Socrates a distinguished gas-bag in comparison with Confucius and Mencius.''[63] Here Pound not only defended his use of Chinese characters in the *Cantos*, but also expanded Fenollosa's old thesis: the fundamental difference between the Chinese and the Greek, between the Oriental and the Occidental mode of thinking. As he also explained in *ABC of Reading*, the European tends progressively toward the remote, the general, and the abstract as he attempts to define a simple thing; contrary to this analytical method, the ideogrammic is at once poetic and scientific. In the *Cantos* this particular method does away with many of the grammatical connectives which are essential to logical, sequential, and lineal thinking, while promoting direct, concrete perception of images, facts, and ideas. Defending himself against the common charge of logical gaps and breakdowns, Pound declared: ''The statement is nevertheless complete. All the elements are there.''[64] Noting some critics' grudging admission that he occasionally causes the reader ''suddenly to see'' or that his remark ''reveals the whole subject from a new angle,'' Pound drove his point home: ''I mean to say the purpose of the writing is to reveal the subject. The ideogrammic method consists of presenting one facet and then another until at some point one gets off the dead and desensitized surface of the reader's mind, onto a part that will register.'' In short, his aim was revelation, ''a just revelation irrespective of newness or oldness.''[65]

In 1944 Pound wrote: ''For forty years I have schooled myself, . . . to write an epic poem which begins 'In the Dark Forest,' crosses the Purgatory of human error, and ends in the light, 'fra i maestri di color che sanno.' ''[66] True to this Dantean scheme the light imagery does recur, culminating in a series of revelations. Canto 51 opens with a hymn to light: ''Shines / in the mind of heaven God / who made it / More than the sun / in our eye.'' Beginning with 耀 (*yao*[4])—glory, brightness—which unfolds the Chinese History Cantos, there appear numberless ideograms suggesting light. In Cantos 74, 85, 91, and 93 顯 (*hsien*[3])—manifest—is presented, whereas Canto 84 introduces the ideogram showing the sun and the moon in embrace, 明 (*ming*[2])—bright, clear, intelligent. And Canto 98 couples both ideograms, celebrating the peaceful reign of Emperor Yong Tching:

> Iong Ching, Canto 61
>   of the light of 顯 hsien
>   明 ming,
> by the silk cords of the sunlight,
> Chords of the sunlight (*Pitagora*)
>   non si disuna (xiii)
> Splendor

As we all know, the *Cantos* are incomplete, *Drafts and Fragments* (110–17) indicates Pound's desperate efforts to bring his lifework to completion. Even here the light imagery persists, as in Canto 115: "A blown husk that is finished / but the light sings eternal / a pale flare over marshes / where the salt hay whispers to tide's change," and as in Canto 116: "a little light / in great darkness" and "A little light, like rushlight / to lead back to splendour." Once, when challenged on his ability to devise an ending, Pound reportedly produced a sheet of paper "bearing sixteen ideograms locked into a square" for the last canto. His first Chinese quatrain, according to Kenner, consisted of the sixteen ideograms he found most interesting, such as *ching*[4], "respect for the kind of intelligence that enables grass to grow grass"; *chien*[4], the luminous eye with a pair of legs; and *hsien*[3], the sun's silk "manifest."[67] At the end of his long career Pound, a modern Odysseus, was still determined to see light as Dante did at the end of his journey. But there is little doubt that Pound's light reflected what he had received from China, what he called his "new Greece."

EPILOGUE

The Beat Generation:
Salinger, Kerouac,
and Snyder

In 1954, while surveying the postwar literary situation in America, Malcolm Cowley noted a fairly large group of young writers waging "a dogged sort of rebellion" against not just the old literary standards but the old way of life as a whole. Often heavy-drinking, pot-smoking, promiscuous, and fast-driving, these young writers preferred to call themselves "the beat generation," to use the phrase coined by Jack Kerouac, author of *On the Road* yet to be published. They and the rest of their generation had two things in common. As Cowley pointed out, "they had no interest in politics, even as a spectator sport, and they were looking for something to believe, an essentially religious faith that would permit them to live at peace with their world."[1] An astute observer of the changing literary situation since World War I, Cowley knew what he was talking about. Moreover, he was serving as a publisher's editor in charge of Kerouac's novel. In spite of his usual insights, Cowley could not but be puzzled by this new generation. Though open-minded, he was an outsider; and the group itself, the generation itself, had yet to find its own identity.

By 1957, when Kerouac's long-awaited, much revised novel finally appeared, the scene had begun to emerge in a more definable perspective. Gilbert Millstein, writing for the *New York Times*, hailed its publication as "a historic occasion," not dissimilar to that of Hemingway's *The Sun Also Rises* in the 1920s.[2] Millstein compared this new generation, the beat generation, to the lost generation—a gesture which, to hostile observers, amounted to granting a status neither *On the Road* nor the new generation deserved. Norman Podhoretz vehemently rejected the legitimacy of such a comparison. To him, the Bohemianism of the 1920s signified primarily "a movement created in the name of civilization," with its ideals of intelligence, cultivation, and spiritual refinement; whereas the Bohemianism of the 1950s with its cult of primitivism and spontaneity was "more than a cover for hostility to intelligence," resulting from "a pathetic poverty of feeling as well."[3]

Podhoretz's objection notwithstanding, this juxtaposition of the lost and the beat generations was unavoidable because of their similarities and differences. What both postwar generations shared was an overall spirit of rebellion against the establishment. But the beat generation was far more radical, rejecting on the one hand the intellectual legacy of the old, an uneasy coalition of academic conservatives and political liberals, and on the other, those middle class values which the parent generation had come to embrace with religious zeal.[4] As Lawrence Lipton declared in his preface to *The Holy Barbarians*: "It is not the anti-Babbitt caper of the twenties. Nor the politically oriented alienation of the thirties. The present generation has taken note of all these and passed on beyond them to a total rejection of the whole society, and that, in present-day America, means the business civilization. The alienation of the hipsters from the squares is now complete."[5] While approving this act of willing alienation or deliberate withdrawal, Kenneth Rexroth, a sort of father figure to the young writers on the West Coast, also pointed out that the new generation, rejecting the official highbrow culture, chose the creative act as the only defense against the ruins of the world. Whatever might befall this generation, Rexroth was certain about one thing as he concluded: "Social disengagement, artistic integrity, voluntary poverty—these are powerful virtues and may pull them through, but they are not the virtues we tried to inculcate—rather they are the exact opposite."[6]

Rexroth was an insider as Cowley was an outsider; yet they both concurred in their view of the young generation's interest in religion. Relating how he came to find a new meaning in his own coinage *beat* (a jazz term meaning "poor, down and out, deadbeat, on the bum, sad, sleeping in subways"), Kerouac referred to the vision he had had in 1954, while in his hometown church—"the vision of the word Beat as being to mean beatific . . . There's the priest preaching on Sunday morning, all of a sudden through a side door of the church comes a group of Beat Generation characters in strapped raincoats like the I. R. A. coming in silently to 'dig' the religion . . . I knew it then."[7]

This religious interest was another characteristic which distinguished the beat from the lost generation. In the earlier generation Eliot's conversion had been received as something reactionary and even scandalous. In the later generation, however, interest in religion was virtually a universal phenomenon, and nothing to be ashamed of. In their search for wisdom, the kind of religious wisdom which would promise to bring life and art into their original intimacy, many beat writers turned to the East. Here again we may recall O'Neill, Eliot, and Pound, but their study of Eastern thought was the exception rather than the rule. The new generation was more like that of Emerson, Alcott, Thoreau, and Whitman, which eagerly turned to India's philosophy and religion; or more like the subsequent generation, of Adams, Bigelow, Lowell, Fenollosa, and

Hearn, which journeyed to the East in search of nirvana. As Rexroth said: "They are all interested in Far Eastern art and religion; some even call themselves Buddhists."[8]

Indeed, no other recent generation has turned to the Orient, especially to Zen Buddhism, more excitedly than this one; it was as though the whole generation had gone on its pilgrimage. Alan W. Watts explained this religious fervor, this Zen craze, in terms of various factors: the writings of Dr. Suzuki; the war with Japan; the anthologies of Zen stories; the appeal of Zen arts to the "modern" spirit in the West; the attraction of a nonconceptual, experiential philosophy in a climate of scientific relativism; and the appeal of the mystical naturalism of Zen to those in search of the reintegration of man and nature as well as to those immobilized in the moral absolutism of the Hebrew-Christian universe. From this broad intellectual perspective Watts defined the beat mentality: "It is a younger generation's nonparticipation in 'the American Way of life,' a revolt which does not seek to change the existing order but simply turns away from it to find the significance of life in subjective experience rather than objective achievement."[9] So the beat generation turned to Zen Buddhism; more than anything else, Zen seemed to promise the liberation of the mind from conventional thought.

As Watts pointed out here and elsewhere,[10] Zen Buddhism is no monopoly of Japan. Originating in India, it was transmitted to China, where having absorbed Taoism, it came to be called *ch'an* for its emphasis on *dhyana* (meditation); to Korea; and then to Japan, where it became known under the name of Zen and nurtured Japanese culture. In the evolution of the Mahayana school, Zen Buddhism thus represented the culmination of several cultural traditions—Indian, Chinese, Korean, and Japanese—and, in a way, the quintessence of the Oriental religious and philosophical imagination. Thus the beat generation, by responding to Zen, turned toward the Orient, as is evinced in Salinger, Kerouac, and Snyder, to name three of its representative writers.

Although J. D. Salinger (b. 1919) has never been labeled a beat writer, his *Catcher in the Rye*, according to Lipton, was "to be found everywhere on the bookshelves of the beat." As he explained, 'It is not difficult for the beat youth to identify itself with the book's hero, Holden Caufield. He not only *sounds* right to them but the things he says are often the things they say."[11] Lipton made this observation in 1959, and we may wonder what he would have said of Salinger's subsequent Glass family saga, which is full of Zen. If Salinger and the beat writers had anything in common, it was their interest in Zen Buddhism.

One could of course dismiss the matter summarily, as George Steiner did, by concluding that Salinger simply catered to the ignorance and shallowness of his young audience. "He suggests to them," Steiner wrote, "that formal ignorance, political apathy and a vague *tristesse* are positive virtues. They open the heart to mystic intimations of love. This is where his cunning and somewhat shoddy use of Zen comes in. Zen is in fashion." Most critics, however, taking the matter more seriously, have recognized its central significance in Salinger's art. Tom Davis designated Zen as "the dominating force in most of his later fiction," though he felt that its influence was a negative one. Salinger was "deeply—perhaps harmfully—influenced by Zen," he argued. "Zooey," and the entire Glass family saga for that matter, according to Davis, is less satisfactory than some of Salinger's early stories, partly because of its "easy marriage of East and West." "And if Salinger's central concern is the 'search for love,' then 'Zooey' reveals a kind of love which is a strained synthesis of East and West and, in the end, a kind of love which is unsatisfactory." Ihab Hassan was more positive when he wrote: "Two of the cardinal assumptions in Salinger's work find expression in the Buddhist ideas of tanha, or blind self-demandingness, and of moksa, a state of liberation achieved by the kind of impersonal compassion which 'The Parable of the Mustard Seed' exemplifies." Referring to Zen experience as "a certain harmony between our imaginative and spiritual responsiveness to all things," Hassan continued: "It becomes evident that these qualities of Zen define some of the interest which Salinger has constantly kept at heart, and that Zen itself, in Salinger's work, makes up to an odd way of criticizing contemporary failures."[12]

Although Salinger's interest in Zen reportedly began as early as 1946,[13] it did not yield anything immediately tangible in his writings. *The Catcher in the Rye* (1951) had only one passing reference to an Eastern view of sex as a physical and spiritual experience. In *Nine Stories* (1953) only "Teddy," which originally appeared in the *New Yorker* for January 31, 1953, mentioned Japanese haiku poetry, reincarnation, and meditation, among other things. With "Raise High the Roof Beam, Carpenter" (1955), the second of the Glass family stories, however, began a steady flow of Oriental references and allusions, culminating in "Seymour: An Introduction" (1959). That is, Salinger's interest in Zen surfaced slowly over nearly a decade as he came to conceive of his Glass family as a fictional unit.

True, some of the Glass children did appear as early as 1948–49, Seymour in "A Perfect Day for Bananafish," Walt indirectly in "Uncle Wiggily in Connecticut," and Boo Boo in "Down at the Dinghy." But there were no signs yet that they were in any way related to one another. Moreover, none of these three characters, none of these three stories, revealed any significant relation to Zen Buddhism or the Orient. Rather in "Teddy," a story unrelated to any of these, Salinger's interest finally began to emerge. Apparently a psychic and a mystic as well as a child prodigy, Teddy complained that "it's very hard to meditate and live a spiritual life in America." Full of Zen, he denounced logic as the curse of apple-eaters, the first thing to get rid of. "I grew my own body. Nobody else did it for me. So if I grew it, I must have known *how* to grow it. Unconsciously, at least. I may have lost the *con*scious knowledge of how to grow it sometime in the last few hundred thousand years, but the knowledge is still *there*, because—obviously—I've used it. . . . It would take quite a lot of meditation and emptying out to get the whole thing back—I mean the conscious knowledge." In all this Teddy anticipated Seymour, as Salinger himself must have realized. Realizing this, he resuscitated Teddy, so to speak, in the person of the already deceased Seymour, and made Walt and Boo Boo his younger brother and sister. The familly kept growing as Salinger added Buddy, Seymour's living spokesman, Waker, Zooey, Franny—seven gifted children born to the retired vaudevillians Les and Bessie Glass. Salinger's initial decision to resuscitate Teddy was a momentous one because he had to abide by this self-imposed condition, for better or for worse.

With Seymour dead, Buddy away teaching in college, Boo Boo married, Walt killed in action, and Waker also away as a Catholic missionary, Zooey and Franny are the only ones at home. The most extraordinary of these extraordinary brothers and sisters is the oldest, Seymour, who, though he committed suicide long ago, in 1948, still remains the central figure—a sort of guru, master, and saint dispensing his own brand of wisdom to whoever needs it.

In "Seymour: An Introduction" Buddy calls his late brother "Semitic-Celtic Oriental," because, born to a Jewish father and an Irish mother, he also embodies Oriental wisdom, a blend of three religious traditions—Hindu, Buddhist, and Taoist.[14] And through Buddy, through Zooey, Seymour comes to help Franny with her first spiritual crisis. The task first falls on Zooey, her actor brother. Failing, however, he enters Seymour and Buddy's room wherefrom he phones Franny. As he does he notes a series of quotations written on the beaverboard which begins: "You have the right to work, but for the work's sake only. You have no right to the fruits of work. Desire for the fruits of work must never be your motive in working. Never give way to laziness, either." Impersonating Buddy, he urges: "The only thing you can do now, the only religious thing you can do, is act. Act for God, if you want to—be *God's* actress, if you want to. What could be prettier? You can at least try to, if you want to—there's nothing wrong in *trying*." Zooey also urges his sister to put stupid audiences out of her mind: "That's none of your business, Franny. An artist's only concern is to shoot for some kind of perfection, and *on his own terms*, not anyone else's." Here Zooey is paraphrasing the central doctrine of the *Gita*, no doubt distilled through his own acting experience. In impersonating Buddy he gradually becomes Seymour.

While discussing Seymour, Buddy declares that his late brother was "virtually all things," "all *real* things to his brothers and sisters"—"our blue-stripped unicorn, our double-lensed burning glass, our consultant genius, or portable conscience, our superego, and our one full poet," "our rather notorious 'mystic' and 'unbalanced type' " and "a *mukta*, a ringding enlightened man, a God-knower." To create such a hero was hard enough, but to create him out of the dead, someone who had committed suicide, was even harder. Once he set out on this task Salinger must have realized its enormous difficulty.

Through Buddy, Salinger filled out the later career of the original "Wise Child" of the radio show. Outwardly, Seymour was worldly enough. A Ph.D. from Columbia, he taught English, joined the army, married the girl he had met while in the service, underwent analysis, and committed suicide at the age of thirty-one while vacationing with his wife in Florida. Nothing so unusual for a one-time child prodigy. Inwardly, however, he was altogether extraordinary. A born seer, he possessed marvelous capacities. As a child he had excelled in various games; in marble-shooting, for instance, he was unbeatable, though his playing was "maddeningly irregular." At the same time he was steeped in Oriental lore, freely commenting on Laotzu, Chuangtzu, the Cheng brothers, Vivekananda, and other figures.[15] All his life drawn to Chinese and Japanese poetry, "in ways that he was drawn to no other poetry in the world," he himself produced 184 incomparable "double haiku" poems, which in Buddy's opinion would secure him a place in the literary Pantheon.

There was yet another side to Seymour, unfathomable and unaccountable. When a boy, he threw a stone to a girl called Charlotte simply because "she looked so beautiful sitting there in the middle of the driveway with Boo Boo's cat." When asked about his future plans after his military service, he shocked everyone with the statement that he would be "a dead cat"—referring to a Zen story in which a master called a dead cat the most valuable thing in the world because "no one could put a price on it." As he confided in his diary, certain things would leave permanent marks on him, that is, physically. Once he grabbed Charlotte's yellow cotton dress which he loved because "it was too long for her," and it left a lemon-yellow mark on the palm of his right hand. "Oh, God, if I'm anything by a clinical name, I'm a kind of paranoiac in reverse. I suspect people of plotting to make me happy."

212

Seymour's suicide represents the ultimate of these unforgettable and paradoxical words and deeds which make him what he is—guru, master, and saint, a rarity in modern American literature. All of Buddy's efforts eventually come up against this ultimate fact, the suicide of his brother whom he loves to the point of adulation. He admits that he must go on several more years before he is ready to discuss the details of Seymour's suicide.[16] In order to make his hero, Seymour, a convincing character, Salinger, too, must face the same task. And this task he has not yet tackled. Whatever his difficulty, one thing is certain: without Zen, Salinger could not possibly have conceived of resurrecting his dead hero in the first place.

Near the end of *The Catcher in the Rye* Holden dreams about going out West and working at a filling station. He would pretend to be one of those deaf-mutes, so as to be left alone; with his earnings he would build a little cabin near the woods and live there for the rest of his life. Later on he would marry a beautiful girl, a deaf-mute like himself; if they had children, they would hide them somewhere; they would buy them books and teach them how to read and write by themselves. Salinger developed this theme of childhood innocence into a theme of primal innocence, an ideal common to Taoism and Zen Buddhism. As Buddy stated paradoxically: "But my life itself couldn't very conceivably be less Zenful than it is, and what little I've been able to apprehend—I pick that verb with care—of the Zen experience has been a by-product of following my own rather natural path of extreme Zenlessness." That was Seymour's advice, he pointed out. The crux of this advice was that the ideal of Zen is not to be Zenful but rather to be Zenless—in other words, to be utterly natural, no more no less.

Holden's dream is interesting for another reason. It also presaged the pattern of Salinger's own life: a series of withdrawals which has made him a virtual recluse. All sorts of speculations have been ventured about what motivated his withdrawals. Warren French suggested that Salinger's seclusion resulted from his "inability to make the social adjustments expected of mature members of society."[17] But it would seem that in following his own preference Salinger was also following the age-old ideal of the East: a hermit's passion for anonymity. Whatever the reason, Salinger, in his own way, was living out the pattern of his generation: disengagement.

Holden concludes in the above confession: "If we had any children, we'd hide them somewhere. We could buy them a lot of books and teach them how to read and write by ourselves." Zooey also, impersonating Buddy, relays Seymour's message to his sister: "An artist's only concern is to shoot for some kind of perfection, and *on his own terms*, not anyone else's.'' Behind them all is Salinger talking to himself. Denouncing the recent unauthorized publication of his uncollected early short stories, Salinger broke his more than two-decade-long silence: ''There is a marvelous peace in not publishing. It's peaceful. Still publishing is a terrible invasion of my privacy. I like to write. I love to write. But I write just for myself and my own pleasure.'' He then admitted that he was working on a new work and indicated that he would dictate the terms of its release.[18] Apparently, Salinger has been working in his deliberate, perfectionist way. This new work may be about the Glass family, especially Seymour's suicide; or it may be about something else. Whichever the case, it will be interesting to see what role the Orient plays in it.

In many ways Jack Kerouac (1922–69) was the exact opposite of Salinger. Known as King of the Beats, he never shunned publicity, though he too said he wanted to live in the woods à la Thoreau. A Canadian Catholic born in Lowell, Massachusetts, this Columbia dropout was footloose, criss-crossing the continent in his frantic quest for kicks. Matching this life-style was his writing, free-wheeling, often sentimental, lyrical, and ecstatic. In what he called spontaneous prose he wrote the Legend of Duluoz, a series of Galsworthian, Proustian, and Wolfean novels centering on his soul's progress. Whatever we may think of his fantasy of being another Shakespeare or another Joyce, Kerouac was very serious about his chosen craft. As his nine-year-long struggle over *On the Road* attests, his dedication to art was almost religious. After all, it was Kerouac who not only coined the term *beat* for his generation but also sublimated it into *beatific*. If this religious devotion was one thing Kerouac shared with Salinger, there was still another, his interest in the Orient, especially in Buddhism.

In 1959, Alan W. Watts wrote of Kerouac and his fellow writers in terms of what he called beat Zen: ''Beat Zen is a complex phenomenon. It ranges from a use of Zen for justifying sheer caprice in art, literature, and life to a very forceful social criticism and 'digging of the universe' such as one may find in the poetry of Ginsberg, Whalen and Snyder, and, rather unevenly, in Kerouac, who is always a shade too self-conscious, too subjective, and too strident to have the flavor of Zen.'' In the following year Margaret E. Ashida seriously questioned Kerouac's response to Zen. Principal traits of his art, such as the aimlessness, the itch, and the lack of self-containment and self-control, had little to do with Zen, she argued. ''Kerouac's major characters—his 'angel hipsters,' his 'Bodhisattvas'— share this basic confusion of Zen gone awry.'' She ascribed his fellow beat writers' failure to convey the Zen spirit to their own inability to absorb Zen, to the difficulty of verbalizing about Zen, or to its basic incompatibility with Western culture.[19]

This seems rather odd in view of Kerouac's repeated insistence that he was interested in the original Buddhism, not Zen. In his *Paris Review* interview of 1967 Kerouac said: "What's really influenced my work is the Mahayana Buddhism, the original Buddhism of Gotama Sakyamuni, the Buddha himself of the India of old . . . Zen is what's left of his Buddhism, or Bodhi, after its passing into China and then into Japan. The part of Zen that's influenced my writing is the Zen contained in the haiku. . . . But my serious Buddhism, that of ancient India, has influenced that part in my writing that you might call religious, or fervent, or pious, almost as much as Catholicism has. Original Buddhism referred to continual conscious compassion, brotherhood, the *dana paramita* meaning the perfection of charity." When asked why he had not written about Jesus as he had about Buddha, Kerouac retorted: "All I *write about* is Jesus. I am Everhard Mercurian, General of the Jesuit Army."[20] That is, to Zen, "a gentle but goody goofy form of heresy," Kerouac preferred what he called his serious Buddhism, the original Buddhism of Gotama Sakyamuni—primarily for the latter's view of life as pain and suffering, and also for his teaching of charity and compassion. Apparently, this was where Kerouac found the essential affinity between Buddhism and Catholicism. There at least he saw no difference between Buddha and Jesus.

According to Ann Charters, Kerouac began reading Buddhist writings in late January 1954, stimulated by Allen Ginsberg's interest in Zen, goaded by Neal Cassady's interest in Edgar Cayce's view of reincarnation, and inspired by Thoreau's interest in Hindu philosophy. With his characteristic fury he plunged into Oriental studies, ranging from Buddhist sutras and Vedic Hymns to Confucius. At the same time he began to practice meditation. It was Buddhism that brought him the kind of consolation he needed at the time of personal and literary despair.[21] (He was still revising *On the Road* while *Visions of Cody, Doctor Sax, Maggie Cassidy*, and *The Subterraneans* remained in manuscript form awaiting publication.) His intense absorption in the next two years resulted in *Some of the Dharma*, a compilation of his notes; *Buddha Tells Us*, a version of the *Surangama Sutra*; *Wake Up*, a life of Buddha; and *The Scripture of the Golden Eternity*. With all this in mind, no doubt, Ginsberg dedicated *Howl* (1956) to Kerouac, along with others, calling him a "new Buddha of American prose."

Indeed, none of Kerouac's novels written up to 1954, such as *The Town and the City, Visions of Cody, Doctor Sax*, and *The Subterraneans*, makes any significant mention of Buddhism, or of the Orient. Even *On the Road*, which he was then revising, has only a few scattered Buddhist references, but none vital to its structure or meaning. All his works written after 1954, on the other hand, are full of Buddhism, with its familiar terms and doctrines. *Mexico City Blues* (written in 1955), a series of choruses recording Kerouac's Mexican experience, is high on Buddhism as it is high on drugs; *Visions of Gerard* (written in 1956), a tribute to his long dead saintly brother, is as Buddhistic as it is Catholic. But most Buddhistic and at the same time most "beat" of all his writings is *The Dharma Bums* (written in 1957), a celebration of the San Francisco Renaissance in particular and the beat generation in general.

When the novel came out in 1958, most reviewers found it superior to *On the Road*, stylistically and thematically. Whereas *On the Road* never went beyond its quest for excitement, *The Dharma Bums* gained religious dimensions as Ray Smith, with his new friend Japhy Ryder, left the madding crowd and scaled the Matterhorn, then sat all alone in midnight meditations in the South Carolina woods, and then alone faced solitude on Mt. Desolation—in short, the bums in search of truth, as the novel's title suggests. If *On the Road* belonged to Kerouac's "beat" period, then *The Dharma Bums* represented his "beatific" period.

This fundamental difference between *On the Road* and *The Dharma Bums* derives from the difference between their narrators, Sol Paradise and Ray Smith, in relation to their respective heroes, Dean Moriarty and Japhy Ryder. In Dean Moriarty Kerouac created an archetypal hero for his generation—the demonic type of hero who is reckless, merciless, mad, and monomaniacal in pursuit of his dream, his obsession. In Japhy Ryder, on the other hand, Kerouac created another archetypal hero for his generation, one in search of wisdom. A one-time logger, mountain climber, poet, college graduate, and above all an Oriental scholar, Japhy Ryder stands in sharp contrast to Dean Moriarty. If the one forever chases after excitement, the other seriously seeks religious wisdom, in his case, Zen.

It is in Japhy's company or rather under his guidance that Ray gets initiated, accepting as his models Han-shan and Shih-te, famous Zen lunatics of T'ang China. It is also against Japhy's Zen that Ray pits his own brand of Buddhism, while absorbing, among other things, Zen's openness toward nature. Even after Japhy's departure for Japan, Ray continues his search. Though Sol eventually becomes disillusioned with his hero, Ray remains grateful for his hero's guidance. This difference clearly indicates Kerouac's shift of allegiance from the one to the other archetypal hero, from the "mad Ahab" to the Dharma Bum. Without Zen, there would be no Japhy; without Japhy, there would be no *Dharma Bums*.

By the summer of 1960, according to Charters, Kerouac was no longer interested in Buddhism.[22] This seems to be borne out by *Big Sur* (written in 1961), which marked the beginning of his last phase. In this account of his nightmarish experience in Bixby Canyon there are still Buddhist references and allusions, but they are now powerless to ward off a deepening sense of disillusionment. At this emotional nadir Kerouac repeatedly sees the Cross, not Avalokitesvara, his favorite Buddhist deity of mercy. "I lie there in cold sweat wondering what's come over me for years my Buddhist studies and pipesmoking assured meditations on emptiness and all of a sudden the Cross is manifested to me—My eyes fill with tears." Already anticipated here is what he is later to say in *Satori in Paris* (written in 1965): "But I'm not a Buddhist, I'm a Catholic—revisiting the ancestral land that fought for Catholicism against impossible odds yet won in the end."

There seems to be something ambivalent about Kerouac's attitude toward the Orient. That this sense of ambivalence may have come from deeper sources than his intellectual convictions is suggested in his *Book of Dreams* (1960), a record of his dreams over the period 1952–60. In one dream he finds himself a prisoner in the hands of Oriental captors; in another he comes under fire from the surrounding Orientals; in a third he tracks Orientals to a vast underground cave full of Oriental war prisoners: "If I don't watch out they'll roast me for supper because there's no food down here." And in a fourth, as in other dreams, he narrowly escapes castration at the hand of the great Oriental Kalifa. Yet it is invariably Buddha or Buddhism that comes to his rescue, according to Kerouac's own interpretation. On one occasion something tells him to wake up from a dream in which he climbs a cliff he dreads to descend: "This is the Sign from Buddha's Compassion at last"; and on another occasion he describes his dream experience: "I'M GOING DOWN THE STONE STEPS of the great Buddhist World Cave saying to watchers on the parapet 'It's inward suicide'—and going down the Holy Hall ways with followers, to the big Reclining Face & the swarming dark full of light irradiating from the Center—there's nowhere to go but inward—The Cave of the World, the Cave of Reality beyond conceptions of sun, air, etc., contains the Well of Shining Reality." What emerges from these two dozen Oriental and Buddhist references, most of them in the second half of the book, is a pattern of attraction and revulsion which may point to something deep in Kerouac's psyche.

Despite his protestations, there is much Zen in Kerouac. He himself admitted its influence on his haiku poems. (According to Ginsberg, Kerouac is "the only one in the United States who knows how to write haikus. The only one who's written any good haikus."[23]) There is also much Zen in his theory of spontaneous prose. Although he had been

217

practicing it before 1954, its formulation evolved along with his Buddhist studies, culminating in his nine-point manifesto of 1958, "Essentials of Spontaneous Prose."[24] In point 4 "Scoping" he declared: "Not 'selectivity' of expression but following free deviation (association) of mind into limitless blow-on-subject seas of thought, swimming in sea of English with no discipline other than rhythms of exhalation and expostulated statement, like a fist coming down on a table with each complete utterance, bang! (the space dash)—Blow as deep as you want—write as deeply, fish as far down as you want, satisfy yourself first, then reader cannot fail to receive telepathic shock and meaning—excitement by same laws operating in his own human mind." In stressing the uninhibited, uninterrupted, natural flow of the mind as the central principle of automatic writing Kerouac was unmistakably Zen; and in denying any major role to consciousness in the process of writing he subverted the conventional notion of fiction as a craft, an art. In theory and practice the end result would be the "confessional" novel, a usual label for Kerouac's writings.

This is where Kerouac parts company with Salinger, in spite of their common interest in Buddhism. While Zen Buddhism, with its emphasis on discipline, reinforced Salinger's passion for perfection, it urged Kerouac in the opposite direction. Zen, with its contrary emphasis on spontaneity, helped liberate him from the conventional. *The Town and the City*, his debut piece of 1950, was a conventional novel in every sense. But beginning with *On the Road* and finally with *The Dharma Bums* Kerouac came to discover his own style, inspired to a significant degree by Buddhism.

By now it is a matter of common knowledge that Japhy Ryder, Kerouac's hero in *The Dharma Bums*, is the poet Gary Snyder. There he was hailed as the discoverer of "the great Dharma Bums of the all—," namely, Han-shan and Shih-te, "the big hero of the West Coast" and "a great new hero of American culture."[25] There was something prophetic about this. Ten years later, Thomas Parkinson wrote of Snyder: "He has created a new culture." Always accessible and outspoken, he has been deeply involved with ecological and other movements. This public exposure as something of a culture hero, however, apparently has not interfered with his poetic productivity. In an assessment of twentieth-century American poets Kenneth Rexroth called him "the best informed, most thoughtful, and most articulate of his colleagues," and also "an accomplished technician . . . who has developed a sure and flexible style capable of handling any material he wishes."[26] Critics would agree that Snyder is the best poet to come out of the San Francisco Renaissance and one of the best poets of the beat generation.

Unlike Salinger and Kerouac, Snyder is a native of the West Coast, born to radical and agnostic parents of pioneer stock. His early contact with American Indians led to an academic study of anthropology. While in college, he began writing poetry under the influence of Eliot, Pound, Whitman, D. H. Lawrence, and Kenneth Rexroth, among others. When he also became interested in Buddhism he took up Oriental studies and translated Han-shan's poems.[27] As Snyder himself said: "I became interested in Buddhism at the end of my college career. It led me to leave graduate school, where I was doing advanced work in anthropology and linguistics. I left it to pursue the Dharma, which had become more interesting to me. That was when I had begun to read Suzuki. But almost at the same time I had my first experience with peyote, it was with Indians. So my spiritual career has been half in the realm of peyote and shamanism, American Indian contacts, nature mysticism, animism, long hair and beads, and the other half concerned with the study of Sanskrit and Chinese and the traditional philosophy of the Orient."[28] From this it is clear that his interest in the Orient and his interest in American Indians were inextricably bound, nurturing and shaping his poetry as well as his career.

There is nothing dilettantish about Snyder's interest in the Orient. Although he lived in Japan for several years, studying and practicing Zen, he went beyond Japanese culture, embracing Chinese and Indian. His position as a Buddhist he clarified thus: "When I say that my practice is Zen but my position is within Vajrayana, it is because Vajrayana, of all the sophisticated and learned religious traditions in the world today that I know of, seems to me to be the only one that has tradtional continuous links that go back to the Stone Age. Actually, Hinduism, Shaivism, has that, too. It's a tradition that has never made that cut between the pagan and the present dispensation. Buddhism itself cuts off the earlier dispensation, but Tantrism brings it back in again. These are the religious insights and practices that belong to the paleolithic hunters at the beginning. This is the *real* nature mysticism."[29] If this primitivism lured Snyder from Christianity to Amerindian culture and Buddhism, it was also the matrix of his threefold concerns: religion, poetics, and econoactivism. And from this primitivistic perspective he also defined the primary function of poetry and the poet in modern society: "Poetry must sing or speak from authentic experience. Of all the streams of civilized tradition with roots in the paleolithic, poetry is one of the few that can realistically claim an unchanged function and a relevance which will outlast most of the activities that surround us today. Poets, as few others, must live close to the world that primitive men are in: the world, in its nakedness, which is fundamental for all of us—birth, love, death; the sheer fact of being alive."[30] A similar notion has been voiced by various modern poets, including Eliot. With Snyder, however, this is no mere theory, no mere conviction; he brings experience of the authentically primitive into his poetry.

A student of Japanese and Chinese, Snyder translated some poetry from these languages, and more importantly, he absorbed it. Indeed, the Orient pervades his poetry in ways ranging from the obvious to the subtle, from the conscious to the unconscious. Take one of his short poems entitled "Hiking in the Totsugawa Gorge": "pissing / watching / a waterfall."[31] In humor we momentarily regain the innocence, spontaneity, and naturalness which we lost as we grew out of our childhood. In both form and spirit this poem appropriates Japanese haiku; it is authentic haiku, to be sure.

Rexroth called Snyder's vision essentially elegiac—"more akin to the great elegiac poets of Sung China"; and Wai-lim Yip compared him to the T'ang poet Wang Wei in philosophy, tone, and style.[32] Whatever the case, there is little doubt that Snyder's poetic sensibility is more Chinese than Japanese. There is "Mid-August at Sourdough Mountain Lookout," the first piece in *Riprap & Cold Mountain Poems*:

> Down valley a smoke haze
> Three days heat, after five days rain
> Pitch glows on the fir-cones
> Across rocks and meadows
> Swarms of new flies
>
> I cannot remember things I once read
> A few friends, but they are in cities
> Drinking cold snow-water from a tin cup
> Looking down for miles
> Through high still air.

Although based on the poet's own experience as a forest lookout, the poem is typically Chinese in its progression from the natural to the human. The first stanza, almost nothing but nouns, could easily pass for a literal translation of some Chinese stanza. For that matter, the second stanza sounds equally familiar, especially the last three lines, the poem's focal point, which ring with an echo of Tao Yuan-ming's famous lines: "Plucking chrysanthemums by the eastern hedge, I gaze afar at the southern hill."[33]

There is another poem from the same lookout experience, entitled "August on Sourdough, a Visit from Dick Brewer." Following the description of a friend who "hitched a thousand miles / north from San Francisco" for an overnight visit, the poem continues:

Next morning I went with you
               as far as the cliffs,
Loaned you my poncho—the rain across the shale—
You down the snowfield
               flapping in the wind
Waving a last goodbye   half hidden in the clouds
To go on hitching
               clear to New York;
Me back to my mountain and far, far, west.
                        (*The Back Country*)

The poem combines friendship and separation, two recurring motifs in classical Chinese poetry. In situation and sentiment the poem evokes something familiar; the concluding passage quoted above especially brings to mind Li Po's poem "A Farewell to Mêng Hao-jan on His Way to Yang-Chou." Snyder's poem can be enjoyed without this kind of knowledge, but it unquestionably gains in poetic dimensions if we know Li Po's original and also Pound's version, "Separation on the River Kiang."[34]

In many of his poems Snyder celebrates love as intrinsic to nature's process. There is nothing prudish about these love poems, ranging from the erotic to the mystical, as in "Bedrock": "On the bedrock, gently tilting, / sky and stone, / teach me to be tender."[35] Such a Lawrentian poetic treatment of love should not be at all surprising in view of his interest in Tantric Buddhism, which makes sexual ecstasy part of its spiritual discipline. Yet he is no Romantic who believes that love dies in marriage. Quite the contrary, marriage, to him, marks the beginning of another cycle, deeper, richer, and more lasting as it eventually leads to the creation of another life. This new genesis is the theme of "No Matter, Never Mind":

The Father is the Void
The Wife   Waves

Their child is Matter.

Matter makes it with his mother
And their child is Life,
              a daughter.

The Daughter is the Great Mother
Who, with her father/brother Matter
              as her lover,

Gives birth to the Mind.
              (*Turtle Island*)

In 1952, while working as a lookout on the Crater Mountain, Snyder jotted down in his journal: "If one wished to write poetry of nature, where an audience? Must come from the very conflict of an attempt to articulate the vision   poetry & nature in our time." Since then he has established himself as a foremost nature poet of contemporary America. In his paper "The Wilderness" (1971) Snyder defined his position in these unequivocal terms: "But the voice that speaks to me as a poet, what Westerners have called the Muse, is the voice of nature herself, whom the ancient poets called the great goddess, the Magna Mater. I regard that voice as a very real entity. At the root of the problem where our civilization goes wrong is the mistaken belief that nature is something less than authentic, that nature is not as alive as man is, or as intelligent, that in a sense it is dead, and that animals are of so low an order of intelligence and feeling, we need not take their feelings into account."[36] Here Snyder was merely restating what he had said in "Piute Creek":

> . . . A million
> Summers, night air still and the rocks
> Warm. Sky over endless mountains.
> All the junk that goes with being human
> Drops away, hard rock wavers
> Even the heavy present seems to fail
> This bubble of a heart.
> Words and books
> Like a small creek off a high ledge
> Gone in the dry air.
> (*Riprap & Cold Mountain Poems*)

Such an ecstatic response to nature is one of Snyder's gifts as man and as poet, and this inborn capacity was undoubtedly reinforced by his long exposure to the Orient, where nature has always been accepted as the ultimate norm of art and life. Quite candidly he mentions his own natural mystical experience about a community or unity of all living creatures. In another lookout journal (1953) he wrote down: "Don't be a mountaineer, be a mountain. And shrug off a few with avalanches."[37] This sense of identity he reaffirmed in "By Frazier Creek Falls":

> This living flowing land
> is all there is, forever
>
> We *are* it
> it sings through us

We could live on this Earth
without clothes or tools!
(*Turtle Island*)

Snyder is a poet much traveled, much experienced, and learned in his own way. Over the last twenty years he has been working on *Mountains and Rivers Without End*. This ongoing project owes its title, conception, and structure to the Orient. The two Chinese characters which represent "mountains" and "rivers," taken together mean "nature" in Far Eastern tradition. As Snyder himself explained in 1959: "Since 1956 I've been working on a long poem I'm calling 'Mountains and Rivers Without End' after a Chinese sidewise scroll painting. It threatens to be like its title. Travel, the sense of journey in space that modern people have lost. . . . The dramatic structure follows a certain type of *No* play."[38] When completed according to his ambitious plans, it may well be Snyder's *chef-d'oeuvre*. In view of his declared intentions and also his finished sections, it would seem that the Orient will continue to loom large in *Mountains and Rivers Without End*.

What seems clear now is that *Mountains and Rivers* is the autobiography of a mid-twentieth-century American poet who said once: "I tried to make my life as a hobo and worker, the questions of history & philosophy in my head, and the glimpses of the roots of religion I'd seen through meditation, peyote, and 'secret frantic rituals' into one whole thing."[39] This poetic autobiography centers on Snyder's ceaseless attempt to "hold history and wilderness in mind"[40]—a hobo in search of the dharma.

Snyder's twofold interest, Amerindian lore and Buddhism, finally finds its focus in *Mountains and Rivers* in the section "The Hump-Backed Flute Player." Here he clarifies his two primary sources of wisdom, represented by Kokopilau and Hsuan Tsang, respectively. Kokopilau, a minor Amerindian deity, sows the seeds packed in the hump on his back and creates warmth with his flute music; and Hsuan Tsang, a seventh-century Chinese Buddhist monk, undertook a long and perilous pilgrimage to India in search of the dharma and brought home, among other things, the Buddhist doctrine of the Void. As Snyder says: "he carried / 'emptiness' / he carried / 'mind only.' " (It was this pilgrimage that turned him into a folk hero, the hero of the *Hsi yu chi*, one of the great classic Chinese novels.) Celebrated travelers, both figures apparently had a special appeal for Snyder. In the section "The Blue Sky" he combines both in the figure of "Old Man Medicine Buddha," the archetypal healer, and thereby justifies his personal conviction about the poet's function as a shaman.[41]

> The Blue Sky
> The Blue Sky
> The Blue Sky
> is the land of

OLD MAN MEDICINE BUDDHA

It is in this capacity as a poet-shaman that Snyder has been involved with the ecological movement. On one occasion he said: "I am a poet. My teachers are other poets, American Indians, and a few Buddhist priests in Japan. The reason I am here is because I wish to bring a voice from the wilderness, my own constituency. I wish to be a spokesman for a realm that is not usually represented either in intellectual chambers or in the chambers of government."[42] He pointed out that the current environmental crisis has been building up for a millennium in Western culture, as in any culture which "alienates itself from the very ground of its own being." As he wrote in *Myths & Texts*: "All America hung on a hook / & burned by men, in their own praise." Yet unlike many of his fellow activists, Snyder does not indulge in hysterics; confident with the wisdom he has absorbed from both the American Indian and the Oriental, he urges us to restore the primitive within us and without. He remains convinced that this is where he can fulfill his proper role, the poet-shaman's role as healer. His attempt "to hold history and wilderness in mind" echoes Thoreau's attempt in *Walden* to combine the hardiness of savages and the intellectualness of civilized men. For his answer Thoreau turned to the Orient and then to the Maine woods, where he could learn the ways of Indians. A century later Snyder comes closer to realizing this dream by bringing both together in his poetry and in his person.

Their varying backgrounds and achievements notwithstanding, Salinger, Kerouac, and Snyder have one thing in common: Their heroes—guru-saint Seymour Glass, Dharma bum Japhy Ryder, archetypal hobo Han-shan—all are alienated from the mainstream of American society. Peripheral figures or outsiders without any recognized status, they stand in sharp contrast to the "organization man" our official culture tends to idolize. From their particular cases it becomes a little clearer why their generation, whether deliberately or desperately, took up drugs, took to the road, or turned toward the Orient.

But such figures are not new in American literature. As we may recall, Hearn branded himself a "civilized nomad," a Bohemian fleeing from his genteel Victorian world. Nor were the writers of the lost generation any exception. Pound and Eliot chose to be expatriates; O'Neill was haunted by memories of sailors, drifters, and denizens of saloons—all failures by conventional standards; even Babbitt urged leisure and meditation, while calling America "the paradise of the half-educated." More or less the same was true of the Transcendental generation, however shocking it may sound. Whitman preferred to be a loafer—as his scandalous frontispiece of the first edition of *Leaves of Grass* made abundantly clear. Thoreau, in his essay "Walking" (1862), defined himself as a "saunterer"—a sort of idler or vagabond. And Emerson, by now perhaps the most venerated and venerable of all American writers, was a rebel in his own day; worse still, he considered himself an idler. In 1836 he wrote in defense: "The scholar works with invisible tools to invisible ends, so passes for an idler, or worse, brain-sick, defenceless to idle carpenters, masons, and merchants." Again, in 1840, "I have been writing with some pains essays on various matters as a sort of apology to my country for my apparent idleness."[43]

This congenial group of idlers, saunterers, and loafers have in time come to be accepted as the Transcendentalists. They seemed idle only in that they would not budge an inch until they heard "the highest command," as Emerson declared in his essay "The Transcendentalist" (1843). No mere idlers, they were all seekers, very serious ones at that. No one expressed this paradox more defiantly than Thoreau. In the above-mentioned essay he, playing his usual etymological game with the word *saunter*, preferred "sainte terre" to "sans terre." Defining a saunterer as "a Holy-Lander," he then concluded: "For every walk is a sort of crusade, preached by some Peter the Hermit in us, to go forth and reconquer this Holy Land from the hands of the Infidels." Loafer that he was, Whitman never tired of celebrating his soul. Similarly, Fenollosa dreamed of his "millennial man," and Hearn of his "perfect sphere." Their footloose Yankee contemporaries, too, once across the Pacific, turned into pilgrims in search of nirvana. This spirit of search led Babbitt to delineate the humanist as an ideal modern, O'Neill to pursue his ever-elusive Taoist paradise, Eliot and Pound to articulate their utopian visions. The beat generation also matured into the beatific generation. Salinger's hero, no mere freak, was a guru-saint; Kerouac's hero, no mere bum, was a Dharma bum, a bum in search of truth; and Snyder's hero, no mere hobo, was a Zen lunatic. It is in this radical transformation of these generations, their heroes, and their visions that the Orient played a crucial role, as we have so far observed.

And as we have also observed, these American writers often invoked explorers. Adams and Pound invoked Ulysses; Adams and O'Neill challenged Marco Polo. More often than not, however, they invoked and identified with Columbus. Hearn hoped to become "a literary Columbus." O'Neill set this play *The Fountain* in the age of Columbus, that

225

great age of discovery. Emerson, while crossing the Atlantic in 1833, reflected: "But to be Columbus, to steer WEST steadily day after day, week after week, for the first time, and wholly alone in his opinion, shows a mind as solitary and self-subsistent as any that ever lived."[44] At that point of his career Emerson himself, cut off from *terra firma* for the first time, was alone on his path toward the unknown future. Whitman spelled out this sense of identification once and for all in his oft-revised poem "Prayer of Columbus." If this poem sealed his personal identification with the great explorer, "Passage to India," likewise, registered the collective, national identification with his heroic search for a western passage to the Orient. America was discovered on his attempted passage to the Orient. The Orient, Columbus, and America have thus become an inseparable triad in the American imagination, the American psyche, as Fenollosa suggested by pairing his occasional poems "The Discovery of America" and "East and West."

In invoking Columbus these writers are not alone. As the discoverer of America he has inevitably stirred the imagination of other American writers over the generations, such as Barlow, Irving, Miller, and MacLeish. Undoubtedly Columbus reigns supreme in American mythology, easily overtowering other figures. No wonder that James, a contemporary of those Yankee pilgrims to Japan, named the hero of his novel *The American* Christopher Newman, though his pilgrimage tended toward the Old World. Through his voyages of discovery Columbus prepared the way for what Crèvecoeur called "a new race of men." In so doing he himself became the first American, so to speak, to lead those "western pilgrims, who are carrying along with them that great mass of arts, sciences, vigour, and industry which began long since in the east."

When Crèvecoeur wrote this in 1782, he probably had in mind the old theory of the course of empire that human civilization progressed as it spread from east to west. The young Emerson incorporated this notion of the westward advance of civilization into his poetic exercise "Improvement" (1820), read before the Pythologian Society at Harvard. In it Emerson wrote that Improvement began in Greece and Rome, and then, with Columbus, crossed the Atlantic in favor of his beloved America: "Oer climes oer ages Empire holds his way / Still [canceled] westward where Destiny's strange pathway lay."[45] And in "Indian Superstition," his exhibition poem of the following year, Emerson more confidently stated that America would deliver its message of liberty to India, the fallen "Queen of the East." With both poems he in his own way reaffirmed the inseparable triad: Columbus, America, India. That is perhaps why in his trans-Atlantic reflection of 1833 he wrote out the word *west* in capital letters.

226

Nor was Thoreau indifferent to Columbus. (One of his early college essays was about Columbus.)[46] And in the essay "Walking" he wrote: "I must walk toward Oregon, and not toward Europe. And that way the nation is moving, and I may say that mankind progress from east to west." Turning as usual to nature, he noted that the sun "appears to migrate westward daily, and tempt us to follow him." "He is the Great Western Pioneer whom the nations follow." Recalling the rich mythical associations grown over the west, Thoreau added: "Columbus felt the westward tendency more strongly than any before. He obeyed it, and found a New World for Castile and Leon." With characteristic insight Thoreau discerned his so-called western impulse behind the westward movement, America's collective endeavors to complete Columbus's passage to India.

Throughout the first half of the nineteenth century, from the time Lewis and Clark reached the shores of the Pacific to the time Oregon and California were added to the union, this notion of a passage to India remained uppermost in the minds of leading advocates of the westward movement. Senator Thomas H. Benton, of Missouri, wrote that Jefferson was "the first to propose the North American road to India, and the introduction of Asiatic trade on that road," and that with this in mind he had sent Lewis and Clark on their famous mission. And Benton himself declared that the future lay with the Pacific, and access to the Orient would become a symbol of freedom and national glory for America. As he summed up in his senate speech of 1825 favoring military occupation of Oregon: "There is the East; there lies the road to India."[47]

Blatantly commercial and political as they were, Benton and his fellow expansionists were just as obsessed with this passage to India as Columbus was. "So rich and compelling was the notion that it remained for decades one of the ruling conceptions of American thought about the West," as Henry Nash Smith pointed out. Whitman's poem "Passage to India" was the sublimation of this popular obsession into the poetical, spiritual realm. If, as Thoreau suggested, this "western impulse" is instinctive with mankind, it should seem doubly so with the American. In the same context Smith called this notion of a passage to India "the oldest of all ideas associated with America."[48] Indeed, it may well be the oldest of all American myths.

For this reason American Orientalism has been no mere exoticism, no mere escapism, no mere dilettantism, but has constituted an authentic part of the American experience; for the same reason American literary Orientalism has been more than a fashion, more than a cult, more than a trend, and has sustained a tradition of remarkable continuity, vitality, and variety. As a literary tradition it has inspired many of our writers and has, in

227

turn, been enriched by them. Having survived many other movements and traditions, it shows no signs of exhaustion; on the contrary, all indications are that it will persist.

This seems odd, to say the least, inasmuch as our ever-increasing contact has shrunk the world, obliterating many of the old barriers between East and West, and inasmuch as the extensive research by specialists in the humanities and social sciences has all but dispelled the romantic aura around the Orient—those stereotyped images of the Orient as something exotic, fabulous, and mysterious. As the entire Orient, in its determined modernization, has turned to the Occident for guidance, the response of these American writers seems anachronistic, reactionary, and ironic, especially because the Orient they have turned to for inspiration is exclusively the archaic, traditional Orient, the philosophical, religious, and spiritual Orient. To that extent these American writers and their European counterparts have shared the same longing for the source of light: *Ex oriente lux*. What is unique about these American writers, however, is their "western impulse." Not only have they turned to the Orient; they have also returned to the Orient. And this return has been to the source of life, or "the house of maternity," as Whitman put it in his poem "Facing West from California's Shores." There he also noted "the circle almost circled": "Now I face home again, very pleas'd and joyous." With these words Whitman confirmed the essential truth of Crèvecoeur's prophecy about the Americans' being "the western pilgrims" destined to "finish the great circle."

American literary Orientalism still looks back to that old genre of the philosophic or allegorical voyage which flourished over the centuries since More's *Utopia*. This genre, we may recall, brought together four traditions old and new: allegory, utopianism, Orientalism, and travel literature. In this genre, which ultimately centers on man's voyage of discovery and quest for self-knowledge, the Orient has invariably served as the mirror-image of the Occident, a sort of symbolic mirror in which it can see itself best. Now these American writers, with their western impulse, have added a new meaning, a sense of return, to man's quest for self-knowledge. With this sense of return, it has become the quest for wholeness. In this sense, too, Kipling was surely wrong when he said: "Oh, East is East, and West is West, / And never the twain shall meet." They have met, are meeting, and will continue to meet, because they are divided only to strive for their original wholeness, as these American writers bear witness.

Notes

NOTES TO *Prologue: Orientalism as a Literary Tradition*

1. Quoted in H. G. Rawlinson, "India in European Literature and Thought," in *The Legacy of India*, ed. G. T. Garratt (Oxford, 1951), p. 8.

2. Quoted in Rawlinson, pp. 18–19.

3. Ibid., p. 26. For a fuller account, see Arthur Christy, "The Sense of the Past," in *The Asian Legacy and American Life* (New York, 1945), pp. 7–8.

4. For a general discussion of these three traditions in connection with Orientalism, see Christy, pp. 10–16, and also William A. Eddy, *Gulliver's Travels* (Oxford, 1923), pp. 8–50. Incidentally, Christy quotes the opening sentence of the *New Atlantis*: "We sailed from Peru, where we had continued for the space of one whole year, for China and Japan, by the South Sea, taking with us victuals for twelve months; and had good winds from the east, though soft and weak, for five months space and more."

5. Rawlinson, pp. 28–30.

6. William W. Appleton, *A Cycle of Cathay* (New York, 1951), p. 92.

7. Quoted in G. F. Hudson, "China and the World," in *Legacy of China*, ed. Raymond Dawson (Oxford, 1964), p. 358.

8. H. G. Creel, *Confucius and the Chinese Way* (New York, 1960), p. 256.

9. Quoted in Creel, p. 261.

10. For an English version of the Chinese original, *Chao shih ku-earh* by Chi Chün-hsiang, see Liu Jung-en, *The Orphan of Chao* (*Six Yüan Plays* [Baltimore, 1972]). Included in the Jesuit J. B. du Halde's *Description of the Chinese Empire and of Chinese Tartary* (1736), this Prémare translation also inspired William Hatchett's play *The Chinese Orphan* (1741). For a discussion of Voltaire's adaptation, see Leonard C. Pronko, *Theater East and West* (Berkeley and Los Angeles, 1967), pp. 35–38.

11. See Arthur O. Lovejoy's article "The Chinese Origin of a Romanticism," *JEGP* 32 (January 1933):1–20.

12. Rawlinson, p. 32.

13. Quoted in Rawlinson, p. 32.

14. Quoted in Christy, p. 40.

15. For a study of this phase, see Earl Miner, *The Japanese Tradition in British and American Literature* (Princeton, 1966).

16. Franklin to George Whitefield, July 6, 1749, *Benjamin Franklin: Representative Selections*, ed. Chester E. Jorgenson and Frank Luther Mott (New York, 1962), p. 198.

17. Franklin to Mrs. Sarah Bache, January 26, 1784, ibid., p. 461.

18. J. P. Rao Rayapati, *Early American Interest in Vedanta* (New York, 1973), p. 59.

19. Creel, p. 5.

20. Henry Nash Smith, *Virgin Land: The American West as Symbol and Myth* (New York, 1957), p. 22.

21. J. Hector St. John Crèvecoeur, *Letters from an American Farmer* (Garden City, N.Y., n.d.), p. 49.

NOTES TO *One: Emerson*

1. H. C. Goddard observed that the whole movement was "in no inconsiderable measure a renaissance" (*Studies in New England Transcendentalism* [New York, 1908], p. 108).

2. Entry of December 7, 1851, *The Journals of Bronson Alcott*, ed. Odell Shepard (Boston, 1938), p. 259.

3. W. T. Harris, "Emerson's Orientalism," in *The Genius and Character of Emerson*, ed. F. B. Sanborn (Boston, 1885), pp. 372–73; Protap Chunder Mozoomdar, "Emerson as Seen from India," ibid., p. 371; and John Jay Chapman, *Emerson and Other Essays* (New York, 1898), p. 46. Immediately following this, however, Chapman wrote: "The whole of his mysticism is to be found in *Nature*, written before he knew the sages of the Orient, and it is not impossible that there is some real connection between his own mysticism and the mysticism of the Eastern poets."

4. Frederic Ives Carpenter, *Emerson and Asia* (Cambridge, Mass., 1930), pp. 15, 13. See also idem, *Emerson Handbook* (New York, 1953), pp. 210–15.

5. Arthur Christy, *The Orient in American Transcendentalism* (New York, 1932), pp. 61–183. In addition to Emerson, Christy also discusses Thoreau and Alcott.

6. Stephen Whicher, *Freedom and Fate* (Philadelphia, 1953), p. 151. It should be noted that Whicher makes no sufficient distinction between Hinduism and Buddhism.

7. Man M. Singh, "Emerson and India" (Ph.D. diss., Pennsylvania State University, 1947), as summarized in Carpenter, *Emerson Handbook*, pp. 210–11.

8. In his doctoral dissertation, "Emerson and Indian Thought" (Wayne State University, 1973), Shukla attempts to show that Emerson's major doctrines are pervaded by Indian thought. Rayapati, on the other hand, concludes that the early American interest in Vedic literature was "of a passing nature," and that Emerson's early interest, likewise, was of slight significance (*Early American Interest in Vedanta* [New York, 1973], pp. 91, 93–101).

9. See Cameron's introductory essay, "Young Emerson's Orientalism at Harvard," *Indian Superstition* (Hanover, N.H., 1954), pp. 13–38.

10. Carpenter, *Emerson and Asia*, p. 235n; and Lin Yutang, *The Wisdom of Laotse* (New York, 1948), pp. 5–6, 13–14.

11. See, for instance, Alan W. Watts, *The Way of Zen* (New York, 1959), pp. 3–28, 81–93 passim, 100, 134.

12. See Van Meter Ames, *Zen and American Thought* (Honolulu, 1962), chapters 1 ("America and Zen") and 5 ("Emerson: American Bodhisattva"); Robert Detweiler, "Emerson and Zen," *American Quarterly* 14 (Fall 1962):422–38; and Donald D. Eulert, "Matter and Method: Emerson and the Way of Zen," *East-West Review* 3 (Winter 1966–67):48–65.

13. See Carpenter, *Emerson and Asia*, pp. 161–94; and Christy, pp. 137–54. See also J. D. Yohannan, "Emerson's Translations of Persian Poetry from German Sources," *American Literature* 14 (January 1943):407–20; and idem, "The Influence of Persian Poetry on Emerson's Work," *American Literature* 15 (March 1943):24–41.

14. Entry of 1845, *The Journals of Ralph Waldo Emerson*, ed. Edward Waldo Emerson and Waldo Emerson Forbes (Boston, 1909–14), 7:126. For Emerson's reponse to China, see Carpenter, *Emerson and Asia*, pp. 232–46; and Christy, pp. 123–37.

15. As Odell Shepard suggested, it appears that Alcott was the only Concord Transcendentalist who had read Laotzu (Alcott, *Journals*, p. xxiii). According to Professor David G. Hoch, Alcott made notes on the *Tao Tĕh King*, tr. John Chalmers (London, 1868), in volume 44 (1869) of his journals, from pages 762 to 771 (letter of February 19, 1981). By 1869, needless to say, Thoreau was gone, and Emerson had already finished his lifework.

16. Entry of December 22, 1839, *Journals*, 5:355; and entry of 1855, ibid., 8:568.

17. In his essay "Nominalist and Realist" (1844) Emerson wrote: "I am faithful again to the whole over the members in my use of books. I find the most pleasure in reading a book in a manner least flattering to the author. I read Proclus, and sometimes Plato, as I might read a dictionary, for a mechanical help to the fancy and the imagination. I read for the lustres, as if one should use a fine picture in a chromatic experiment, for its rich colors."

18. Entry of February 9, 1848, Alcott, *Journals*, p. 202. This appears in connection with his comment on Emerson's reading of Montaigne: "As I read I discern all along my friend's debt to this author. But how happens it that Emerson first found him out? Simply because he found himself there." Cf. Emerson in 1847: "*Scholar, Centrality.* 'Your reading is irrelevant.' Yes, for you, but not for me. It makes no difference what I read. If it is irrelevant, I

read it deeper. I read it until it is pertinent to me and mine, to Nature, and to the hour that now passes'' (*Journals*, 7:256–57).

19. Entry of January 18, 1850: "Sexual qualities seem as needful to the propagation of thought as of human beings, nor do I like any man who never reminds me of the graces proper to women. It is these qualities that we love in a friend. The best of Emerson's intellect comes out in its feminine traits, and were he not as stimulating to me as a woman, and as racy, I should not care to see and know him intimately nor often'' (Alcott, *Journals*, p. 221).

20. Entry of 1857: " 'Masterly inactivity,' 'wise passiveness';—see how much has been made of that feather stolen from the plume of Carlyle by Calhoun and others'' (*Journals*, 9:135). Emerson's "wise passiveness" may recall Wordsworth's following lines in "Expostulation and Reply'': "That we can feed this mind of ours / In a wise passiveness.'' For the Taoist emphasis on this virtue, see the *Tao Te Ching*, chapters 43 and 76.

21. Entry of 1849, *Journals*, 8:56; entry of August 18, 1828, ibid., 2:248; and entry of October 13, 1835, ibid., 3:553.

22. Cf. H. H. Waggoner: "It was of course not simply poetic maturity but intellectual and (I suspect) psychic too that came to Emerson only in his and the century's third decade'' (*Emerson as Poet* [Princeton, 1974], p. 99).

23. Entry of April 4, 1820, *Journals*, 1:21–22. More than a half century later Emerson repeated this statement in his address at the Japanese banquet of August 2, 1872.

24. On the basis of Emerson's early journals, Carpenter reached the same conclusion: "During this time the estimates that he was making of Oriental civilization have been seen to vary between fascination and aversion'' (*Emerson and Asia*, p. 9).

25. Entry of December 19, 1820, *The Journals and Miscellaneous Notebooks of Ralph Waldo Emerson*, ed. William H. Gilman and others, Vol. 1 (Cambridge, Mass., 1960), 48.

26. Entry of July 13, 1822, *Journals*, 1:164; and entry of October 1827, ibid., 2:217.

27. Entry of March 1825, ibid., 2:63.

28. Entry of February 1830, ibid., 2:295; and entry of December 10, 1830, ibid., 2:323.

29. Entry of January 16, 1837, ibid., 4:185; and entry of March 5, 1838, ibid., 4:403–4.

30. Entry of August 14, 1866, Alcott, *Journals*, p. 383. For Alcott's projected "Mankind Library,'' see Christy, pp. 240–42.

31. See Edward C. Lindeman, "Emerson's Pragmatic Mood,'' *American Scholar* 16 (Winter 1946–47):57–64. Stressing Emerson's psychological orientation, he concludes: "There was in all his thought an allegiance to the experimental approach to life, and it was this fidelity to an unfinished but promising world which guarantees his permanent place in American life and thought.'' Incidentally, Lindeman doubts Emerson's debt to Oriental metaphysics.

32. "Emerson,'' *Interpretations of Poetry and Religion* (New York, 1900), p. 218. Cf. Emerson in "Natural History of Intellect'': "My metaphysics are to the end of use.''

33. Entry of 1833, *Journals*, 3:235; and entry of November 15, 1834, ibid., 3:362.

34. With reference to Indian philosophy, Heinrich Zimmer writes: "But the primary concern—in striking contrast to the interests of the modern philosphers of the West—has always been, not information, but transformation: a radical changing of man's nature and, therewith, a renovation of his understanding both of the outer world and of his own existence; a transformation as complete as possible, such as will amount when successful to a total conversion or rebirth'' (*Philosophies of India* [New York, 1958], p. 4).

35. Cf. W. T. Stace: "Buddhism and the higher forms of Hinduism are essentially mystical because the enlightenment experience is their source and centre. . . . Mysticism, which is a major component in Indian religions, is only a minor strand in Christianity, Islam, and Judaism'' (*Mysticism and Philosophy* [Philadelphia, 1960], p. 342).

36. Entry of September 24, 1836, *Journals*, 4:98; entry of March 26, 1839, ibid., 5:179; and entry of April 1826, ibid., 2:95. Emerson writes about picking up "unawares the Master Key'' "after waiting mostly in the vestibule,'' and also about arriving at "one of those general ideas which not only epitomize whole trains of thought, but cast a flood of new light upon things inscrutable before.''

231

NOTES TO PAGES 32–38

37. Christy, p. 65.

38. Cf. Dale Riepe: "That Emerson was deeply influenced by Indian thought cannot be doubted. Furthermore it must be said that his writing would have been different if he had not known it" ("Emerson and Indian Philosophy," *Journal of the History of Ideas* 28 [January–March 1967]:122).

39. *Journals*, 3:489.

40. The italicized passage, which does not appear in the journal entry of March 19, 1835, is meant to paraphrase a brief statement in the original: "I become happy in my universal relations" (*Journals*, 3:452). And the oft-ridiculed "transparent eyeball" grew out of the parenthetical phrase "leaving me my eyes," which is found in both versions. Cf. D. T. Suzuki on Zen enlightenment: "The subject feels as if living in a crystal palace, all transparent, buoyant, and royal. But the end has not yet been reached, this being merely the preliminary condition leading to the consummation called satori" (*Zen Buddhism*, ed. William Barrett [Garden City, N.Y., 1956], p. 102).

41. The first two phrases appear in an entry of May 26, 1837 (*Journals*, 4:248–49), and the third appears in his essay "The Transcendentalist" (1843).

42. Entry of 1841, *Journals*, 5:569. While conceding that Emerson was "a mystic only in the very loosest sense of the term," Patrick F. Quinn points out that "it is scarcely desirable to call Emerson's philosophy, whether in whole or part, mysticism" ("Emerson and Mysticism," *American Literature* 21 [January 1950]:414).

43. Watts, pp. 36, 16.

44. Huston Smith, *The Religions of Man* (New York, 1965), pp. 198–200.

45. Ibid., pp. 204–7.

46. Entry of May 26, 1837, *Journals*, 4:248; and entry of 1851, ibid., 8:211.

47. For an attempt to view this question in terms of Romantic polarity, see Joel Porte, "Emerson, Thoreau, and the Double Consciousness," *New England Quarterly* 41 (March 1968):40–50. See also Anna Mac Powell's doctoral dissertation, "The Evolution of Emerson's Concept of Bipolar Unity and Double Consciousness" (Wayne State University, 1982).

48. Entry of February 13, 1831, *Journals*, 2:356–57.

49. Ibid., 3:454. In the entry of November 3, 1838, he also wrote: "If my wife, my child, my mother, should be taken from me, I should still remain whole, with the same capacity of cheap enjoyment from all things" (ibid., 5:115).

50. Entry of October 1, 1848, ibid., 7:511. For Alcott's interest in the *Gita* as "the best of all reading for wise men," see his various journal entries for May 1846.

51. *The Song of God: The Bhagavad-Gita*, tr. Swami Prabhavananda and Christopher Isherwood (New York, 1951), p. 84. Krishna also declares: "The Lord is everywhere / And always perfect: / What does He care for man's sin / Or the righteousness of man?" (p. 59).

52. Entry of October 13, 1836, *Journals*, 4:115–17.

53. Entry of January 1825, ibid., 2:41–42; "On Showing Piety at Home," *Young Emerson Speaks*, ed. Arthur C. McGiffert (Boston, 1938), p. 17; and "Self-Culture," ibid., p. 99.

54. Emerson used this metaphor as early as 1835, though with somewhat different connotations. In the entry of March 23 he pointed out that the most powerful men in the community had no theory of business: "They skate so fast over a film of ice that it does not break under them" (*Journals*, 3:458.)

55. Suzuki, p. 257. For Zen on the question of time and eternity, see p. 267.

56. Letter to Aunt Mary (Moody Emerson), June 10, 1822; see James Elliot Cabot, *A Memoir of Ralph Waldo Emerson* (Boston, 1887), 1:81. In an entry of the same year Emerson called himself "the pampered child of the East" (*Journals*, 1:108).

57. For his first recorded use of "mine Asia," see the entry of January 8, 1837 (ibid., 4:182).

58. Ibid., 8:36–37.

59. Goddard, p. 109.

60. The East-West Philosophers' Conference, which has met at the University of Hawaii several times since 1939, is, in Charles A. Moore's words, "dedicated to the search for

greater mutual understanding between the Eastern and Western philosophical traditions and to the effort to discover avenues of progress toward a significant synthesis of the ideas and ideals of the Orient and the Occident'' *(Essays in East-West Philosophy* [Honolulu, 1951], p. vii). For an assessment of Emerson in this light, see Kurt Leidecker, ''Emerson and East-West Synthesis,'' *Philosophy East and West* 1 (July 1951):40–50.

61. For their readings, see Carpenter, *Emerson and Asia*, pp. 110–23, and Christy, pp. 164–70. See also K. R. Chandrasekharan, ''Emerson's *Brahma*: An Indian Interpretation,'' *New England Quarterly* 33 (December 1960):506–12.

62. Cf. Perry Miller: ''In the final form, I think it fair to say, Emerson's debt to the Orient is much less than the title suggests: this is not a rendition of anything in the *Bhagavad-Gita*; it is New England's old Puritanism decked out in Oriental imagery'' *(The American Transcendentalists* [Garden City, N.Y., 1957], p. 219). After an extensive discussion of the poem, H. H. Waggoner calls it ''Emerson's strongest expression of his religious intuitions, intuitions he found inexpressible except in the form of paradoxes deriving from the Medieval and Renaissance tradition of 'negative theology' '' (p. 160).

63. Stace lists paradoxicality as one of the major characteristics of mystical experience (pp. 131–32).

64. Christy, pp. 164, 170.

NOTES TO *Two: Thoreau*

1. See Henry Nash Smith, ''Emerson's Problem of Vocation—A Note on 'The American Scholar,' '' *New England Quarterly* 12 (March–December 1939):52–67.

2. Jung writes: ''But we must not forget that only a very few people are artistic in life; that the art of life is the most distinguished and rarest of all the arts'' *(Modern Man in Search of a Soul,* tr. W. S. Dell and Cary F. Baynes [New York, 1939], p. 127).

3. On August 10, 1853, Thoreau wrote with reference to Alcott: ''He observed that he had got his wine [Emerson] and now he had come after his venison [Thoreau]'' *(The Journal of Henry David Thoreau,* ed. Bradford Torrey and Francis Allen [Boston, 1949], 5:365). For a full-scale comparison, see Joel Porte, *Emerson and Thoreau: Transcendentalists in Conflict* (Middletown, Conn., 1966).

4. Entry of March 21, 1853, *Journal,* 5:36.

5. William Ellery Channing, *Thoreau, The Poet-Naturalist,* ed. F. B. Sanborn (Boston, 1902), p. 50.

6. Entry of June 24, *The Journals of Ralph Waldo Emerson,* ed. Edward Waldo Emerson and Waldo Emerson Forbes (Boston, 1909–14), 9:522.

7. Entry of May 31, *Journal,* 1:261; entry of March 23, 1842, ibid., 1:343–44; and entry of 1851, ibid., 2:145.

8. ''The American Scholar.''

9. Arthur Christy, *The Orient in American Transcendentalism* (New York, 1932), p. 65.

10. Quoted in Christy, p. 202.

11. Channing, p. 50.

12. Thoreau's contributions to the series are ''The Laws of Menu'' (January 1843), ''Sayings of Confucius'' (April 1843), ''Chinese Four Books'' (October 1843), and ''The Preaching of Buddha'' (January 1844).

13. Mark Van Doren, *Henry David Thoreau* (Boston, 1916), p. 95.

14. Christy, pp. 185–233. For recent studies of Thoreau's Orientalism, see Walter Harding and Michael Meyer, *The New Thoreau Handbook* (New York, 1980), pp. 113–14.

15. Sherman Paul, *The Shores of America* (Urbana, Ill., 1958), pp. 69–75. Paul's earlier study, *Emerson's Angle of Vision* (Cambridge, Mass., 1952), makes little mention of Emerson's Orientalism.

16. William Bysshe Stein, ''The Hindu Matrix of *Walden:* The King's Son,'' *Comparative Literature* 22 (Fall 1970):303–18. See also his articles ''Thoreau's *Walden* and the

Bhagavad Gita," *Topic,* no. 6, Fall 1963, pp. 38–55; "Thoreau's First Book: A Spoor of Yoga," *ESQ,* no. 41, 4th Quarter 1965, pp. 4–25; and "The Yoga of 'Sounds' in *Walden,"* *Literature East & West* 16 (1972):1111–35.

17. D. T. Suzuki, *Zen and Japanese Culture* (New York, 1959), pp. 342–44; and Van Meter Ames, *Zen and American Thought* (Honolulu, 1962), p. 81.

18. Lin Yutang, *The Importance of Living* (New York, 1937), p. 128n; and idem, *The Wisdom of Laotse* (New York, 1948), pp. 7–8.

19. Paul, pp. 74n, 228n; and Lyman V. Cady, "Thoreau's Quotations from the Confucian Books in *Walden," American Literature* 33 (March 1961):20–32.

20. T. Y. Chen, "Thoreau and Taoism," in *Asian Response to American Literature,* ed. C. D. Narashimhaiah (New York, 1972), pp. 406–16. In this connection, see also Gary Simon, "What Henry David Didn't Know about Lao Tzu: Taoist Parallels in Thoreau," *Literature East & West* 17 (1973):253–71, and Kichung Kim, "On Chuang Tzu and Thoreau," ibid., 275–81.

21. See Chapter 1, n. 15. It must be pointed out that Thoreau knew the term *Tao* from his Confucian sources. In the section "The Taou" of his "Chinese Four Books" (1843) he made several excerpts, such as "Sincerity is the *Taou* or way of heaven. To aim at it is the way of man." See *The Writings of Henry D. Thoreau: Early Essays and Miscellanies,* ed. Joseph J. Moldenhauer, Edwin Moser, and Alexander C. Kern (Princeton, 1975), pp. 148–49.

22. Paul, pp. 70–75.

23. For Emerson's renewed interest in the *Gita,* see his *Letters,* ed. Ralph L. Rusk (New York, 1939), 3:288. His first journal reference to the *Gita* appears in an entry of March 1845 (*Journals,* 7:29). For Alcott's reading of it, see his *Journals,* ed. Odell Shepard (Boston, 1938), especially the entries for May 1846. However, Thoreau's first journal reference appears in the entry of June 26, 1852—a warning to those who attempt to date such matters solely on the basis of his journals.

24. Immediately following this, Thoreau expresses his hope that "the collected scriptures or sacred writings" of several nations, "the Scripture of mankind," will eventually be made available. Most certainly he had in mind his own contributions to the "Ethnical Scriptures" in the *Dial.* In the journal entry of May 8, 1846, Alcott, mentioning Emerson's visit, wrote: "We talked about the *Bhagvat Geeta,* and of printing of the 'Bible of Mankind.' " (*Journals,* p. 180). For his "Mankind Library" project, see Christy, pp. 240–41.

25. In this connection Shanley refers to Thoreau's journal passage of May 6, 1851: "Like some other preachers, I have added my texts—derived from the Chinese and Hindoo scriptures—long after my discourse was written." See *The Making of Walden* (Chicago, 1957), p. 30.

26. Emerson, "Introduction," *Nature.*

27. Entry of April 9, 1840, *Journals,* 5:381.

28. Emerson, "Spirit," *Nature.*

29. See, for example, the *Tao Te Ching,* chapters 8, 55, and 78.

30. Christy, p. 193; and Paul, pp. 352, 353n (the brackets are Paul's).

31. Having found no source for this fable, all Thoreau scholars now assume that it was original with him. In response to my query Professor Barend A. van Nooten writes that the tale would not be out of place in one of the Hindu scriptures, though he doubts its existence (letter of December 26, 1972). Cf. Emerson in "Illusions": "Well, 't is all phantasm; and if we weave a yard of tape in all humility and as well as we can, long hereafter we shall see it was no cotton tape at all but some galaxy which we braided, and that the threads were Time and Nature."

32. *Journal,* 1:92; and ibid., 2:315.

33. Entry of September 11, 1851, ibid., 2:491; entry of October 4, 1851, ibid., 3:41–42; entry of November 17, 1855, ibid., 8:26; and entry of December 15, 1859, ibid., 13:29.

34. As has already been noted, T. Y. Chen points out the similarity between Thoreau's fable of the artist of Kouroo and Chuangtzu's of the royal carpenter Ch'ing. For Chuangtzu's other examples, see Arthur Waley, *Three Ways of Thought in Ancient China* (Garden

City, N.Y., n.d.), pp. 15–16, 47–48. For a discussion of the underlying principle, see his introduction to *The Way and Its Power* (New York, 1958), pp. 58–59.

35. For the significance of the *Gita* in the Vedanta, see S. Radhakrishnan, *The Hindu View of Life* (New York, n.d.), pp. 18–19. For a general discussion of the *Gita*, see Chapter 9.

36. Edward Rose, " 'A World with Full and Fair Proportions': The Aesthetics and the Politics of Vision," *The Western Thoreau Centenary: Selected Papers* (Logan, Utah, 1963), p. 46; and Walter Harding, *The Variorum Walden and the Variorum Civil Disobedience* (New York: 1968), p. 288.

37. The parable appears in the *Mundaka Upanishad*, 3:1, and also in the *Svetasvatara Upanishad*, 4:6. For Tagore's comment, see *The Religion of Man* (New York, 1931), p. 135.

38. *The Bhagvat-Geeta*, tr. Charles Wilkins (London, 1785), pp. 104–5. This edition, which Thoreau used for *A Week*, is now available in a facsimile reproduction with George Hendrick's introduction (Delmar, N.Y., 1972).

39. Letter of November 20, 1849; *Familiar Letters*, ed. F. B. Sanborn (Boston, 1906), p. 175. Cf. "My power of observation and contemplation is much increased. My attention does not wander. The world and my life are simplified" (entry of November 7, 1855); "I was silent; I reflected; I drew into my mind all its members, like the tortoise; I abandoned myself to unseen guides. Suddenly the truth flashed on me." (entry of January 28, 1858).

40. Entry of October 1837, *Journals*, 4:315–16.

41. This passage from "Solitude" on conscious doubleness, together with several others, leads Richard Maurice Bucke to the conclusion that Thoreau, though not an actual exemplar of Cosmic Consciousness, is "yet well on the way thereto" (*Cosmic Consciousness* [Philadelphia, 1905], pp. 244–46). This is especially interesting in view of what Bucke has to say of Emerson: "He was perhaps as near Cosmic Consciousness as it is possible to be without actually entering that realm. He lived in the light of the great day, but there is no evidence that its sun for him actually rose" (ibid., p. 240). Cf. D. T. Suzuki: "There is one who is busily engaged in work and there is another who is not working and quietly unmoved observes all that goes before him. This way of thinking is not Zen. In Zen there is no such separation between worker and observer, movement and mover, seer and the seen, subject and object" (*Zen Buddhism*, ed. William Barrett [Garden City, N.Y., 1956], p. 243). Cf. Swami Nikhilananda on two kinds of samadhi, or enlightenment experience: "In this samadhi one retains consciousness of the individual soul, the body, and the world, and at the same time sees them all as permeated by Brahman, or pure consciousness. In the other samadhi, the I-consciousness is totally obliterated, and there no longer remains any distinction between knower, knowledge, and the object of knowledge" (*Hinduism* [Madras, 1968], p. 127). For Patanjali's distinction, see Chapter 9, n. 40.

42. Richard Drinnon, "Thoreau's Politics of the Upright Man," *Massachusetts Review* 4 (Autumn 1962):135.

43. For an attempt to discern a similar dialectical pattern in Thoreau's career, see Winfield E. Nagley, "Thoreau on Attachment, Detachment, and Non-Attachment," *Philosophy East and West* 3 (January 1954):307–20.

NOTES TO *Three: Whitman*

1. Gay Wilson Allen, *Walt Whitman Handbook* (New York, 1957), p. 450; and H. H. Waggoner, *American Poets* (Boston, 1968), pp. 150–61.

2. John Townsend Trowbridge, *My Own Story: With Recollections of Noted Persons* (Boston, 1903), p. 367.

3. Quoted in William Sloane Kennedy, *Reminiscences of Walt Whitman* (London, 1896), p. 78. In the *Brooklyn Daily Times* for November 16, 1857, Whitman defended Emerson's poem "Brahma": "Some of the papers are poking fun at Emerson on account of the unintelligibility of his little Mystic Song entitled 'Brahma' in the new Atlantic Monthly.

The name of the poem is a facile key to it; Brahma, the Indian Deity, is the absolute and omnipresent god, besides whom all is illusion and fancy, and to whom everything apparent reverts in the end. This pantheistic thought Emerson expresses, not only clearly, but with remarkable grace and melody'' (*I Sit and Look Out*, ed. Emory Holloway and Vernolian Schwarz [New York, 1932], p. 64).

4. Thoreau to H. G. O. Blake, December 7, 1856, *Familiar Letters*, ed. F. B. Sanborn (Boston, 1906), p. 296.

5. For these early views of Whitman's Orientalism, expressed by Conway, Guthrie, Carpenter, Mercer, and others, see Allen, *Walt Whitman Handbook*, pp. 457–62.

6. Malcolm Cowley, Introduction, *Leaves of Grass*, First (1855) Edition (New York, 1968), pp. x–xiii.

7. Quoted in Frederic Ives Carpenter, *Emerson and Asia* (Cambridge, Mass., 1930), p. 250.

8. V. K. Chari, *Whitman in the Light of Vedantic Mysticism* (Lincoln, Nebr., 1964), p. 106.

9. Summarized in Gay Wilson Allen, *The New Walt Whitman Handbook* (New York, 1975), pp. 263–64.

10. T. R. Rajasekharaiah, *The Roots of Whitman's Grass* (Rutherford, N.J., 1970), pp. 440–41.

11. For attempts to relate Whitman to Taoism, see Edward Carpenter, *Days with Walt Whitman* (London, 1906), pp. 100–1, and Walter Karl Malone, ''Parallels to Hindu and Taoist Thought in Walt Whitman'' (Ph.D. diss., Temple University, 1964).

12. For the only obvious reference, see lines 1098–100 in the first edition, or lines 1102–4 in the final edition.

13. *The Complete Writings of Walt Whitman*, ed. Richard Maurice Bucke and others (New York, 1902), 9: pt. 1, no. 7.

14. Namely, ''The House of Friends,'' ''Resurgemus,'' and ''Blood-Money,'' all collected in *Walt Whitman: The Early Poems and Fiction*, ed. Thomas L. Brasher (New York, 1963).

15. Richard Maurice Bucke, *Cosmic Consciousness* (Philadlephia, 1905 ed.), pp. 178–96. In the same place Bucke also writes that this new sense ''must have come to him in June, 1853 or 1854, at the age, that is, of thirty-four or thirty-five'' (pp. 187–88). For a general discussion of Whitman's mysticism, see Allen, *Walt Whitman Handbook*, pp. 241–54.

16. William James, *The Varieties of Religious Experience* (New York, 1958), pp. 80–82, 304. James lists ineffability, noetic quality, transiency, and passivity as four major characteristics of mystical experience.

17. Evelyn Underhill, *Mysticism* (New York, 1955), pp. 238, 255, 192. Underhill quotes from Whitman's ''Prayer of Columbus.'' In this study she makes no special reference to either Emerson or Thoreau.

18. W. T. Stace, *Mysticism and Philosophy* (Philadelphia, 1960), pp. 174, 15–16. Stace is especially valuable for his full use of Eastern documents.

19. Heinrich Zimmer, *Philosophies of India* (New York, 1958), pp. 43–45. He also uses the term *liberation*.

20. See Stace, p. 81; Underhill, p. 272; and Edward Carpenter, pp. 55, 51. For Bucke's discussion of Carpenter, see *Cosmic Consciousness*, pp. 196–209.

21. *Walt Whitman's Workshop*, ed. Clifton Joseph Furness (Cambridge, Mass., 1928), pp. 185–86. In his introduction Furness also writes that Whitman's ''conception of the function of the creative imagination was practically identical with the religious intuition of the Quaker faith'' (p. 13).

22. See, for example, S. K. De, *Sanskrit Poetics as a Study of Aesthetics* (Berkeley and Los Angeles, 1963); Mai-mai Sze, *The Tao of Painting* (New York, 1956); and D. T. Suzuki, *Zen and Japanese Culture* (New York, 1959). See also Thomas Munro, *Oriental Aesthetics* (Cleveland, 1965).

23. Quoted in *Walt Whitman's Workshop*, p. 188. In this connection Furness also quotes

Thomas Donaldson: "Mr. Whitman worked in a desultory manner. For days he would not write. . . . 'You know, in writing poetry, the machine won't always work . . . usually I have to wait to until it does.' . . . I do not believe, and this is strengthened by the fact that he so intimated it, in relation to a minor poem, that, when Mr. Whitman started a theme in verse, or prose, he had the remotest idea when he would make port, or how he would land. He said to me, 'I just let her come, until the fountain is dry' " (*Walt Whitman, the Man* [New York, 1896], pp. 74, 75, 125). Quoting Morris's account, Kennedy also notes: "It thus appears that Walt Whitman's method of composition resembled that of Emerson, his envelopes answering to Emerson's commonplace-books" (*Reminiscences of Walt Whitman*, pp. 24–25).

24. In his essay "The Poet" (1844) Emerson wrote:

> It is a secret which every intellectual man quickly learns, that beyond the energy of his possessed and conscious intellect he is capable of a new energy (as of an intellect doubled on itself), by abandonment to the nature of things; that beside his privacy of power as an individual man, there is a great public power on which he can draw, by unlocking, at all risks, his human doors, and suffering the ethereal tides to roll and circulate through him; then he is caught up into the life of the Universe, his speech is thunder, his thought is law, and his words are universally intelligible as the plants and animals. . . . As the traveller who has lost his way throws his reins on his horse's neck and trusts to the instinct of the animal to find his road, so much we do with the divine animal who carries us through this world.

25. In his note: "He evidently thinks that behind all faculties of the human being, as the sight, the other senses and even the emotions and the intellect stands the real power, the mystical identity, the real I or Me or You" (*Complete Writings*, 9: pt.1, no. 28).

26. *Uncollected Poetry and Prose*, ed. Emory Holloway (New York, 1921), 2:66. This statement appears in Manuscript Notebook I (1847?).

27. With specific reference to these similar observations Chari writes: "The similarity between these ideas and the utterances of the Gita and the Upanishads is unmistakable; the Indian scriptures might have possibly been the sources for Emerson as well as Thoreau" (p. 74).

28. *Walt Whitman's Workshop*, p. 200.

29. *Complete Writings*, 9: pt. 2, no. 10. Whitman's self-induced mental flight seems akin to what parapsychologists call astral flight. Interesting in this connection is the series of visions Jung experienced in a state of unconsciousness following his heart attack. See his *Memories, Dreams, Reflections* (New York, 1965), pp. 289–90, 295.

30. Leo Spitzer, " 'Explication de Text' Applied to Walt Whitman's 'Out of the Cradle Endlessly Rocking,' " *ELH* 16 (Spring 1949):229–49.

31. Emory Holloway, *Whitman: An Interpretation in Narrative* (New York, 1926), p. 162.

32. For this episode in the beginning sections of the epic, see C. Rajagopalachari, *Ramayana* (Bombay, 1971), pp. 15–16. Cf. Krishna Chaitanya: "The episode about how the poem arose is no mere anecdote, but a profound parable of the creative process" (*A New History of Sanskrit Literature* [London, 1962], p. 171). For the significance of the episode, see also Barbara Stoler Miller, "The Original Poems: Vālmīki-Rāmāyana and Indian Literary Values," *Literature East & West* 17 (1973):163–69.

33. In his notes on "Indian Epic Poetry," an article which appeared in the *Westminister Review* for October 1848, Whitman duly refers to both the *Ramayana* and the *Mahabharata* as "two most ancient Indian poems," along with their respective authors, Valmiki and Vyasa (*Complete Writings*, 9: pt. 3, no. 25). Incidentally, the article makes no mention of this episode about the krauncha birds.

34. *Leaves of Grass*, ed. Sculley Bradley and Harold W. Blodgett (New York, 1973), pp. 242–43n.

35. In the writings of Emerson and Thoreau Japan appears far less frequently than India and China—an understandable fact in view of its isolationist policy prior to 1868. Thoreau

wrote in 1853: "The whole enterprise of this nation, which is not an upward, but a westward one, toward Oregon, California, Japan, etc., is totally devoid of interest to me. . . . What end do they propose to themselves beyond Japan? What aims more lofty have they than the prairie dogs?'' (Thoreau to H. O. G. Blake, February 27, *Familiar Letters*, p. 210). Emerson, on the other hand, had lived long enough to see Japan's emergence on the international scene. In "Progress of Culture," his second Phi Beta Kappa speech of 1867, he noted that Oriental wisdom—Indian, Chinese, and Japanese—was now "part of our own." And five years later, in his address at a Japanese banquet, he showed his knowlege of Japanese arts, national character, and interest in education.

36. *Eureka* is a different case, however. For an interesting approach to it from an Oriental perspective, see D. Ramakrishna, "Poe's *Eureka* and Hindu Philosophy," *ESQ*, no. 47 (1967), pp. 28–32.

37. See Allen, *Walt Whitman Handbook*, p. 354; Chari, p. 88; and Rajasekharaiah, p. 335. Citing this and other poems, however, Tony Tanner writes: "But just from these moments of doubt and worried silence we can extract a hint of the possible dangers and limitations of the naive vision: i.e. its inability to assimilate discordant facts, its vulnerability to the harsher textures of existence, the likelihood of its being irrecoverably bruised and stunned by the darker side of human life whenever it should happen to stumble upon it" (*The Reign of Wonder: Naivety and Reality in American Literature* [Cambridge, 1965], pp. 73–74.

38. Introduction to the London edition (*Walt Whitman's Workshop*, p. 150).

39. James E. Miller, Jr., *Walt Whitman* (New York, 1962), pp. 92–97; and Cowley, pp. xiv–xx.

40. Underhill writes: "Now it [the transcendental self] seizes upon the ordinary channels of expression; and may show itself in such forms as *(a)* auditions, *(b)* dialogues between the surface consciousness and another intelligence which purports to be divine, *(c)* visions, and sometimes *(d)* in automatic writings. In many selves this automatic activity of those growing but largely subconscious powers which constitute the 'New Man,' increases steadily during the whole of the mystic life" (pp. 240–41).

41. George R. Carpenter, *Walt Whitman* (New York, 1924), p. 55.

42. Quoted in Carpenter, *Emerson and Asia*, p. 250.

43. Chari, pp. 120–27.

44. Rajasekharaiah, p. 392.

45. Preface of 1876.

46. Horace L. Traubel, *With Walt Whitman in Camden* (Boston, 1906), 1:156.

47. Cowley, p. xxx.

48. Chari, p. 116.

49. Gay Wilson Allen, *A Reader's Guide to Walt Whitman* (New York, 1970), pp. 202, 207.

50. *Walt Whitman's Workshop*, p. 201. The brackets are Furness's.

51. Mircea Eliade, *Myths, Dreams, and Mysteries*, tr. Philip Mairet (New York, 1967), p. 44.

52. The same sailing imagery also appears in Whitman's note for an abortive lecture on Hegel: "It [the soul] escapes utterly from all limits, dogmatic standards and measurements and adjusts itself to the ideas of God, of space, and to eternity, and sails them at will as oceans, and fills them as beds of oceans" (*Complete Writings*, 9: pt. 2, no. 175). Cf. Plotinus to Flaccus: "I applaud your devotion to philosophy: I rejoice to hear that your soul has set sail, like the returning Ulysses, for its native land—that glorious, that only real country—the world of unseen truth" (quoted in Bucke, p. 101).

53. Whitman wrote to Ellen O'Connor: "As I see it now I shouldn't wonder if I have unconsciously put a sort of autobiographical dash in it" (quoted in Bradley and Blodgett, p. 420n.) Cf. Bucke: "It was written about 1874–75, when the condition of the poor, sick, neglected spiritual explorer was strikingly similar to that of the heroic geographical explorer shipwrecked on the Antillean Island in 1503, at which time and place the prayer is supposed to be offered up" (p. 192).

54. To quote Mrs. Gilchrist further: "You too have sailed over stormy seas to your goal—surrounded with mocking disbelievers—you too have paid the great price of health—our Columbus" (quoted in Bradley and Blodgett, p. 421n.).

NOTES TO *Four: Yankee Pilgrims in Japan*

1. Samuel Eliot Morison quotes the following passage from Columbus's own copy of Marco Polo's *Travels:* "The king of the Island [Japan] hath a mighty palace all roofed with finest gold, just as our churches are roofed with lead. The windows of that palace are all decorated with gold; the floors of the halls and of many chambers are paved with golden plates, each plate a good two fingers thick. There are pearls in the greatest abundance." (*Admiral of the Ocean Sea* [Boston, 1942], p. 237).

2. Goncourt and Wilde are quoted in Earl Miner, *The Japanese Tradition in British and American Literature* (Princeton, 1966), pp. 66 and 86, respectively.

3. *Selections from Cotton Mather*, ed. Kenneth B. Murdock (New York, 1926), p. 307.

4. Chapter III, "The Pacific," *Moby Dick*. For a discussion of Melville's interest in the Orient, see James Baird, *Ishmael* (Baltimore, 1956).

5. He was approached for the assignment while serving as U.S. Consul in Liverpool. In his journal for December 28, 1854, Hawthorne also wrote: "The world can scarcely have in reserve a less hackneyed theme than Japan" (quoted in Miner, p. 18).

6. Lawrence W. Chisolm, *Fenollosa: The Far East and American Culture* (New Haven, 1963), pp. 36–37.

7. For Morse's career, see Frederick W. Coburn, "Morse, Edward Sylvester," *DAB* (1934), and also Dorothy G. Wayman, *Edward Sylvester Morse* (Cambridge, Mass., 1942).

8. For an account of this group of Americans, see Van Wyck Brooks's lead essay in *Fenollosa and His Circle* (New York, 1962), pp. 1–68. Brooks compares Morse to a magnet in this regard.

9. In his entry of October 6, 1877, Morse wrote: "I gave my first lecture in a course of three on Evolutionism to-night in the large college hall. A number of professors and their wives and from five hundred to six hundred students were present, and nearly all of them were taking notes. It was an interesting and inspiring sight. . . . The audience seemed to be keenly interested, and it was delightful to explain the Darwinian theory without running up against theological prejudice as I often did at home" (*Japan Day by Day* [Boston, 1917] 1:339–40).

10. For his career, see John F. Fulton, "Bigelow, William Sturgis," *DAB* (1929).

11. Quoted in Brooks, p. 26. According to Brooks, it was Morse who persuaded Bigelow to accompany him to Japan.

12. This "Ingersoll lecture on the Immortality of Man" was published as *Buddhism and Immortality* (Boston, 1908).

13. One of Bigelow's notes on the conversations he and Fenollosa had with Archbishop Keitoku reads: "The real object of life is to acquire freedom from the ties that limit consciousness by connecting it with the material world (to the law of which it habitually conforms). The real object of religion is to facilitate the acquisition of such freedom" (quoted in Brooks, p. 52). For Henry Adams's comment on Bigelow's interest in Buddhism, see Chisolm, pp. 107–8.

14. Adams to John Hay, July 9, 1886, *Letters of Henry Adams (1858–1891)*, ed. Worthington Chauncey Ford (Boston, 1930), p. 366.

15. *Henry Adams: The Middle Years* (Cambridge, Mass., 1958), pp. 290–93.

16. Cf. Motoshi Karita: "Adams was only interested in pleasure seeking" ("Henry Adams in Japan," *Studies in English Literature*, English Number [1962], p. 147).

17. Adams to Hay, July 24, 1886, *Letters*, pp. 371–72.

18. Adams to Hay, July 9, 1886, ibid., pp. 366–69.

19. Ibid., p. 367.

20. Adams to Elizabeth Cameron, August 13, 1886, ibid., p. 373.

21. Adams to Hay, August 25, 1886, ibid., pp. 377–78. Apparently, Adams was referring to Marquis Nabeshima, late Lord of Hizen (Saga Prefecture). Both Hizen and Satsuma were famous for their potteries.

22. Karita, p. 149.

23. Adams to Hay, July 9, 1886, *Letters*, p. 367.

24. La Farge also quotes from the Taoist Chuangtzu's story about the Yellow Emperor and a shepherd boy: "My sight is now better, and I continue to dwell outside of the points of the compass" (*An Artist's Letters from Japan* [New York, 1897] p. 116), and in *Reminiscences of the South Seas* he returns to the same passage: "And at the thought of dropping him [the sun], the old Taoist wish of getting outside the points of the compass comes over me, the feeling that leads me to travel. Can we never get to see things as they are, and is there always a geographical perspective?" ([Garden City, N.Y., 1916] p. 67).

25. *The Education of Henry Adams* (New York, 1931), pp. 369–72.

26. See Royal Cortissoz, "La Farge, John," *DAB* (1933).

27. Although the statue has been popularly named *Grief*, Adams himself called it *Peace of God*, and La Farge called it *Kwannon*. For the circumstances surrounding the statue from conception to execution, see M. K. Bequette, "Adams, La Farge, Saint-Gaudens and *Grief*," *Forum* 12 (1975):2–7. Cf. La Farge: "Hence, also, the difficulty, I had almost said the impossibility, of finding a designer to-day capable of making a *monument:* say, for instance, a tomb, or a commemorative, ideal building—a cathedral, or a little memorial. There is no *necessity* in such forms of art, nothing to call into play the energies devoted to usefulness, to getting on, to adaptation, to cleverness, which the same Taoist says is the way of man, while integrity is the way of God" (*An Artist's Letters from Japan*, p. 106).

28. Related in Adams to Hay, June 11, 1886, *Letters*, p. 366.

29. Adams to Hay, July 24, 1886, ibid., p. 372.

30. Adams to Cameron, September 8, 1891, ibid., pp. 525–26.

31. Ernest Samuels, *Henry Adams: The Major Phase* (Cambridge, Mass., 1964), pp. 56–57.

32. The episode which inspired Adams's poem is found in *The Questions of King Milinda*, tr. T. W. Rhys Davids, Pt. 1 (Oxford, 1890), 204–6. According to Samuels, Adams read Max Müller's version, "Mâlunkya-putta and Buddha," in *Natural Religion* ([London, 1889], pp. 105–8). For Samuels's extended discussion of the poem, see *Henry Adams: The Major Phase*, pp. 58–64.

33. Adams to Hay, October 20, 1886, quoted in Samuels, *Henry Adams: The Middle Years*, p. 312.

34. Adams to Charles Milnes Gaskell, December 12, 1886, *Letters*, p. 382.

35. Samuels, *Henry Adams: The Middle Years*, p. 321.

36. Hay to Sir John Clark, ibid., p. 321.

37. Adams to Cameron, May 19, 1889, *Letters*, p. 398.

38. Samuels, *Henry Adams: The Middle Years*, p. 414.

39. For an analysis of Adams's failure in this light, see Lynn White, Jr., "Dynamo and Virgin Reconsidered," *American Scholar* 27 (Spring 1958):183–94. White concludes: "We have been too easily impressed by the dualities of Descartes and by the majestic symbols of his disciple, Henry Adams. Closely observed, experience does not in fact fall into neat opposing categories—spirit and matter, religion and technology, man and cosmos, cathedral and powerhouse. Reality is more complex than this, and its parts more intricately interlocked. Man is a bit cosmic; the cosmos is a bit humane; and the free man may worship without despair."

40. For his career, see Raymond S. Dugan, "Lowell, Percival," *DAB* (1933).

41. Chamberlain to Hearn, January 10, 1893, *Letters from Basil Hall Chamberlain to Lafcadio Hearn*, ed. Kazuo Koizumi (Tokyo, 1936), pp. 2–6.

42. Hearn to Chamberlain, January 1895, *The Life and Letters of Lafcadio Hearn*, ed. Elizabeth Bisland (Boston, 1906), 2:200; Hearn to Chamberlain, February 1895, ibid., p. 208; and B. H. Chamberlain, *Things Japanese* (London, 1905), pp. 166n, 66. Chamberlain on *The Soul of the Far East*: "With a dazzling array of metaphysical epigrams, this distinguished Bostonian attacks the inner nature of the Japanese soul, whose hallmark he

discovers in 'impersonality.' Nothing on earth—or elsewhere—being too profound for an intellect so truly meteor-like in its brilliancy'' (p. 66).

NOTES TO *Five: Fenollosa*

1. For a full-length study of his career, see Lawrence W. Chisolm, *Fenollosa: The Far East and American Culture* (New Haven, 1963).
2. The best historical survey of this subject is George B. Sansom, *The Western World and Japan* (New York, 1950).
3. B. H. Chamberlain, "Foreign Employés in Japan," *Things Japanese* (London, 1905), pp. 181–85.
4. For further information on this matter, see Shinichi Kurihara, *Fenollosa and Meiji Culture*, Japanese text (Tokyo, 1968), especially chapter 5.
5. Chamberlain, "Education," *Things Japanese*, pp. 131–35.
6. Quoted in Chisolm, pp. 50–51.
7. Kurihara, pp. 312–15.
8. Quoted in Van Wyck Brooks, *Fenollosa and His Circle* (New York, 1962), p. 66.
9. Quoted in Chisolm, p. 86.
10. While getting ready for a summer trip to the southern provinces of Japan, Edward Morse wrote in his diary: "We shall see a little of the life of old Japan; I shall add a great many specimens to my collection of pottery; Dr. Bigelow will secure many forms of swords, guards, and lacquer; and Mr. Fenollosa will increase his remarkable collection of pictures, so that we shall have in the vicinity of Boston by far the greatest collection of Japanese art in the world" (*Japan Day by Day* [Boston, 1917], 2:239).
11. Chisolm, pp. 89–93.
12. Ibid., pp. 153–64, 177–95.
13. Ibid., p. 211.
14. "Fenollosa, Ernest Francisco," *DAB* (1931).
15. Mary McNeil, Fenollosa's second wife, wrote fiction and poetry. For further information, see Chisolm, p. 198.
16. Hence Fenollosa's low opinion of Tokugawa art. Cf. Henry Adams: "Fenollosa and Bigelow are stern with us. Fenollosa is a tyrant who says we shall not like any work done under the Tokugawa Shoguns. As these gentlemen lived two hundred and fifty years or thereabouts, to 1860, and as there is nothing at Tokio except their work, La Farge and I are at a loss to understand why we came; but it seems we are to be taken to Nikko shortly and permitted to admire some temples there. On secret search in Murray, I ascertain that the temples at Nikko are the work of Tokugawa Shoguns. I have not yet dared to ask about this apparent inconsistency for fear of rousing a fresh anathema" (Adams to Hay, July 9, 1886, *Letters of Henry Adams 1858–1891*, ed. Worthington Chauncey Ford [Boston, 1930], p. 367).
17. Chisolm, pp. 130–49.
18. For further information, see Hugh Kenner, *The Pound Era* (Berkeley and Los Angeles, 1971), p. 198.
19. See, for instance, Chisolm, pp. 222–23; and Kenner, pp. 197–98.
20. Introductory note to *The Chinese Written Character as a Medium for Poetry* (San Francisco, n.d.), p. 3.
21. Kenner, p. 198.
22. Morse, 2:401–2.
23. Chisolm, pp. 137–39. Chisolm quotes from Mary Fenollosa's diary entry of January 12, 1899: "E[rnest] thinks of nothing but Noh."
24. *The Classic Noh Theatre of Japan* (New York, 1959), p. 27n.
25. Ibid., p. 155.
26. Introductory note to *The Chinese Written Character as a Medium for Poetry*, p. 3.
27. George Kennedy, "Fenollosa, Pound and the Chinese Character," *Yale Literary Magazine* 126 (December 1958):24–36.

28. Emerson, "Language," *Nature*.

29. Cf. George Kennedy: "But the fact is that such images as appear through the sort of analysis illustrated above are not present in the mind of the Chinese reader, because he has never thought of them. They were unknown to the compiler of the etymological dictionary of 100 A.D. It is more than likely that they were unknown to the Chinese poet himself, who used the characters as arbitrary symbols for the words of his poem" (34).

30. Donald Davie, *Articulate Energy* (London, 1955), pp. 33–34. Davie also tests Sidney and other poets in terms of Fenollosa's precepts with the conclusion that Shakespeare "does all that Fenollosa says" (p. 51). For a more recent study of this subject, see Carol Ann Bays's doctoral dissertation, "Ernest F. Fenollosa: New Perspectives in Poetics" (Wayne State University, 1978).

31. Chisolm, pp. 17–19, 133, 198–200. According to Chisolm, some of Fenollosa's ideas were incorporated in his wife's novels; *The Breath of the Gods* (1905) and *The Dragon Painter* (1906) have especially "Fenollosan touches" (p. 199n).

32. Quoted in Chisolm, p. 101.

33. For a summary discussion of the speech, see Chisolm, pp. 127–29. In his article "Chinese and Japanese Traits" Fenollosa wrote: "What now do I mean by individuality? Surely not that sickly cast of thought, that morbid self-consciousness which is sometimes spoken of as the feeling of personality. This has been necessarily absent from creative periods, whether in the East or in the West. I mean by individuality, not the self of which we think, but the self by which we do. It is the power to produce freshly from within, to react and adapt under rapid change of environment. It transcends institution, custom, love of approbation, fear of disapproval, all slowly acting forces of sheer mass. It is spontaneous origination, the salt of social life, the last hope of a race" (*Atlantic Monthly* 69 [June 1892]: 770–71).

34. Chisolm, pp. 22–23

NOTES TO *Six: Hearn*

1. For Hearn's career, see Orcutt W. Frost, *Young Hearn* (Tokyo, 1958); Edward L. Tinker, *Lafcadio Hearn's American Days* (New York, 1924); and Elizabeth Stevenson, *Lafcadio Hearn* (New York, 1961). This chapter is based on my longer study, *An Ape of Gods: The Art and Thought of Lafcadio Hearn* (Detroit, 1964).

2. Hearn to B. H. Chamberlain, April 19, 1893, *The Japanese Letters of Lafcadio Hearn*, ed. Elizabeth Bisland (Boston, 1910), pp. 85–89. See also his letter of March 4, 1894 (ibid., pp. 261–62).

3. Hearn to Chamberlain, February 2, 1894, ibid., pp. 243–44.

4. Cf. Chamberlain: "They [the Japanese, emotionally and intellectually] appear to me far inferior to the European race,—at once less balanced, less tender, and less imaginative" (letter of August 4, 1891, *Letters from Basil Hall Chamberlain to Lafcadio Hearn*, ed. Kazuo Koizumi [Tokyo, 1936], p. 57).

5. Hearn to Chamberlain, July 15, 1894, *Japanese Letters*, p. 341.

6. Chamberlain to Hearn, May 10, 1894, *Letters*, p. 140.

7. Chamberlain to Hearn, July 17, 1894, *More Letters from Basil Hall Chamberlain to Lafcadio Hearn*, ed. Kazuo Koizumi (Tokyo, 1937), p. 142. The Tempo period (1830–44) here stands for Old Japan.

8. Yone Noguchi, *Lafcadio Hearn in Japan* (Yokohama, 1910), p. 128. The circumstances surrounding Hearn's resignation were never clarified, though he himself suspected that it had been engineered by "the politico-religious combination."

9. John Erskine, *Interpretations of Literature* (New York, 1915), 1:ix; and Norman Foerster, review of *Interpretations of Literature, Dial*, (February 3, 1916), pp. 112–14.

10. Takeshi Saito, "English Literature in Japan: A Sketch," in *Western Influences in Modern Japan*, ed. Inazo Nitobe and others (Chicago, 1931), p. 191.

11. Hearn to H. E. Krehbiel, December 1883, *The Life and Letters of Lafcadio Hearn*, ed. Elizabeth Bisland (Boston, 1906), 1:294–95.

12. Chamberlain, *Things Japanese* (London, 1905), p. 264; and Adams to John Hay, July 9, 1886, *Letters of Henry Adams (1858–1891)*, ed. Worthington Chauncey Ford (Boston, 1930), p. 367.

13. *Glimpses of Unfamiliar Japan* (Boston, 1894), 2:656–83.

14. Percival Lowell, *Occult Japan* (Boston, 1894), p. 321; Hearn, *Gleanings in Buddha-Fields* (Boston, 1897), pp. 162–203; Adams to Hay, August 13, 1886, *Letters*, p. 373; and Hearn, *Japan: An Attempt at Interpretation* (New York, 1904), p. 393. Cf. Chamberlain: "Japanese women are most womanly,—kind, gentle, faithful, pretty" (*Things Japanese*, p. 500).

15. Yoshie Okazaki, *Japanese Literature in the Meiji Era*, tr. V. H. Viglielmo (Tokyo, 1955), p. 572. Cf. Earl Miner: "The West and Japan have shared the idea that he [Hearn] has understood Japan as no Westerner ever had before or is likely to again and, in certain rather limited senses, this is true" (*The Japanese Tradition in British and American Literature* [Princeton, 1966], p. 65). Cf. Lawrence W. Chisolm: "Among all the images of Japan projected by Fenollosa's American friends onto the screen of American thinking, Hearn's came closest to conveying the texture and spirit of Japanese life. Japan was the final enthusiasm of Hearn's restless career in search of a peace that his imagination could render beautiful" (*Fenollosa: The Far East and American Culture* [New Haven, 1963], p. 147).

16. "Sayonara," *Glimpses of Unfamiliar Japan*, 2:687.

17. William E. Griffis, *Critic* 46 (February 1905):186. The same reviewer concluded: "This book is destined to live, and to cause searchings of heart among those who imagine that the Japanese soul has been changed in fifty years."

18. Hearn to Mrs. Elizabeth Wetmore (née Bisland), *Life and Letters*, 2:505.

19. Percival Lowell, *The Soul of the Far East* (New York, 1888), p. 226.

20. Interesting in this regard is William W. Clary, *Japan: The Warnings and Prophecies of Lafcadio Hearn* (Claremont, Calif., 1943).

21. Lowell, *The Soul of the Far East*, p. 4.

22. Hearn to Chamberlain, January 14, 1893, *Japanese Letters*, pp. 30–31.

23. Edward Morse, *Japan Day by Day* (Boston, 1917), 2:401–2.

24. See note 22 above.

25. Hearn to Ellwood Hendrick, *Life and Letters*, 2:120.

26. Hearn to Chamberlain, June 19, 1893, *Japanese Letters*, p. 122.

27. "Of the Eternal Feminine," *Out of the East* (Boston, 1895), pp. 85–125. For his lecture on the same topic, see "The Insuperable Difficulty," *Interpretations of Literature* 1:1–6.

28. George Gould, *Concerning Lafcadio Hearn* (Philadelphia, 1908), pp. 175–76.

29. Adams to Hay, August 25, 1886, *Letters*, p. 377.

30. See Lowell, *The Soul of the Far East*, chapters "Nature and Art" and "Art."

31. Cf. John La Farge in "An Essay on Japanese Art": "Japanese composition in ornamental design has developed a principle which separates it technically from all other schools of decoration. This will have been noticed by all who have seen Japanese ornamental work, and might be called a principle of irregularity, or apparent chance arrangement" (Raphael Pumpelly, *Across America and Asia* [New York, 1870], p. 197).

32. Hearn to Chamberlain, *Life and Letters*, 2:39–40. Lowell's original statement reads: "*the degree of individualization of a people is the self-recorded measure of its place in the great march of mind*" (*The Soul of the Far East*, p. 195).

33. Hearn to Chamberlain, January 14, 1893, *Japanese Letters*, pp. 30–33; and Hearn to Hendrick, November 1893, *Life and Letters*, 2:150. For Fenollosa's criticism of Lowell's thesis of personality, see Chisolm, p. 128.

34. See Hearn to Chamberlain, January 14, 1893, *Japanese Letters*, pp. 30–33.

35. Hearn to Chamberlain, January 19, 1893, *Japanese Letters*, pp. 38–40.

36. The article appeared in the *Atlantic Monthly*, April 1896, and was later collected in *Karma*, ed. Albert Mordell (New York, 1918), pp. 110–63.

37. "Ants," *Kwaidan* (Boston, 1904), pp. 215–40. See also his lecture "Beyond Man," *Interpretations of Literature*, 2:220–27.

38. "Reflections," *Japan: An Attempt at Interpretation*, pp. 504–5. Cf. W. E. Hocking:

"In my judgment, we shall have no just estimate of our own social order until we have understood the philosophical bases of this Oriental outlook, in which the lot of the individual is not immersed in, but entwined with, the fortunes of a corporate group or groups, whether the family, the occupational group, or the nation" ("Value of the Comparative Study of Philosophy," in *Philosophy—East and West*, ed. Charles A. Moore [Princeton, 1946], p. 10).

39. "Of Moon-Desire," *Exotics and Retrospectives* (Boston, 1898), p. 177.

40. *Japan: An Attempt at Interpretation*, p. 232. Hearn is cited several times in Ananda Coomaraswamy's *Buddha and the Gospel of Buddhism* (London, 1916). His essays on Buddhism are conveniently collected in Kenneth Rexroth's edition, *The Buddhist Writings of Lafcadio Hearn* (Santa Barbara, Calif., 1977). For an attack on his Buddhist studies, see Arthur Kunst, *Lafcadio Hearn* (New York, 1969), pp. 89–90.

41. "In the Twilight of the Gods," *Kokoro* (Boston, 1896), p. 211.

42. *Victorian Philosophy*, ed. Ryuji Tanabe (Tokyo, 1930), p. 46. For similar views, see S. Radhakrishnan, *Eastern Religions and Western Thought* (Oxford, 1939), and F. S. C. Northrop, *The Meeting of East and West* (New York, 1946).

43. *In Ghostly Japan* (Boston, 1899), p. 200. With this in mind Hearn defined the poet as "a man who is half a woman" (*Life and Literature*, ed. John Erskine [New York, 1917], pp. 24–25).

44. Matthew Josephson, *Portrait of the Artist as American* (New York, 1930), pp. 199–231; and Harry Levin, "The Discovery of Bohemia," in *Literary History of the United States*, ed. Robert E. Spiller and others (New York, 1974), pp. 1070–72.

45. "A Ghost" appeared in *Harper's Magazine*, December 1889, and was later collected in *Karma*, pp. 59–69.

46. The phrase appears in the following passage: "Even in fiction we learn that we have been living in a hemisphere only; that we have been thinking but half-thoughts; that we need a new faith to join past with future over the great parallel of the present, and so to round out our emotional world into a perfect sphere. The clear conviction that the self is multiple, however paradoxical the statement seem, is the absolutely necessary step to the vaster conviction that the many are One, that life is unity, that there is no finite, but only infinite" ("The Idea of Preëxistence," *Kokoro*, pp. 248–49). Using the same phrase, Thoreau wrote in "The Service" (1840): "But the brave man is a perfect sphere, which cannot fall on its flat side and is equally strong every way. . . . Only by resigning ourselves implicitly to the law of gravity in us shall we find our axis coincident with the celestial axis, and by revolving incessantly through all circles acquire a perfect sphericity." Similarly, Emerson wrote in his journal for 1851: "I don't like linear, but spheral people; but discontent merely shows incompleteness as you measure yourself by times and events; as soon as you express yourself, you will round" (*Journals*, ed. Edward Waldo Emerson and Waldo Emerson Forbes [Boston 1909–14], 8:230).

47. Hearn once wrote: "The beauty is really in that psychic truth of the desire to melt into another being—the fable of Salmacis and Hermaphroditus" (Hearn to Chamberlain, May 10, 1984, *Japanese Letters*, p. 308).

Notes to *Seven: Babbitt*

1. For a historical sketch of the controversy, see "The Battle of the Books," in *Literary History of the United States*, ed. Robert E. Spiller and others (New York, 1974), pp. 1135–56. The fact that one contributor appears in both *Humanism and America* and *The Critique of Humanism* indicates the confusing and confused situation. It should also be noted that George Santayana joined the controversy with his *Genteel Tradition at Bay* (New York, 1931).

2. For a study of Babbitt from this perspective, see Louis J. A. Mercier, *The Challenge of Humanism: An Essay in Comparative Criticism* (New York, 1933).

3. Louis J. A. Mercier, in *Irving Babbitt: Man and Teacher*, ed. Frederick Manchester and Odell Shepard (New York, 1941), p. 204.

4. For an epigraph to the volume Babbitt quotes his favorite passage from Emerson's "Ode": "There are two laws discrete, / Not reconciled— / Law for man, and law for thing; / The last builds town and fleet, / But it runs wild, / And doth the man unking."

5. Cf. Henry Hazlitt in "Humanism and Value": "Rousseau and his doctrines have become an obsession with him [Babbitt]—one might almost say a monomania—and they play for him the rôle that the devil and his temptations did for the medieval saint" (*The Critique of Humanism: A Symposium*, ed. C. Hartley Grattan [New York, 1930], p. 94).

6. Paul Elmer More, in *Irving Babbitt: Man and Teacher*, pp. 325–26.

7. "What I Believe: Rousseau and Religion" originally appeared in the *Forum*, February 1930, and was later collected in *Spanish Character and Other Essays* (Boston, 1940).

8. "Humanism: An Essay at Definition" appeared in *Humanism and America*, ed. Norman Foerster (New York, 1930), pp. 25–51.

9. Obviously Babbitt had in mind the *Chung Yung*, or *Doctrine of the Mean*, which Pound later translated under the title *The Unwobbling Pivot*. See Chapter 10.

10. Harry Levin, "Irving Babbitt and the Teaching of Literature," *Refractions: Essays in Comparative Literature* (New York, 1966), pp. 336, 338. The essay was the author's inaugural lecture as the first Irving Babbitt Professor of Comparative Literature at Harvard.

11. For Lévi's recollection of Babbitt at the Sorbonne, see *Irving Babbitt: Man and Teacher*, pp. 34–35.

12. Victor M. Hamm, ibid., p. 314. Hamm also relates More's account of Babbitt's "power of profound meditation." During his last confinement, when his wife suggested that he read detective stories—a hobby of his friend More's—as a way of combatting his pain, Babbitt reportedly said: "Detective stories? Good Lord, no! I can still meditate" (Levin, p. 334).

13. *Irving Babbitt: Man and Teacher*, pp. 332–33. In the same tribute More also mentions that his own early interest centered on the Sanskrit literature of the *Upanishads*, the *Bhagavad-Gita*, and the Vedantic philosophy—in other words, Hinduism.

14. René Wellek, "Irving Babbitt, Paul More, and Transcendentalism," in *Transcendentalism and Its Legacy*, ed. Myron Simon and Thornton H. Parsons (Ann Arbor, 1966), p. 194.

15. William F. Giese, in *Irving Babbitt: Man and Teacher*, p. 5; and Frank Jewett Mather, Jr., ibid., pp. 43–44.

16. C. Hartley Grattan, "The New Humanism and the Scientific Attitude," in *The Critique of Humanism*, p. 28; and Henry-Russell Hitchcock, Jr., "Humanism and the Fine Arts," ibid., p. 215; and Henri Massis, as summarized by Kenneth Burke, "The Allies of Humanism Abroad," ibid., p. 177. Burke designates T. S. Eliot as the link between the New Humanists and *L'Action française*. For Henri Massis's warning against the danger of Orientalism, see his *Defense of the West*, tr. F. S. Flint (New York, 1928).

17. Although Babbitt did not have much to say about Japan, what he said on one occasion is worth noting: "Let us ask ourselves again whether the chances of a clash between America and Japan are likely to diminish if Japan becomes more democratic, if, in other words, the popular will is substituted for the will of a small group of 'elder statesmen.' Any one who knows what the Japanese sensational press has already done to foment suspicion against America is justified in harboring doubts on this point" (*Democracy and Leadership* [Boston, 1924], p. 267).

18. The review originally appeared in the *Atlantic Monthly*, October 1899, and was later collected in *Spanish Character and Other Essays*, pp. 141–49.

19. Although it is difficult to date Babbitt's interest in China, K. T. Mei writes that in 1915, when he went to Harvard "to sit at the feet of this new sage," Babbitt was "already fully informed on Confucius and the early Taoists, though he had not yet said anything about them in print." Mei also points out: "By all odds, [Babbitt] was the first Western writer to appreciate the quintessential humanism of the Confucian teaching and see the affinity of the early Taoists with modern Western apostles of naturalism, thereby establishing the two main opposing views of life that represent and divide the two universal orders of mind" (*Irving Babbitt: Man and Teacher*, pp. 119–20). When Mrs. Babbitt, who was reared in China, reminded him of his lack of firsthand knowledge of the country, he is said

to have maintained that "the five senses do not permit us to the truth—no, nor the deep truth—about a country" (ibid., p. 217).

20. "Romanticism and the Orient" originally appeared in the *Bookman*, December 1931, and was later collected in *On Being Creative and Other Essays* (Boston, 1932), pp. 235–61.

21. "Buddha and the Occident," *The Dhammapada* (New York, 1965), pp. 65–121. The essay once again makes it clear that Babbitt has little sympathy with Taoism or Mahayana Buddhism for that matter. Although agreeing with Babbitt over "the extravagant perversions" of Chinese and Japanese Buddhism, More nevertheless distinguishes Christianity from Buddhism. As he puts it, Jesus offers "a vision of divine purpose at work in the world, an inexhaustible hope,—which the pursuit of the Eightfold Path of the Buddha can never quite attain." "Buddhism, I think," he continues, "at the last may be accepted as a preface to the Gospel, 'lovely in its origin, lovely in its progress, lovely in its end,' and as the most convincing argument withal that truth to be clearly known waits upon revelation" ("Buddhism and Christianity," *The Catholic Faith* [Princeton, 1931], pp. 74–75).

22. Cf. Arthur O. Lovejoy: "[Babbitt] has attained the distinction of having damned a larger number of eminent and long accepted writers than any other modern critics" (quoted in Keith F. McKean, *The Moral Measure of Literature* [Denver, 1961], pp. 60–61). Cf. René Wellek: "Inevitably, we shall come to the conclusion that Babbitt indulged in an imperceptive wholesale condemnation of the whole modern world and modern literature" (p. 186).

23. Babbitt wrote: "In general the humanist will not repudiate either sentimental or scientific naturalism; for this would be to attempt an impossible reaction. His aim is not to deny his age, but to complete it" (*Literature and the American College* [Boston, 1908], pp. 258–59).

24. Cf. Harry Levin: "Babbitt, according to More, was 'greater as a teacher than a writer,' and possibly greatest of all as a talker" (p. 335).

25. Among the contributors were T. S. Eliot, Norman Foerster, Van Wyck Brooks, Austin Warren, Theodore Spencer, Walter Lippmann, Newton Arvin, Harry Levin, Granville Hicks, and Crane Brinton.

26. T. S. Eliot, "Second Thoughts about Humanism," review of Foerster's *American Criticism* (*Selected Essays* [London, 1963] p. 481).

27. Cf. W. T. Stace: "There is no doubt that [scientific] naturalism, with its corollary of the futility of human life, has brought despair into the world. It is the root-cause of the modern spiritual malaise" (*Religion and the Modern World* [Philadelphia, 1952], p. 233). Cf. J. D. Hoeveler, Jr.: "Although the Humanists were often unable to offer a realistic cure for the ills they diagnosed, their diagnosis was always a perceptive one. At their best they offered a thorough critique, a useful alternative to the prevailing liberalism of their generation of thinkers" (*The New Humanism: A Critique of Modern America 1900–1940* [Charlottesville, Va., 1977], pp. vii–viii).

28. Austin Warren writes: "In becoming a citizen of the world he never saw the necessity for ceasing to be an American" (*Irving Babbitt: Man and Teacher*, p. 217). G. R. Elliott also paraphrases Babbit's classroom utterance: "America, now inundated with contemporaneity, must rediscover the noblest heights of thought in the past, the whole long past, Occidental and Oriental, of which she is the inheritor" (ibid., p. 155).

NOTES TO *Eight: O'Neill*

1. Irving Babbitt, *On Being Creative and Other Essays* (Boston, 1932), p. 237.

2. John Henry Raleigh, in his research survey, duly notes O'Neill's "great interest in the Orient and its creeds," though he discusses only two articles in this connection. See *Fifteen Modern American Authors*, ed. Jackson R. Bryer (Durham, N.C., 1970), p. 318.

3. Frederic Ives Carpenter, "Emerson, Asia, and Modern America," *Emerson and Asia* (Cambridge, Mass., 1930), pp. 252–54.

4. *Transcendentalism and Its Legacy*, ed. Myron Simon and Thornton H. Parsons (Ann

Arbor, 1966), pp. 204–13. Cf. Virginia Floyd: "What was possibly his first total exposure to Taoism had a profound—and lasting—effect on him" (*Eugene O'Neill at Work* [New York, 1981], p. 114).

5. For this information I am indebted to Dr. Donald Gallup, curator at the Yale University Library. He also points out: "I find no other references to the play and I doubt that O'Neill ever got around to working on it" (letter of March 30, 1978). According to Floyd, in 1925 O'Neill recorded two ideas for plays dealing with the public and private lives of pre-Christian despotic rulers: the "Lives of Caesars" and the "Career of Shih Huang Ti." See her lengthy discussion of O'Neill's notes for the latter (pp. 114–20).

6. James A. Robinson, *Eugene O'Neill and Oriental Thought: A Divided Vision* (Carbondale, Ill., 1982), pp. 185–86.

7. O'Neill to Richard Madden, September 14, 1928, quoted in Arthur and Barbara Gelb, *O'Neill* (New York, 1960), p. 678.

8. Ibid., p. 798.

9. Ibid., p. 930, as related by Charles Kennedy. He also adds: "We joked over the possibility that perhaps he was rewriting *Marco Millions* in his sleep." Apparently inspired by *Karma* (1918), a play by Blackwood and Violet Pearn, O'Neill wrote in his notebook (1918–20): "Idea for long—reincarnation—oldest civilization, China 1850 (?)—modern times during war—South Sea Island, 1975—Some crises offering a definite choice of either material (i.e. worldly) success or a step toward higher spiritual plane—Failure in choice entails immediate reincarnation and eternal repetition in life on this plane until spiritual choice is made" (Floyd, p. 32).

10. Doris Alexander, "Eugene O'Neill and *Light on the Path*," *Modern Drama* 3 (December 1960):261–62. As her source Alexander refers to O'Neill's letter to Martha Carolyn Sparrow, October 13, 1929, quoted in her doctoral dissertation, "Influence of Psychoanalytical Material on the Plays of Eugene O'Neill" (Northwestern University, 1931), p. 77. Although the Gelbs point out that Carlin (really Terrence O'Carolan) had "a greater effect on O'Neill's philosophy than any other living man," they make no mention of *Light on the Path* (pp. 281–94).

11. Robinson, pp. 50–84. In this connection Robinson also notes the importance of O'Neill's third wife, Carlotta Monterey, an avid student of Chinese culture (pp. 3, 23).

12. Robert Mayo stands for what O'Neill, in his account of the source of *Beyond the Horizon*, calls "a vague, intangible wanderlust." See Barrett H. Clark, *Eugene O'Neill: The Man and His Plays* (New York, 1947), p. 66.

13. Ibid., p. 101.

14. Alexander, "Eugene O'Neill and *Light on the Path*," p. 267.

15. From the above-mentioned letter to Sparrow, October 13, 1929, as quoted in Doris Alexander, "*Lazarus Laughed* and Buddha," *Modern Language Quarterly* 17 (December 1956):359.

16. O'Neill to Barrett H. Clark, 1919, quoted in Clark, *Eugene O'Neill*, p. 59.

17. O'Neill to Arthur Hobson Quinn, quoted in Quinn, *A History of the American Drama* (New York, 1927), 2:199.

18. For an English version, see Robert Payne, "The Peach-Blossom Fountain," *The White Pony* (New York, n.d.), pp. 132–33.

19. For George Jean Nathan's account of this episode, see Clark, *Eugene O'Neill*, pp. 107–9.

20. Based on O'Neill's manuscript revisions of the play, John H. Stroupe writes: "O'Neill's changes again seem to be motivated by one dominant factor: all the alterations serve to emphasize the spirituality of Eastern culture and the crassness of the Western, widening the gulf between the two. At the same time, they heighten the dramatic effect by making the Western figures the corrupting influence upon the East" ("*Marco Millions* and O'Neill's 'Two Part Two-Play' Form," *Modern Drama* 13 [February 1971]:388). See also his earlier article, "O'Neill's *Marco Millions*: A Road to Xanadu," ibid. 12 (February 1970):377–82.

21. Alexander, "*Lazarus Laughed* and Buddha," pp. 357–65. Cf. D. V. K. Raghavacharyulu: "But a more basic resemblance, even though O'Neill himself may not have been

aware of it, is between Lazarus and Krishna. In fact, Krishna alone of the religious heroes, like Lazarus, is immediately concerned with the fear of death, advising Arjuna, who wavers on the field of battle, that death is non-existent" (*Eugene O'Neill: A Study* [Bombay, 1965], p. 83).

22. See note 17 above.

23. Frederick Ives Carpenter, *Eugene O'Neill* (New York, 1964), p. 120.

24. Babbitt wrote: "In general, the primacy accorded to will over intellect is Oriental. The idea of humility that man needs to defer to a higher will, came into Europe with an Oriental religion, Christianity" (*Democracy and Leadership* [Boston, 1924], p. 6).

25. "Working Notes and Extracts from a Fragmentary Work Diary," reprinted in Barrett H. Clark, *European Theories of the Drama* (New York, 1947), p. 530.

26. For a comparison of both trilogies, see Clark, *Eugene O'Neill*, pp. 122–37.

27. Clark, *European Theories of the Drama*, p. 533. In his work diary of 1929 O'Neill justifies his choice of a New England setting: "(New England background best possible dramatically for Greek plot of crime and retribution, chain of fate—Puritan conviction of man born to sin and punishment—Orestes' furies within him, his conscience—etc.)" (p. 531). Inasmuch as O'Neill, while making notes for the "Career of Shih Huang Ti" in May and July 1929, was also working on this trilogy, Floyd suggests that A. E. Grantham's references to the Taoist "mystic island of P'êng lai" and the "wonder-islands" may have inspired O'Neill's description of the "Blessed Islands" (p. 119n).

28. In his study *Ishmael* James Baird writes: "E. S. Craighill Handy, the Pacific ethnologist, has concluded that Tahiti and its neighboring islands were in all probability the center from which Asiatic influences were disseminated throughout Oceania. Thus the culture of all outlying island areas may be traced to Tahiti. As the traits of this 'old' culture are followed beyond Polynesia to the Asiatic mainland, the true prototypes are discovered in Hindu civilization" ([Baltimore, 1956], pp. 174–75). For his remarks on O'Neill in this regard, see pp. 69–70.

29. According to Robinson, *Dynamo* already marked O'Neill's ebbing interest in Eastern mysticism, and his trip to China completed the process. For this reason he has little to say about *Mourning Becomes Electra* (pp. 165–66).

30. Carpenter, *Eugene O'Neill*, pp. 36–43, 79.

31. Quoted in Gelb and Gelb, *O'Neill*, p. 681.

32. Reprinted in *O'Neill and His Plays*, ed. Oscar Cargil and others (New York, 1961), p. 116.

33. Agnes Boulton, *Part of a Long Story* (New York, 1958), p. 200. As O'Neill himself admitted the "dump" in the play combines the three places where he hung out in his early twenties: Jimmy the Priest's, the Hell Hole, and the taproom of the Garden Hotel (Floyd, p. 260).

34. "*The Iceman Cometh*," an interview by Karl Schriftgriesser, *New York Times*, October 6, 1946, sec. 2, p. 1.

35. Ibid., p. 3.

36. In O'Neill's first tentative list of characters Slade appears as Terry [Carlin]: "Who sees and is articulate about real meaning of what is going on—who regrets they can't leave themselves alone—can't forgive themselves for not being what they are not—" (Floyd, p. 261).

37. Citing this particular passage, Robinson writes: "He thereby confesses the futile hypocrisy of his Eastern mask. . . . The Irishman Larry Slade cannot escape his Catholic upbringing, nor can Eugene O'Neill, for his ironic debunking of Larry's mysticism represents an implicit admission of the futility of Oriental approaches for himself" (p. 176).

38. Eliot wrote: "I should like to say that I place his work very high indeed, and *A Long Day's Journey Into Night* seems to me one of the most moving plays I have ever seen" (quoted in *O'Neill and His Plays*, p. 168).

39. For Eugene M. Waith's use of "epiphanies" in this particular context, see "Eugene O'Neill: An Exercise in Unmasking," *Educational Theatre Journal* 13 (October 1961): 182–91. It is worth quoting Waith's conclusion: "This is O'Neill at his best. In these last

plays he gave up his reliance on elaborate theatrical contrivance and attempted no forcing of his muse to rhapsodic heights. As a result his genuine gifts are seen to the best advantage. These plays are a kind of unmasking of their author."

40. For a discussion of this aspect of O'Neill, see Henry F. Pommer, "The Mysticism of Eugene O'Neill," *Modern Drama* 9 (May 1966):26–39. Pommer quotes Mrs. Carlotta O'Neill's response to his inquiry: "The 'speech' you mention was often discussed by O'Neill and me—and led to further conversation of like experiences that were interesting to think of." Agnes Boulton also writes: "At times, however, Gene must have achieved briefly a sense of that expanded consciousness in which the self, forgotten, becomes one with whatever is behind the veil; he speaks of it in a prose poem the next fall, which he gave me as a gift; and perhaps, in those beautiful and moving lines that Edmund speaks near the end of *Long Day's Journey into Night*—" (p. 257). For the role of Oriental mysticism in the shaping of O'Neill's art as "a redemption of the melodramatic form," see Mary Miceli Ryba's doctoral dissertation, "Melodrama as a Figure of Mysticism in Eugene O'Neill's Plays" (Wayne State University, 1977). Noting that Edmund's ecstatic glimpses vanish all too quickly, Robinson writes: "As a non-Oriental, O'Neill can abandon the self and passively experience belonging only 'for a second' before he is 'alone, lost in the fog again.' The play's central symbol, the fog, thickens during the play, pointing to the inescapable confusion and loneliness that were O'Neill's heritage as both a 'haunted Tyrone' and a Western man. And the steady march of Mary and the other Tyrones into the past demonstrates—as does the very act of writing the play—O'Neill's inability to effect escape from history, despite his momentary mystical withdrawals from time" (p. 177).

41. Nancy Wilson Ross, *The World of Zen: An East-West Anthology* (New York, 1960), pp. 313–14.

42. See note 17 above.

43. See note 15 above.

44. *Light on the Path* (Madras, 1975), pp. 15–16. On completing an outline for the play, O'Neill wrote in his Work Diary: "will have to be written in blood—but will be a great play, if done right" (Floyd, p. 292).

45. Alexander, "Eugene O'Neill and *Light on the Path*," p. 260.

NOTES TO *Nine: Eliot*

1. "Second Thoughts about Humanism," *Selected Essays* (London, 1963), p. 481.

2. For Eliot's relationship with Babbitt at Harvard, see Herbert Howarth, *Notes on Some Figures Behind T. S. Eliot* (Boston, 1964), pp. 127–35.

3. Austin Warren, "Continuity in T. S. Eliot's Literary Criticism," in *T. S. Eliot: The Man and His Work*, ed. Allen Tate (New York, 1966), p. 282.

4. "The Humanism of Irving Babbitt," *Selected Essays*, p. 480.

5. Cf. Babbitt in "Buddha and the Occident": "Schopenhauer knew little about the authentic teaching of Buddha, but his error is so fundamental that it is doubtful whether he would have corrected it even if he had been more adequately informed" (*The Dhammapada* [New York, 1965], p. 101).

6. Cf. Robert Sencourt: "Besides, despite all his study, there was something in Indian philosophy he [Eliot] did not quite understand—and never would. It was a matter of temperament" (*T. S. Eliot: A Memoir* [New York, 1971], p. 53). Immediately following his statement quoted here, Eliot continues: "And I should imagine that the same choice would hold good for Chinese thought: though I believe that the Chinese mind is very much nearer to the Anglo-Saxon than is the Indian" (*After Strange Gods* [London, 1934], p. 44).

7. *Christianity and Culture* (New York, 1949), p. 114. In a footnote Eliot also writes that Conrad's *Heart of Darkness* has "a hint of something similar."

8. Ibid., "Appendix," pp. 190–91.

9. This *Paris Review* interview by Donald Hall was later collected in *Writers at Work*, 2d ser., ed. Van Wyck Brooks (New York, 1968), pp. 96–97. Mary Hutchinson, a friend of

Eliot's, who read the poem soon after its completion, said that it was "Tom's autobiography" (Lyndall Gordon, *Eliot's Early Years* [Oxford, 1978], p. 86).

10. In the same interview Eliot explained his French poems as a way out of this impasse: "At that period [between "Prufrock" and "Gerontion"] I thought I'd dried up completely. I hadn't written anything for some time and was rather desperate" (*Writers at Work*, p. 98).

11. See Elizabeth Drew, *T. S. Eliot: The Design of His Poetry* (New York, 1949), chapters "The Mythical Vision" and "The Mythical Method."

12. Raymond Tschumi, quoted in C. D. Narasimhaiah, "Notes towards an Indian Response to T. S. Eliot's Poetry," in *Indian Response to American Literature*, ed. C. D. Narasimhaiah (New Delhi, 1967), p. 122; Stephen Spender, "Remembering Eliot," in *T. S. Eliot: The Man and His Work*, p. 40; and G. Nageswara Rao, "The Upanishad in The Waste Land," in *Asian Response to American Literature*, ed. C. D. Narasimhaiah (New York, 1972), pp. 84–91.

13. "The Fire-Sermon," *Buddhism in Translations*, ed. Henry Clarke Warren (Cambridge, Mass., 1953), pp. 351–53.

14. Eliot to Bertrand Russell, October 15, 1923. Quoted in Russell, *Autobiography*, vol. 2 (London, 1968), 173.

15. For this fable in the *Brihadaranyaka Upanishad*, 5:2, see *The Upanishads*, tr. Swami Prabhavananda and Frederick Manchester (New York, 1957), p. 112.

16. F. O. Matthiessen, *The Achievement of T. S. Eliot* (Boston, 1935), p. 51.

17. Cleanth Brooks, *Modern Poetry and the Tradition* (Chapel Hill, N.C., 1939), p. 165.

18. Drew, pp. 64, 78, 89–90.

19. Narasimhaiah, pp. 124–30; and Rao, pp. 84–91.

20. Narasimhaiah, p. 133.

21. Kamal Wood, "The Poetry of the Way and the Poetry of Arrival: A Comparative Study of Some Images in *Four Quartets* and The Upanishads," in *Asian Response to American Literature*, pp. 76–83.

22. Harold E. McCarthy, "T. S. Eliot and Buddhism" *Philosophy East and West* 2 (April 1952):39; and Russell T. Fowler, "Krishna and the 'Still Point': A Study of The *Bhagavad-Gita*'s Influence in Eliot's *Four Quartets*," *Sewanee Review* 79 (July–September 1971):408. Interesting in this regard is Eloise Knapp Hay's view that in his later poems, especially *Four Quartets*, Eliot uses Buddhism in support of Christian experience. See her study *T. S. Eliot's Negative Way* (Cambridge, Mass., 1982), pp. 67, 69, 93, 187–88.

23. *The Song of God: Bhagavad-Gita*, tr. Swami Prabhavananda and Christopher Isherwood (New York, 1951), p. 75.

24. Eliot expresses the same thought in the concluding lines of his poem "To the Indians Who Died in Africa": "Let those who go home tell the same story of you: / Of action with a common purpose, action / None the less fruitful if neither you nor we / Know, until the moment after death, / What is the fruit of action."

25. Helen Gardner, *The Art of T. S. Eliot* (New York, 1959), p. 173n.

26. "Dante" (1929), *Selected Essays*, p. 258.

27. *Criterion* 16 (January 1937):290.

28. Fowler, 411, 423.

29. Review for the *Adelphi*, as quoted in Neville Braybrooke, *T. S. Eliot: A Critical Essay* (n.p., 1967), p. 46.

30. "The 'Pensées' of Pascal" (1931), *Selected Essays*, p. 405. Gordon provides Eliot's reading list in mysticism during the period 1908–14 (pp. 141–42). For a study of this aspect of Eliot, see Fayek M. Ishak, *The Mystical Philosophy of T. S. Eliot* (New Haven, 1970), and Nadine Dyer, "T. S. Eliot: 'A Taste for Mysticism' " (Ph.D. diss., Wayne State University, 1983).

31. In Eliot's radio talk on Charles Williams, as quoted in Kristian Smidt, *Poetry and Belief in the Work of T. S. Eliot* (Oslo, 1949), p. 156. Smidt also refers to the "rare moments of inattention and detachment" Eliot mentions in his essay on Marston (*Selected Essays*, p. 232).

32. Gardner, pp. 185–86; and Sencourt, p. 189.

33. W. T. Stace, *Mysticism and Philosophy* (Philadelphia, 1960), p. 173. With reference to another passage from "East Coker" beginning with "In order to arrive at what you do not know," Stace also writes: "There are mystical overtones in the poetry of Eliot which seem to go beyond mere rhetoric" (p. 254). Cf. Kristian Smidt: "I merely contend, then, that Eliot's supreme visions are not concretely and specifically Christian. They are as closely akin to those of Oriental as to those of European mystics" (p. 160).

34. Quoted in Willian Turner Levy and Victor Scherle, *Affectionately, T. S. Eliot* (Philadelphia, 1968), p. 41.

35. *The Song of God: Bhagavad-Gita*, p. 56.

36. In connection with Eliot's repeated use of "Fare forward"—in "Animula," *Murder in the Cathedral, Four Quartets*, and *The Cocktail Party*. See David E. Jones, *The Plays of T. S. Eliot* (Toronto, 1960), pp. 219-20.

37. Philip R. Headings, *T. S. Eliot* (New York, 1964), p. 114.

38. Grover Smith, *T. S. Eliot's Poetry and Plays* (Chicago, 1965), p. 220.

39. Headings, p. 153. He continues: "The compound of psychic content from Eastern and Christian religions seen in *The Cocktail Party* suggests Eliot's earlier poetic usage of such elements from as early as *The Waste Land* to the later *Four Quartets* and *The Family Reunion*, and it is also paralleled outside religious institutionalism in published writings and rituals of Freemasonry."

40. See Chapters 1–3. In view of what Eliot had to say about Patanjali, it is interesting to note the latter's distinction of two kinds of samadhi: savitarka and nirvitarka, savichara and nirvichara. See Swami Prabhavananda and Christopher Isherwood, *How to Know God: The Yoga Aphorisms of Patanjali* (New York, 1969), pp. 55–57.

41. *The Song of God: Bhagavad-Gita*, p. 48.

42. Headings, p. 163.

43. The following discussion of Eliot as a critic of society and culture is based on my article "The *Gita*, the *Comedy*, and Eliot," *English Language and Literature*, nos. 51–52 (1974), pp. 227–47.

44. Headings, p. 136. See also Sencourt, p. 189.

45. See, for instance, Henry W. Wells, "The Bhagavad Gita and the Divine Comedy," *Literary Half-Yearly* 9 (January 1968):37.

46. S. Radhakrishnan, *The Hindu View of Life* (New York, n.d.), p. 76.

47. Allan H. Gilbert points out that this sense of justice lies at the heart of the *Comedy* (*Dante's Conception of Justice* [Durham, N.C., 1925], p. 144).

48. For a discussion of the caste system, see R. P. Masani, "Caste and the Structure of Society," in *The Legacy of India*, ed. G. T. Garratt (Oxford, 1951), pp. 124–61. For a forceful defense of the caste system, see Ananda Coomaraswamy, "What Has India Contributed to Human Welfare?" *The Dance of Shiva* (New York, 1957), pp. 3–21.

49. In his address "Catholicism and International Order" (1933) Eliot, urging restoration of "the classical conception of wisdom," concludes: "There must always be a middle way, though sometimes a devious way when natural obstacles have to be circumvented; and this middle way will, I think, be found to be the way of orthodoxy; a way of mediation, but never, in those matters which permanently matter, a way of compromise" (*Essays Ancient and Modern* [New York, 1936], p. 141).

50. For Eliot's view that harmony with nature "must be re-established if the truly Christian imagination is to be recovered by Christians," see *A Choice of Kipling's Verse* (New York, 1943), p. 33. In insisting on man's harmony with the elemental process of nature Eliot is primitivistic. From this anthropological point of view he readily acknowledges the significance of Lawrence's primitivism: "The struggle to recover the sense of relation to nature and to God, the recognition that even the most primitive feelings should be part of our heritage, seems to be the explanation and justification of the life of D. H. Lawrence, and the excuse for his aberrations" (*Christianity and Culture*, p. 49). For Eliot's view of natural law as a bridge between theology and behavior, see Roger Kojecky, *T. S. Eliot's Social Criticism* (New York, 1971), pp. 145–56, 177–78, 182–83.

51. In the *Definition of Culture* Eliot also observes: "But when I speak of the family, I have in mind a bond which embraces a longer period of time than this: a piety towards the

dead, however obscure, and a solicitude for the unborn, however remote. Unless this reverence for past and future is cultivated in the home, it can never be more than a verbal convention in the community. Such an interest in the past is different from the vanities and pretensions of genealogy; such a responsibility for the future is different from that of the builder of social programmes" (*Christianity and Culture*, pp. 116–17). In this regard it may not be irrelevant to recall what Eliot has to say about the Cacciaguida episode in the *Paradiso* ("Dante," *Selected Essays*, p. 264).

52. Pointing out that Eliot's idea of a graded society has "a kind of Utopian sanction, which makes criticism difficult or impossible," Raymond Williams concludes: "If Eliot, when read attentively, has the effect of checking the complacencies of liberalism, he has also, when read critically, the effect of making complacent conservatism impossible" (*Culture and Society 1780–1950* [Garden City, N.Y., 1960], p. 260).

NOTES TO *Ten: Pound*

1. T. S. Eliot, *After Strange Gods* (London, 1934), pp. 43–45. The lectures were delivered in 1933 at the University of Virginia.

2. This interview by Donald Hall appeared in the *Paris Review*, 28 (1962) and was later collected in *Writers at Work*, 2d ser., ed. Van Wyck Brooks (New York, 1968), p. 48.

3. "The Renaissance," *Literary Essays*, ed. T. S. Eliot (New York, 1968), p. 215.

4. Noel Stock, *The Life of Ezra Pound* (New York, 1970), p. 176.

5. In this connection Earl Miner emphasizes Pound's early interest in the Impressionists in general and James McNeill Whistler in particular. See *The Japanese Tradition in British and American Literature* (Princeton, 1966), pp. 108–12.

6. "Vorticism" (1914) is reprinted in part in *Ezra Pound*, ed. J. P. Sullivan (Baltimore, 1970), pp. 51–54.

7. Pound, in *Writers at Work*, p. 49.

8. Hugh Kenner, *The Pound Era* (Berkeley and Los Angeles, 1971), p. 197.

9. See Pound to William Carlos Williams, December 19, 1913, and Pound to Amy Lowell, April 30, 1914, in *The Letters of Ezra Pound: 1907–1941*, ed. D. D. Paige (New York, 1950), pp. 27 and 36, respectively.

10. Pound in *Writers at Work*, p. 49.

11. "How to Read" (1927 or 1928), *Literary Essays*, pp. 25–27.

12. Kenner, *The Pound Era*, p. 204.

13. For the information on Fenollosa's notes of July 3, 1900, I am indebted to Professor Hugh Kenner. For comments on Pound's translation, see Achilles Fang, "Fenollosa and Pound," *Harvard Journal of Asiatic Studies* 20 (June 1957):227, and Wai-lim Yip, *Ezra Pound's "Cathay"* (Princeton, 1969), p. 140. In his use of "Kiang" for the Yangtze, Pound shares company with James Legge and Arthur Waley.

14. Pound to Felix E. Schelling, June 1915, *Letters*, p. 61.

15. Introduction (1928), *Ezra Pound: Selected Poems*, ed. T. S. Eliot (London, 1948), p. 14.

16. John Gould Fletcher, "The Orient and Contemporary Poetry," in *The Asian Legacy and American Life*, ed. Arthur Christy (New York, 1945), p. 154; and Kenner, *The Pound Era*, p. 199.

17. Introduction, *Ezra Pound: Selected Poems*, p. 12.

18. Pound to Harriet Monroe, January 31, 1914, *Letters*, pp. 30–31.

19. Miner, p. 137.

20. For a summary account of the episode, see Arthur Waley, *The Nō Plays of Japan* (New York, n.d.), pp. 179–80. Waley's own translation of *The Tale of Genji* did not begin to appear until 1925.

21. Waley, *Nō Plays of Japan*, p. 304. For Waley's own version, see p. 182. Incidentally, in a footnote, Pound thanks Waley for correcting a number of orthographical mistakes and also assisting him out of "various impasses where my own ignorance would have left me."

NOTES TO PAGES 185–199

22. T. S. Eliot, *Ezra Pound: His Metric and Poetry* (1917), reprinted in part in *Ezra Pound*, p. 79.

23. W. B. Yeats's introduction to *The Classic Noh Theatre of Japan* (New York, 1959), p. 151. For Yeats's debt to the Orient in general, see William York Tindall, "Transcendentalism in Contemporary Literature," in *The Asian Legacy and American Life*, pp. 177–86.

24. For its significance in Fenollosa's career, see Chapter 5.

25. See note 14 above. This is the first letter in the volume to bear Chinese characters.

26. Pound to John Quinn, January 10, 1917, *Letters*, p. 101.

27. For an analysis of the essay, see Chapter 5.

28. Pound to Schelling, June 1915, *Letters*, p. 61; Pound to Quinn, January 10, 1917, *Letters*, pp. 101–2; and Pound to Margaret C. Anderson, [?January 1917], ibid., p. 107.

29. Pound to Katue Kitasono, March 11, 1937, ibid., p. 292; and Pound to W. H. D. Rouse, October 30, 1937, ibid., p. 298.

30. For a discussion of this subject, see Kenner, *The Pound Era*, pp. 445–59.

31. Quoted in H. G. Creel, *Confucius and the Chinese Way* (New York, 1960), p. 281.

32. Fung Yu-lan, *A Short History of Chinese Philosophy*, tr. Derk Bodde (New York, 1960), pp. 182–83.

33. Prolegomena, *The Chinese Classics*, tr. James Legge (Hong Kong, 1960), 1:29. The Pauthier reference here is Legge's.

34. *ABC of Reading* (New York, 1960), p. 58.

35. "Immediate Need of Confucius," *Impact: Essays on Ignorance and the Decline of American Civilization*, ed. Noel Stock (Chicago, 1960), pp. 197–205; and *Guide to Kulchur* (New York, 1968), pp. 79–80. Eliot also had the opening paragraphs of the *Ta Hsieh* in mind when he wrote in *The Rock*: "If humility and purity be not in the heart, they are not in the home: and if they are not in the home, they are not in the City." With specific reference to this passage Pound observed that "Eliot's use of Confucius in *The Rock* (section 5), is worth noting" (*Impact*, p. 200n).

36. Legge, p. 55.

37. Fung, p. 166.

38. *Guide to Kulchur*, p. 24.

39. Fung, pp. 41–42.

40. *Guide to Kulchur*, pp. 214–16; and Pound to Katue Kitasono, March 11, 1937, *Letters*, p. 292.

41. Kenner, *The Pound Era*, p. 520.

42. See Kenner, *Gnomon* (New York, 1958), p. 88; and Dembo, *The Confucian Odes of Ezra Pound* (London, 1963), pp. 89–90. Dembo concludes: "The original perhaps calls for dialect, since the Confucian reading is that it represents the deterioration of human relations among the peasantry as a direct result of royal corruption, but Pound's reply, energetic though it may be, is something less than satisfactory."

43. Dembo, p. 5.

44. Cf. Kenner: "[Pound] may have supposed for a long time that Kung's *tao* and Lao Tse's were different words" (*The Pound Era*, p. 458n).

45. Fung, pp. 294–95.

46. *Guide to Kulcher*, pp. 15–16, 29.

47. George Dekker, for example, called it "a colossal failure" (*Sailing after Knowledge: The Cantos of Ezra Pound* (1963), reprinted in part in *Ezra Pound*, p. 314.

48. Pound, in *Writers at Work*, pp. 56–57; and quoted by Daniel Cory, "Ezra Pound: A Memoir," reprinted in part in *Ezra Pound*, pp. 374–76.

49. Quoted in Ronald Bush, *The Genesis of Ezra Pound's Cantos* (Princeton, 1976), p. 5.

50. Ibid., p. 74.

51. The Chinese character (hsin[4]) at the end of Canto 34 in the current American edition was added twenty years later (Kenner, *The Pound Era*, p. 432n).

52. For Pound's rendition of the whole passage, see p. 193. Angela Chih-ying Jung [Palandri] also stresses the importance of this concept in the *Cantos*. See her doctoral dissertation, "Ezra Pound and China" (University of Washington, 1955).

53. Pound to Hubert Creekmore, February, 1939, *Letters*, pp. 322–23.

54. Kenner, *The Pound Era*, p. 222.

55. Ibid., p. 432. Identifying both poems, Achilles Fang observes: "The rest of Canto 49 seems to be transcribed from Fenollosa's stray notes on Chinese poetry" ("Fenollosa and Pound," p. 232).

56. Kenner, *The Pound Era*, pp. 456, 434.

57. For a study of Taoism in this context, see Holmes Welch, *Taoism: The Parting of the Way* (Boston, 1965).

58. Pound to T. S. Eliot, February 1, 1940, *Letters*, p. 336. Then Pound added: "That I think I have conveyed to you by now??"

59. Earl Davis, *Vision Fugitive: Ezra Pound and Economics* (Lawrence, Kans., 1968), p. 31.

60. Ibid., pp. 116–17.

61. Ibid., p. 98.

62. "A Retrospect," *Literary Essays*, p. 4, "Vorticism" (1914), reprinted in part in *Ezra Pound*, p. 57; and *Guide to Kulchur*, p. 266.

63. Pound to Katue Kitasono, November 15, 1940, *Letters*, p. 347.

64. *Guide to Kulchur*, p. 48.

65. Ibid., p. 51. For a provocative study of Pound from this particular perspective, see Max Nänny, *Ezra Pound: Poetics for an Electric Age* (Bern, 1973). In the conclusion he writes: "By introducing the iconic or mosaic 'image' and 'ideogramic method' into the most highly literate culture of the West, American culture, Pound posed an intellectual and emotional challenge to Western literate man that had a similar explosive effect on literature and thought as the technique of montage had on the film and the Cubist revolution had on painting" (pp. 112–13).

66. *Impact*, p. 15.

67. Kenner, *The Pound Era*, p. 535. For a discussion of this quatrain, see Angela [Chung] Palandri, "Homage to a Confucian Poet," *Paedeuma* 3 (Winter 1974):301–4.

NOTES TO *Epilogue*

1. Malcolm Cowley, *The Literary Situation* (New York, 1954), p. 241.

2. Gilbert Millstein, "Book of the Times," *New York Times*, September 5, 1957, sec. 1, p. 27.

3. Norman Podhoretz, "The Know-Nothing Generation" (1958), in *A Casebook on the Beat*, ed. Thomas Parkinson (New York, 1961), pp. 201–12. For a similar view of the beat as "a spectacular instance of the flight from emotion," see Herbert Gold, "The Beat Mystique," ibid., pp. 247–56.

4. Bruce Cook, *The Beat Generation* (New York, 1971), pp. 10–11.

5. Lawrence Lipton, *The Holy Barbarians* (New York, 1959). For his elaboration on this aspect, see especially chapter 14, "Lost Generation, Flaming Youth, Bohemian Leftist, Beat Generation—Is There a Difference?"

6. Kenneth Rexroth, "Disengagement: The Art of the Beat Generation" (1957), in *A Casebook on the Beat*, pp. 179–93.

7. Jack Kerouac, "The Origins of the Beat Generation" (1959), ibid., p. 75.

8. Rexroth, "Disengagement," ibid., p. 191.

9. Alan W. Watts, *Beat Zen Square Zen and Zen* (San Francisco, 1959), pp. 3–9. See also Van Meter Ames, "Current Western Interest in Zen," *Philosophy East and West* 10 (April–July 1960):23–33. Harvy Cox finds six patterns in the young East-turners of the 1970s: they are (1) seeking simple human friendship in a fraternal or communal setting; (2) looking for a way of experiencing life directly and immediately, not conceptually; (3) looking for authority figures, such as guru, swami, and master; (4) looking for more naturalness, a kind of unspoiled purity, or lost innocence; (5) trying—mostly the women among them—to get away from the seemingly total male domination of the Western faith;

and (6) concerned with health, ecology, and conservation of our dwindling natural resources (*Turning East: The Promise & Peril of the New Orientalism* [New York, 1977], pp. 101–3).

10. See, for instance, Alan W. Watts, *The Way of Zen* (New York, 1959).

11. Lipton, p. 230.

12. George Steiner, "The Salinger Industry" (1959), in *Salinger*, ed. Henry Anatole Grunwald (New York, 1963), p. 83; Tom Davis, "J. D. Salinger: 'The Sound of One Hand Clapping'" (1963), *Wisconsin Studies in Contemporary Literature* 4 (Winter 1963):41–47; and Ihab Hassan, "J. D. Salinger: Rare Quixotic Gesture," in *Salinger*, pp. 152–53. See also Bernice and Sanford Goldstein, "Zen and Salinger," *Modern Fiction Studies* 12 (Autumn 1966):313–24, and idem, "Bunnies and Cobras: Zen Enlightenment in Salinger," *Discourse* 13 (Winter 1970):98–106.

13. Jack Skow, "Sonny: An Introduction" (1961), in *Salinger*, p. 14.

14. Buddy says parenthetically: "Would it be out of order for me to say that both Seymour's and my roots in Eastern philosophy—if I may hesitantly call them 'roots'— were, are, planted in the New and Old Testaments, Advaita Vedanta, and classical Taoism?"

15. See Salinger's piece, "Hapworth 16, 1924," *New Yorker*, June 19, 1965, pp. 32–113.

16. Cf. Gerald Rosen: "The question of Seymour's life and suicide is a fascinating one and the Glass stories are, for the most part, a record of the Glass children's response to it, and, apparently, their struggles to let go of it—they (including Buddy) seem to be slowly coming to realize that they are 'holding on' to Seymour in the same way that Holden attempts to hold on to Allie, and the Zen student holds on to his koan" (*Zen in the Art of J. D. Salinger* [Berkeley, Calif., 1977], p. 37).

17. Warren French, *J. D. Salinger* (New York, 1963), pp. 32–33.

18. Apparently Salinger phoned to the *New York Times* from his retreat in Cornish, New Hampshire, as reported in the *Detroit Free Press*, November 4, 1974. See also "J. D. Salinger Speaks about His Silence," *New York Times*, November 3, 1974, sec. 1, p. 1.

19. Watts, *Beat Zen Square Zen and Zen*, pp. 9–10; and Margaret E. Ashida, "Frogs and Frozen Zen," *Prairie Schooner* 34 (Fall 1960):199–206.

20. Kerouac, in *Writers at Work*, 4th ser., ed. George Plimpton (New York, 1976), pp. 378–79.

21. For a detailed account of his interest in Buddhism, see Ann Charters, *Kerouac* (San Francisco, 1973), especially chapters 19 and 20. See also Dennis McNally, *Desolate Angel: Jack Kerouac, the Beat Generation, and America* (New York, 1979), pp. 178–98.

22. Charters, pp. 323, 337.

23. Allen Ginsberg, in *Writers at Work*, 3d ser., ed. George Plimpton (New York, 1967), p. 318.

24. "Essentials of Spontaneous Prose," in *A Casebook on the Beat*, pp. 65–67.

25. Echoing this, Watts observed that Snyder is "in the best sense, a bum" (*Beat Zen Square Zen and Zen*, p. 17). He also wrote: "For Gary is tougher, more disciplined, and more physically competent than I, but he embodied these virtues without rubbing them in, and I can only say that a universe which has manifested Gary Snyder could never be called a failure" (*In My Own Way: An Autobiography* [New York, 1972], p. 309).

26. Thomas Parkinson, "The Poetry of Gary Snyder," *Southern Review* 4 (Summer 1968):617; and Kenneth Rexroth, *American Poetry in the Twentieth Century* (New York, 1971), p. 177.

27. For his career, see Bob Steuding, *Gary Snyder* (Boston, 1976), pp. 17–21.

28. Dom Aelred Graham, *Conversations: Christian and Buddhist* (New York, 1968), p. 59.

29. Ibid., p. 74. Snyder writes elsewhere: "Buddhist Tantrism, or Vajrayana as it's also known, is probably the finest and most modern statement of this ancient shamanistic-yogic-gnostic-socioeconomic view: that mankind's mother is Nature and Nature should be tenderly respected; that man's life and destiny is growth and enlightenment in self-disciplined freedom; that the divine has been made flesh and that flesh is divine; that we not only should but *do* love one another" (*Earth House Hold* [New York, 1969], p. 105).

30. *Earth House Hold*, p. 118.
31. *Regarding Waves* (New York, 1970), p. 74.
32. Rexroth, *American Poetry in the Twentieth Century*, p. 178; Wai-lim Yip, cited in Steuding, p. 45.
33. For an English rendition of the entire poem, see "Drinking Songs," Robert Payne, *The White Pony* (New York, n.d.), p. 138. Snyder himself said of the poems in *Riprap & Cold Mountain Poems*: "I tried writing poems of tough, simple short words, with the complexity far beneath the surface texture. In part the line was influenced by the five- and seven-character line Chinese poems I'd been reading, which work like sharp blows on the mind" (*The New American Poetry*, ed. Donald M. Allen [New York, 1960], p. 421).
34. For Pound's version, see Chapter 10.
35. *Turtle Island* (New York, 1969), p. 64. See also his poem "Beneath My Hand and Eye the Distant Hills, Your Body" in *The Back Company* ([New York, 1968], pp. 108–9).
36. *Earth House Hold*, p. 4; and *Turtle Island*, p. 107.
37. *Earth House Hold*, p. 21.
38. *The New American Poetry*, p. 421.
39. Ibid.
40. This phrase appears in Snyder's own statement: "As poet I hold the most archaic values on earth. They go back to the late Paleolithic: the fertility of the soil, the magic of animals, the power-vision in solitude, the terrifying initiation and re-birth, the love and ecstasy of the dance, the common work of the tribe. I try to hold both history and wilderness in mind, that my poems may approach the true measure of things and stand against the unbalance and ignorance of our times" (*Six Poets of the San Francisco Renaissance*, ed. David Kherdian [Fresno, Calif., 1967], p. 52).
41. For a helpful discussion of both sections, see Steuding, pp. 99–109.
42. "The Wilderness," *Turtle Island*, p. 106. The paper was originally read in a seminar at the Center for the Study of Democratic Institutions, Santa Barbara, California.
43. Entry of January 22, *The Journals of Ralph Waldo Emerson*, ed. Edward Waldo Emerson and Waldo Emerson Forbes (Boston, 1909–14), 4:6; and entry of October 7, ibid., 5:469.
44. Entry of January 7, ibid., 3:12–13.
45. Introductory essay, *Indian Superstition*, ed. Kenneth Walter Cameron (Hanover, N.H., 1954), pp. 21–23.
46. The essay was written at the same time Thoreau withdrew from the Harvard Library Irving's *Voyages of Columbus*, January 8, 1834 (John Aldrich Christie, *Thoreau as World Traveler* [New York, 1965], p. 307). Christie also writes: "His memory of Columbus' feeling upon first sensing a land breeze after the long voyage repeatedly colored his own responses to the sweet wafts from the Concord meadows" (p. 120).
47. Henry Nash Smith, *Virgin Land: The American West as Symbol and Myth* (New York, 1957), p. 23. In this connection Smith also discusses Asa Whitney, who proposed a Pacific railway (pp. 30–34).
48. Ibid., pp. 22, 19.

Index

262

Professor Yu received his undergraduate education from Seoul National University in Korea, and the Ph.D. degree from Brown University. He has twice been awarded a Fulbright Lectureship to Korea, and is currently in the English department at Wayne State University. Among his publications are *An Ape of Gods: The Art and Thought of Lafcadio Hearn*, *Natsume Soseki*, and *Akutagawa: An Introduction*.

The manuscript was edited by Barbara Lamb. The book was designed by E. J. Frank. The typeface for the text is Mergenthaler's VIP Times Roman, based on a design by Stanley Morison in 1932. The typeface for the display is Mergenthaler's VIP Trump, based on a 1954 design by Georg Trump. The text is printed on 55-lb. S. D. Warren's '66 Antique text paper. The book is bound in Holliston Mills' Natural Finish Cloth over binder's boards.

Manufactured in the United States of America.